Anonymous

Short Stories and Lessons on the Festivals, Fasts and Saints' Days of the Protestant Episcopal Church

Anonymous

Short Stories and Lessons on the Festivals, Fasts and Saints' Days of the Protestant Episcopal Church

ISBN/EAN: 9783337336677

Printed in Europe, USA, Canada, Australia, Japan

Cover: Foto ©Lupo / pixelio.de

More available books at **www.hansebooks.com**

SHORT

STORIES AND LESSONS

ON

THE FESTIVALS, FASTS, AND SAINTS' DAYS,

OF THE

𝔓𝔯𝔬𝔱𝔢𝔰𝔱𝔞𝔫𝔱 𝔈𝔭𝔦𝔰𝔠𝔬𝔭𝔞𝔩 𝔠𝔥𝔲𝔯𝔠𝔥.

FIRST AMERICAN EDITION.

NEW-YORK:
H. B. DURAND, No. 11 BIBLE HOUSE.
1866.

ADVERTISEMENT.

The aim of the following admirable little work, is to increase the interest of the children of the Church, in her holy appointments and services, by bringing before them, in an attractive form, generally under the guise of a brief and pertinent story, the Festivals and Fasts which mark the ecclesiastical year.

Being an English work, the liberty has been used of adapting its language to our own Book of Common Prayer, and the wants of our children generally; and the belief is entertained, that the work itself will be found of such intrinsic merit, marked interest, and usefulness, as fully to justify its introduction to American Churchmen.

NEW YORK, June, 1856.

CONTENTS

	PAGE
ADVERTISEMENT,	3
ADVENT SUNDAY,	7
CHRISTMAS DAY,	15
FEAST OF THE EPIPHANY,	27
ASH WEDNESDAY,	35
GOOD FRIDAY,	41
EASTER EVEN, OR THE RETROSPECTION,	51
EASTER DAY,	65
ASCENSION DAY,	79
WHIT-SUNDAY,	89
TRINITY SUNDAY,	101
S. ANDREW'S DAY,	115
S. THOMAS'S DAY,	123
S. STEPHEN'S DAY,	137
S. JOHN EVANGELIST'S DAY,	145
THE INNOCENTS' DAY,	151
FEAST OF THE CIRCUMCISION,	163
CONVERSION OF S. PAUL,	173
THE PURIFICATION OF THE VIRGIN MARY, OR THE PRESENTATION OF CHRIST IN THE TEMPLE,	181
S. MATTHIAS' DAY,	195
THE ANNUNCIATION,	207
S. MARK'S DAY,	213
S. PHILIP AND S. JAMES'S DAY,	219
S. BARNABAS' DAY,	233
S. JOHN BAPTIST'S DAY,	239
S. PETER'S DAY,	249

CONTENTS.

	PAGE
S. James's Day,	259
S. Bartholomew's Day,	273
S. Matthew's Day,	289
S. Michael and All Angels', or Michaelmas Day,	297
S. Luke's Day,	303
S. Simon and S. Jude's Day,	317
All Saints' Day,	825

Advent Sunday.

COLLECT.

ALMIGHTY GOD, give us grace that we may cast away the works of darkness, and put upon us the armour of light, now in the time of this mortal life, in which Thy SON JESUS CHRIST came to visit us in great humility; that in the last day, when He shall come again in His glorious Majesty to judge both the quick and dead, we may rise to the life immortal, through Him Who liveth and reigneth with Thee and the HOLY GHOST, now and ever. AMEN.

> "When, as before the Judge's throne
> The heavens and earth shall flee,
> CHRIST with His angels shall come down,
> The books shall opened be." *

ONE morning, during the latter part of November, two children were employing themselves in a large nursery garden near the city of E——; the boy, a sturdy little fellow, might have been ten, and his sister two years younger. They were the children of Philip Malton, who was the head gardener, and the basket they carried between them was full of bulbs, which they were taking to their father at a distant part of the garden. As they returned from thence, the following conversation passed between them.

"Harry," said little Katie, "do you know what is a talent?"

"Yes," replied the boy, with a little self-impor-

* Hymns on the Catechism. Stanford & Swords, 1850.

tance, "a talent is a piece of money, Katie; don't you remember the Parable of the Talents, which we read in the Bible, a verse each, by turns, to mother, last Sunday evening?"

"I recollect that, Harry; but just now, I heard the minister say, when father was telling him how he missed poor John Gray, that he had made good use of the talents God had given him; now you know old John was very poor, so Mr. Howard could not have meant money."

"Then I don't quite understand it, Katie," replied the boy, with a puzzled look, "but suppose we ask father, or the master, when we go to school."

"What are you talking so earnestly about, my little friends?" said a kind voice at their side, and turning, they saw it was Mr. Howard. The children were silent for a minute, and then Harry replied, "Katie was asking me the meaning of a talent, sir, and I told her it was a piece of money. But she says, you spoke just now of poor John Gray, as having used his talents well, and we all know he was very poor; will you please to tell us the meaning of it, sir?"

"Yes, my boy," replied the clergyman, "you were right in saying that a talent is a piece of money, but the word has another meaning, and it was in the latter sense I used it, in speaking of John Gray. A talent means any of the good gifts with which God has so abundantly blessed us, and which we must use in his service: time, health, and riches, are all talents given us by the Almighty, to Whom we must one day render a strict account of the manner in which we have employed them; if to His honour and glory, we shall receive the reward promised to faithful servants, but if we have wasted and misused these blessings, we shall be punished. You both know the Parable of the Talents, I suppose : our blessed Lord therein teaches us this great truth."

"But can children use talents in the service of God, and what can we do, sir?" said Katie.

"Yes, many things, my child, but great works are not expected from little children, yet all can serve God; look here," said Mr. Howard, stopping opposite a fruit tree, "nature teaches us a lesson; when spring comes, your father will look for blossoms from this apple tree, and in summer he will expect fruit, but from the little bulb lying at the foot of this tree, he only expects the modest snowdrop, because he knows that the Creator has assigned to each its duties in the vegetable kingdom, and he only looks for fruit according to the gifts bestowed by God. Still, he gives the same care and attention to the lowliest plant as to the highest tree in the garden; he does not cut down the apple tree because it is now leafless, nor will he root up the snowdrop because it does not bear apples; but if, after all his tender care, the tree produces no fruit, or the little plant no blossom, he will destroy it, and bestow his labor on those plants and trees which will produce good fruits. And thus, my children, does the great God deal with us: this world is His garden, and we are the plants; He has given to each different gifts or talents, to some knowledge, to others health or riches, and to many, both or all three of these blessings, and there is one talent which is given to every one, time, which we must not waste, but employ in his service. Our blessed LORD tells us that much will be required from those who have received much."

"But, sir," said Harry, "you spoke just now of John Gray; what were his talents? he was very poor; his health was bad, and he was no scholar, for he could not read better than I can, though he was an old man, and I am but a boy."

"John Gray was simple in the things of this world, but he was wise unto salvation," replied Mr. Howard, very gravely, "and that is true wisdom, Harry: he never lost an opportunity of doing good to those with whom he associated, and the ties of kindred and friendship are talents to be used to the honour and glory of GOD. Can little Katie tell me what next Sunday will be?"

"Advent Sunday," replied the child; "governess showed me the Collect yesterday, and she said it was the beginning of the Christian year."

"Very true, my child, I am glad you remember what you are taught. Advent signifies coming, and the four Sundays which precede Christmas are called Advent Sundays, because they prepare us for the Anniversary of the Birth of the Holy JESUS; and the services appointed by the Church for these Sundays, also remind us of the second coming of our LORD to judgment, when all must give an account of the manner in which they have employed the talents entrusted to them. We shall then be rewarded or punished according as we have done good or evil. In that awful day every secret of our hearts will be revealed; GOD always knows our thoughts, but then they will be known to all the world. Believing as we all do, that 'GOD will judge the world in righteousness by that Man Whom He hath ordained' (that is, by JESUS CHRIST), we ought to spend all our lives in preparation for that great and awful day. In the Collect for the first Sunday in Advent, we pray that GOD will 'give us grace to cast away the works of darkness, and put upon us the armour of light,' by which we mean that He will enable us to live a holy life, to be wise unto salvation, and sanctified as his faithful children. Will you try and think of this when you repeat the Collect?" Mr. Howard now left his little friends, who thanked him for his kind explanation.

And what fruits did the seed sown in these young hearts produce? From the mind and thoughts of Harry, Mr. Howard's words soon passed away; he was a boy of great natural ability, and his quickness of intellect attracting the attention of a gentleman, who occasionally saw him in the garden, he was placed by this kind friend in his counting-house as a clerk, and in course of time, Harry rendered himself so valuable as an assistant, that he was taken by his patron into partnership. But how did the young man use these talents? Not to the honour of GOD. His wealth was expended in a manner which he imagined would increase his own importance; he sought not the praise of GOD but the praise of men. And had Katie also forgotten the good pastor's teaching? Not so; the words sunk into her heart, and even in early life she endeavoured to promote the welfare of all with whom she associated, and thus serve GOD. She still lived with her aged mother, her only surviving parent, in the little village; Harry occasionally came to see them, but not often, for his early home had lost all its charms, and he loved the bustle and excitement of a city. Katie sometimes reminded her brother of the account he must one day give of the talents entrusted to him, but he would not brook advice, and then she could only pray for him. She was very much beloved by all her neighbours, for her gentle ways and genuine kindness, and many who would not receive reproof from others, listened with untiring patience to Kate Malton's mild admonition and good advice. One morning, she received a letter written in a hand which was unknown to her, and upon reading the contents, she found that her brother was dangerously ill, and his friend, who gave her the information, entreated she would lose no time in hastening to see Harry. She found him laid on a bed of sickness, unconscious of all around him; now of what avail was his fine intellect or the wealth he had gathered, and the many comforts which surrounded him? They were powerless to guard him from pain or death; he had brought forth no fruits of righteousness, and had the awful sentence, " cut it down, why cumbereth it the ground?" then gone forth, he would have found " no place for repentance."

But Almighty GOD heard the prayers which Katie poured forth for her erring brother, and the fever abated.

It was a long time before Harry recovered, but he was not insensible of the mercy of GOD in giving him still more time for repentance: he shuddered when he considered how near he had been to the grave, beyond which there is "no wisdom, nor device, nor knowledge," and he thought of the gentle warnings his kind sister had given, and which he had so often despised.

The young man rose from his bed of sickness with a firm purpose to endeavour, by GOD's grace, to make a better use of his talents; and when, after a few years, they were left orphans, Katie went and lived with her brother, and their mutual earnest endeavour was to employ the good things with which GOD had blessed them to the honour and glory of His Holy Name.

Christmas Day.

COLLECT.

ALMIGHTY GOD, Who hast given us Thy only begotten SON to take our nature upon Him, and as at this time to be born of a pure Virgin; Grant that we being regenerate, and made Thy children by adoption and grace, may daily be renewed by Thy HOLY SPIRIT; through the same our LORD JESUS CHRIST, Who liveth and reigneth with Thee and the same SPIRIT, ever one GOD, world without end. AMEN.

IT was Christmas Eve, the vigil of that day of holy rejoicing, upon which the SAVIOUR of the world was born. The streets of London, even though it was already dark, were thronged with foot passengers, many of them making purchases of good things against the morrow. The shops were gaily dressed with holly, and lighted up in honour of the approaching festival; here and there a church bell was heard, as if to remind men of the cause of this universal gladness, and many of those whose hearts dwelt with gratitude on the Mercy of our Redemption, were hastening in different directions towards the house of prayer.

For why on this evening were children returning to their parents, and brothers and sisters long separated, meeting again within their happy home? Why had the postman so many letters of love and congratulation to carry from those who could not come? Why was the rich man gladly giving of his abundance, and opening his heart and his purse to almost every petitioner? Why did the poor feel so sure of receiving kindness and meeting with sympathy? The world was about to hail the return of that day upon which the heavenly strain was first heard, " Glory be to God in the highest, and on earth peace, good-will toward men."

Heavy snow had fallen during the day, and boys were busy in all directions sweeping the steps of doors; for now it was freezing fast, and before morning, would be dangerous. "Mother," said a little ragged boy, as he put his head in the door of a poor room, where scarcely any fire lighted the hearth, "I shall take my broom and go and sweep the snow from doors, then I shall earn some pence, and we can have a dinner to-morrow."

Edward Baker, for that was the boy's name, earned eighteen pence in this way, and was preparing to go home, when he noticed a large house, the steps of which were still thickly covered with snow; the windows of this house were lighted up by bright fires within, and little forms passed quickly before them from time to time. What a happy Christmas they must be keeping, thought he, as he rang at the door and heard the sound of many happy voices, which he knew were those of children at play.

The servant gave him the required leave, and Edward, after he had finished his work, stood waiting in the passage to be paid. Just then a door opened, and several children ran across the hall, one of them was a young girl who might have been ten years old. Edward thought he had never seen anything so pretty as this child in her white frock, and with her golden hair; she held by the hand her little sister, some years younger than herself, but with the same sweet face and gentle look. The two seemed very fond of each other, and when they played kept close together. "See, Agnes dear," said Ella, who was the elder of the two, "how cold that poor boy looks, do let us go and ask papa if we may give him some of our money, and something nice to eat, he must be very hungry," and the two sisters ran off, hand in hand; they soon returned with the desired permission, and after Edward had dried and warmed himself by the kitchen fire, they brought him into the large room where they were playing, until their father and mother should come to join them. Ella, meanwhile, tied up a parcel of good things for him, little Agnes looking on all the while with a bright smile,- and the other children, who were boys, ran off to obtain leave to give him some of their clothes. Edward saw that the room was dressed with evergreens, and that Ella had twined some of the green laurel leaves into a wreath for the head of her little sister; how happy these little children are, he thought; I wish I were as happy, they are very good, I hope they will always be happy. "Thank you, Miss," he said to Ella, "for all your kindness, mother will be so pleased to see all these nice things, for she is very poor." "I am sure we are very glad to give them to you," said Ella, "I only wish we could do more, don't you, Agnes?" and away they ran to their father again, to tell him that the boy's mother was very poor, and that he was so badly clothed, and to ask him to come and see if he could do anything for them; for it was Christmas, Ella said, and she was so happy, she could not bear that any one should want food and clothes. Mr. and Mrs. Harvey returned with their children to the room where Edward was, and Mr. Harvey, having written down the name of the street where he said his mother lived, promised to call and see him soon, and try to get him some employment; Mrs. Harvey too gave him some nice warm clothes.

With what a light heart did Edward, after thanking his benefactors, return to his mother; he had so much to tell her, so many good things to give her. It was late before they got into bed that night; they sat over the fire, for Edward's money would soon procure a fresh supply, and they did not spare coal, that happy Christmas Eve. "But, mother," said Edward, when he had described the grand house and the beautiful children, "these good things will not last, and we shall be poor again soon: how I wish we were rich too." "You are forgetting, my boy," replied his mother, "Who it was, that for our sakes became poor, and was born as at this time, into the world, 'that we through his poverty might be rich.' The Holy Child JESUS was not born of a mother who could procure for Him earthly comforts, though even these would have been poor compared to the glory which He left for our sake; but he was cradled in a manger, and exposed in tender infancy to the hardships of such a situation. The human life of our LORD and SAVIOUR has sanctified poverty and made it blessed for ever. 'We have not a High Priest Who cannot be touched with the feeling of our infirmities.' 'Foxes have holes, and the birds of the air have nests,' said our LORD afterwards, 'but the Son of Man hath not where to lay His head.' He had but to will it and He would have been attended by legions of angels, but He endured poverty and hardship, that we might learn in whatsoever state we are, therewith to be content; every station of life has its own trials and duties, my boy, and we may be sure that ours is that which the LORD sees good for us; the time will come when it will matter little whether we have been poor or rich in this world, and the great question will be, have we been laying up treasure in heaven, which fadeth not? You see the great GOD has not forgotten us to-night, when we were in need of food and warmth. He has put it into the hearts of some of his people to send us these good things; may He bless them and theirs for their kindness."

*　　*　　*　　*　　*

"How glad I am that GOD sent that poor boy here to-night, papa," said Ella Harvey, as she stood by her father's side, whilst Agnes was seated on his knee; "I like to think how pleased he is now; what a blessed time Christmas is, and how happy we all are:" she kissed her little sister as she spoke, and then ran about for pleasure. "Agnes and I dressed the room, papa," she said, "Agnes held all the boughs for me; she is getting so tall, mamma says she may go to Church to-morrow; she is nearly five years old, you know: what a nice day to begin to go to Church; will you talk to us about Christmas now, please, papa?"

"Yes, if you will all be thoughtful, and remember what a holy subject it is," said Mr. Harvey. "In order rightly to consider the great gift of salvation which was bestowed upon us through the incarnation of the Son of God, we must carry back our thoughts to the time when the world first left its Creator's hands, so fair and beautiful, we read, that 'God saw everything that he had made, and behold it was very good,' but the disobedience of our first parents brought death upon themselves and upon their children after them, and sin and sorrow defiled the creation over which the Holy Ghost had once moved a Spirit of blessing and peace. No sooner, however, did man sin, than the mercy of God prepared a remedy, even before He pronounced the sentence of judgment which Adam and Eve had deserved. He gave them the promise that the seed of the woman should bruise the serpent's head, that is, that one born of a woman should destroy the power of Satan. This promise was renewed to Abraham, whose descendants were God's chosen people—every part of His dealings with them had reference to the expected Messiah; their deliverance from Egyptian bondage prefigured our salvation, and the passage through the Red Sea was a type of the waters of Baptism. The descendants of faithful Abraham had been separated from the Gentile world by peculiar laws and ceremonies, all of which were typical of the Christian dispensation; unto them were committed the Oracles of God, that they might afterwards become witnesses to the Saviour in Whom all the nations of the earth were to be blessed. The Prophet Isaiah and others foretold the manner of our Blessed

Lord's Birth, Sufferings, and Death, so that when 'In the fulness of time God sent forth His Son made of a woman,' no proof was wanting that Jesus of Nazareth was indeed he of whom Moses in the law and the prophets spake. Can you remember some of the verses in prophecy which refer to Christ?" Charles replied, 'Unto us a Child is born, unto us a Son is given, and the government shall be upon His shoulders, and His Name shall be called Wonderful, Counsellor, the Mighty God, the Everlasting Father, the Prince of Peace;' and Ella repeated the verse, 'Behold a virgin shall conceive, and bear a Son, and shall call His Name Emmanuel.' "You are quite right," said Mr. Harvey, "and there is another prophecy which names the place of the Saviour's birth, for we read in the book of the Prophet Micah, 'That out of Bethlehem in Judea shall He come Who shall rule the people of Israel.' I need not tell you," he continued, "that all these inspired words were fulfilled by the circumstance of our Saviour's birth— The Blessed Virgin was of the house and lineage of David: a tax levied by the Roman Emperor called her and her espoused husband, Joseph, to Bethlehem, where the infant Christ was born, nor were express signs from heaven wanting to attest the Divinity of our Lord—multitudes of the heavenly host announced the glad tidings to the Jewish shepherds, whilst a star in the East led the wise men, the first of the Gentile world, to the feet of their Saviour, to Whom, in token of their adoration, they offered kingly gifts. He Who was cradled in a manger at Bethlehem was indeed 'King of kings and Lord of lords,' 'but for our sakes, He left the glory which He had with His FATHER, before the world began,' 'He made Himself of no reputation, and took upon Him the form of a servant, and was made in the likeness of man.' Tomorrow we celebrate the return of this joyful day, and to-night is, as you know, set apart by the Church that we may prepare our hearts for its sacred services."

"Papa," said little Agnes, who had been listening very attentively, "if I had been living at the time of our SAVIOUR's birth, I should like to have taken Him gifts." "And is there no way, my child, in which we can now make an offering to CHRIST?" said Mr. Harvey. "Yes," said Ella, "we may give to the poor for His sake." "True," replied her father, "and our LORD has said, 'That inasmuch as we give to the least of His little ones in His Name, we do it unto Him.'"

A year had passed, snow covered the earth, doors and windows were closed early, and every heart that ever beat with love and kindness was warmer and kinder now, and longed to share with all the world the happiness of the season; and how did Christmas come to the two families we have visited before? It found Edward and his mother living in a warm comfortable room, with all the necessaries and many of the comforts of life, for through the kindness of Ella's father, Edward had been placed as servant boy in a shop, where he received good wages, and his mother had work found for her which added to their weekly store.

It was Christmas Eve again. "Mother," said Edward, "I am going up now to Mr. Harvey's, it is very long since I was there, and I want to take this beautiful piece of holly to Miss Ella, with my duty; I know it will please her." "Do, my boy," said his mother, "and while you are gone, I will make the pudding, and get forward with my work, and we shall have a nice tea together when you come back: we owe all these comforts to the love that GOD put into their hearts last Christmas, so take my duty too, and say I hope that they will have many happy new years."

Edward carried the holly and rang at the bell of Mr. Harvey's house; he asked to see Miss Ella, and the servant opened the door of the large room, and took in his message. Edward thought that he did not hear so many laughing voices this time as he had done before. Ella herself came out to speak to him, she had a quiet smile upon her face, but it was paler than last year; perhaps it was the black dress she wore, that made her look ill, and this time there was no little Agnes by her side.

"Come in, Edward," she said, kindly, "I am so much obliged to you for thinking of me, and bringing the holly; will you help me to place it over the fireplace?" Edward followed her into the room he had admired so much before, and there were her brothers Charles and James, and Freddy, the baby, was running about, all at play, but he missed Agnes from among them, only her chair was placed by Ella, with a piece of holly twined in it.

"Where is Miss Agnes?" said Edward, "I hope

she is well." The children instantly stopped their play and looked sad, and Ella's eyes filled with tears, as she replied in a low voice, " She is keeping Christmas with the holy angels, and we have placed her chair here that we may remember her all the evening, and how happy she made us last year;" and Ella turned away her face and stooped over the little chair, while the tears she tried to repress, fell fast over the bright holly leaves. "We shall be with her again at last, you know," she said, when she had regained her calmness, "it will be only a few years first, and perhaps she can see us now, and knows how we love her. Dear little Agnes, she was very happy when she died : it was three months ago."

Ella had not forgotten a kind present for Edward, and something for his mother: as he walked home, he could not help thinking of her quiet happiness in the midst of her sorrow, for he knew she must have suffered much in parting from her favourite and only little sister. When he said this to his mother, she replied, " A Christian's hope is like the holly in winter, my boy, green when all else withers. Miss Ella knows that her darling is safe with GOD, she is thankful for the happiness that He still leaves her, and she will forget her sorrow that she may make her brothers happy this Christmas night."

O LORD, to-day, for thy dear sake
Our souls to glad thanksgiving wake;
In all thy faithful hearts below
Bid joys of spring eternal flow,
And every primal curse grow bright,
By thinking on Thy blest birth-night.

"In sorrow shalt thou toil for bread,"
So upon man the doom was said ;

To labouring men amid the field,
First was the holy Babe revealed;
And labour now shall lighter be,
So soothed and hallowed, LORD, by Thee.

"In sorrow shalt thou children bear,"
Of such a doom is woman heir;
But GOD, by that one glorious birth,
Our nature took and dwelt on earth.
Mothers no more their pangs shall blame,
By which the world's REDEEMER came.

"Ye for your sins shall surely die,"
All men beneath this sentence lie;
But He Who came this day to save,
He fought with death, He burst the grave,
And when He vanquished in the strife,
Then death became the gate of life.

"He that spared not His own SON, but delivered Him up for us all, how shall He not with Him also freely give us all things?"—*Rom.* viii. 32.

Feast of the Epiphany.

COLLECT.

O GOD, Who by the leading of a star didst manifest Thy Only-begotten Son to the Gentiles; Mercifully grant, that we, who know Thee now by faith, may after this life have the fruition of Thy glorious Godhead; through JESUS CHRIST our LORD. AMEN.

IT was on the 6th of January, 1830, that two little girls stood outside the window of the largest pastry-cook's shop in the town of Ilfracombe, gazing with delighted eyes at the show of twelfth cakes with their snow white sugar covering, and the gay figures with which they were ornamented. The two children had lately come from a retired village, and never having seen anything of this sort before, they were loud in their exclamations of delight. There was a king, the most splendid of all the decorations, and a crown, and a ship. O, how they wished that they might go inside the shop and have a nearer view of those beauties.

At this moment, a young lady who was passing, and overheard what the children said, stopped and spoke to them, and asked them kindly if they knew what day it was.

" Thursday, ma'am," answered the two little girls at once.

" I do not mean the day of the week," continued

the lady. "It is the Feast of the Epiphany, to-day, a holy day in our Church. I am going to teach some little children at the school, and, if you like, you may come with me. You may, perhaps, hear something about the reason why those beautiful cakes were made to-day, and you will be in time to go to the church afterwards."

So the little girls gladly walked by her side, and the lady stopped on her way to the school, at the cottage where the children said their mother lived, that she might know where they were, and not be alarmed at their absence, for they were strangers in the place. Their mother was the wife of a fisherman who lived on the coast of Wales, and she had come to her native town to see her father who was dying. She was glad to think that her little girls had found a kind friend in the strange place, while she was too busy to attend to them, and that they were going to the same school and church where she had been so often when she was a happy child.

When they came to the school, the lady placed them on a bench with some other little girls, and after the doors were shut at ten o'clock, and they had knelt down while the clergyman said a prayer, in which they joined, they took their places, and listened while the lady heard the other children repeat their lessons. The two little strangers, Mary and Sally Jones, stared about at first, but they tried to listen when the lady told them to be very attentive to the collect, for she would talk to them soon about that beautiful star which appeared to the wise men in the East. She used very plain language, that Mary and Sally Jones might understand what she said, and as I am writing for little children, I will repeat her words.

"You all know that at the time our blessed Saviour was born in Bethlehem of Judea, the Jews were the only people who worshipped the true God. They were the Church, or people of God, whom He had chosen for Himself from among other nations. He had given them laws, and sent them holy Prophets, and kings, and instructed them in His divine will; and more than all this, He had promised by the mouth of His servants, the Prophets, that the Saviour of the world should be born of one of their nation. The Jews possessed that part of the Bible which we call the Old Testament, at the time of the birth of our Lord, and therefore they knew in what place, and in what manner the expected Messiah was to appear. If they had had faith in God's Word, they could not have doubted that the lowly Infant of Bethlehem was He 'of Whom Moses in the law, and the Prophets wrote, Jesus of Nazareth, the King of the Jews.' The Saviour was called ' of Nazareth,' because His mother afterwards lived there with her husband Joseph, but He was born at Bethlehem, as was foretold by the Prophet Isaiah; the Jews, however, called Him ' Jesus of Nazareth,' because they would not acknowledge Him as the expected Saviour Who was to be born in Bethlehem, the city of David. The Jewish nation had sunk into a state of sloth and worldliness; they had been conquered by the Romans, a great and powerful people, and they thought little of the Saviour Who was to make atonement for the sin of the world, and desired only a king who should be a victorious leader, and deliver them from their enemies, the Romans. Therefore, when the LORD JESUS CHRIST came unto His own, His own received Him not. We all know how the Jewish people, given over to hardness and unbelief, because they willingly hardened their hearts against the truth, delivered the SAVIOUR of the world to a cruel death, and cried, Crucify Him, crucify Him.

"Alas! they might have known that this was He Who was to be the glory of His people Israel; GOD had given them many proofs whereby they might believe; but they killed the Holy One, and brought upon themselves the most dreadful guilt. You know, too, how the almighty love of GOD turned the wickedness of man into the means of the world's salvation, and by the death of the SON of GOD we became heirs of life everlasting. Yes, we! not only His Disciples who believed in Him, and followed Him while He lived on earth, but we who are descended from those Gentiles who once knew no better than to bow down in prayer to images of wood and stone; for the LORD JESUS, Who came to be 'the light of the Gentiles,' has shed abroad in our land the knowledge of His Gospel, saying to His servants the Apostles, and afterwards to Priests appointed by them, 'Go ye and teach all nations, baptizing them in the Name of the FATHER, and of the SON, and of the HOLY GHOST.'

"We have therefore good reason to keep this holy day with thankful hearts, and celebrate the Epiphany, which means the showing, or manifesting of CHRIST to the Gentiles. But I will tell you now how wonderfully GOD led the first of the Gentile people to the knowledge of their REDEEMER.

"You all know that when the Son of God came into the world, He was marvellously born of the blessed Virgin Mary, and cradled in a rude manger in Bethlehem, because there was no room for His mother in the inn. Now at this time, in a far off country in the east, the people began to look for the appearing of a great King Who was to be born in the country of the Jews. Perhaps some of the words of the Jewish Prophets who had foretold the birth of a Saviour, had reached that distant land; but, at any rate, it is certain that God put it into the hearts of some wise men in the east to seek Him Who was to be the Salvation of all the ends of the earth. A star which they had never before seen, rose in the heavens, and these wise men, taking this as a sign of some wonderful thing, and evidently taught of God, set off on their long journey to Judea. At this time a cruel and wicked king named Herod ruled over the Jewish people, and when he heard the words of the wise men saying, ' Where is He that is born King of the Jews? for we have seen his star in the east, and are come to worship Him;' he was troubled, for he thought that the kingdom and the power might pass away from him to this new King; and so he called together the chief priests and scribes who were acquainted with the Jewish laws and prophecies, not that he might learn about the Messiah, but that he might know the place of His birth and seek to destroy Him: he demanded of them where Christ should be born; and they answered, ' In Bethlehem of Judea, for thus it is written by the Prophets.'

" Then the king called the wise men and spoke deceitfully to them; he inquired what time the star appeared to them, and sent them to Bethlehem to seek for the young Child, telling them to return and let him know where He was to be found, that he too might go and worship Him. So they departed, and you may think how they rejoiced when they saw the beautiful star again, and felt sure that the God of heaven was thus wonderfully guiding their steps aright; and when the star stood still over the house where the holy child JESUS and His mother were, they did not doubt that this was indeed the great King Whom they were seeking, because they found Him in lowliness and poverty; they had faith that He was to be the King of kings, and Lord of lords, for we read that they fell down and worshipped Him, and they offered unto Him gifts of gold, and frankincense, and myrrh, an offering of respect usually made to kings; and then, after being warned of God in a dream not to return to Herod, who was only seeking to destroy the new-born King, they departed into their own country another way.

"You know, I am sure, that Herod afterwards destroyed all the infants who were in Bethlehem, in the hope that He Who was to be the King of the Jews, might perish among the number, but God had warned Joseph and His mother of the wicked king's intention, and they had taken their precious charge into Egypt. You heard all about this upon the Innocents' Day, so I will not speak more of it now.

"It was twelve days after the birth of our blessed SAVIOUR that the wise men came and worshipped Him, and the Epiphany, you will remember, is always twelve days after Christmas Day. The Church of Christ has always joyfully celebrated the anniversary of that day, when the prophecy first began to be fulfilled that the Lord Jesus should be the 'Light of the Gentiles.'

"There was an old custom of making little cakes of spice covered with gold, in memory of the gold, frankincense, and myrrh, which the wise men presented to our Saviour.

"Little by little the greater number of the people have learnt to think more of this custom, than of the great mercy of God in sending salvation to the Gentiles; gay and rich cakes are bought and sold on the sixth of January, and too many people think nothing about the Feast of the Epiphany. There can be no harm in cheerful parties and innocent amusement, but, O, how great harm to our souls if we are content to think *only* of the pleasures of this life, and to forget the solemn truths of which our Church reminds us from time to time by her holy days and seasons. But now we are going to Church, and I hope that none of us will ever pass this day without feeling thankful to God that we have been born in a Christian land, and made members of His Holy Church. Once, our forefathers, who lived in this island, knew nothing of God, and at the time when the wise men from the east were seeking the Saviour, the people of Britain were idolaters, not only worshipping idols, but sacrificing human beings, killing their own children to please their false gods."

While the lady was speaking thus to the children, the bells began to ring for church. It was a cheerful sound, and it was a pleasant sight, too, to see the children winding up the hill which led to the old church, and the rest of the congregation covering the path; behind them rolled the glorious sea, and on either side were beautiful hills, and before them the church, which had stood there for so many hundred years, where generation after generation of their ancestors had been baptized in their infancy, united in holy matrimony at the altar, within whose walls they had been taught and nourished in the faith of Christ, fed with the bread of life, and within whose sacred precincts they had been laid to rest, as one by one they were gathered to their fathers.

The lady meditated on these things as she walked with her little charges, and she remembered the words of that gracious prophecy respecting our Saviour, "He shall see of the travail of His soul and be satisfied." The children too reflected in their own simple way on the blessings of the Epiphany, and when next they passed the tempting window where the gay-looking cakes were displayed, they thought of the wonderful story of the wise men who came from the east, and offered kingly gifts to the Infant Saviour.

Ash Wednesday.

COLLECT.

ALMIGHTY AND EVERLASTING GOD, who hatest nothing that Thou hast made, and dost forgive the sins of all those who are penitent, create and make in us new and contrite hearts, that we, worthily lamenting our sins and acknowledging our wretchedness, may obtain of Thee, the GOD of all mercy, perfect remission and forgiveness, through JESUS CHRIST our Lord. AMEN.

"WE are getting on nicely with our new cottage, neighbour," said John Wilkins to his friend Jones, who looked in to see him, one evening; "we shall be quite tidy in a few days, and we must have a merry evening together; will you and your wife come in too, this day week?"

"Why, that will be Ash Wednesday," said Mrs. Wilkins, who was busy washing outside the door. "We won't ask our friends on a fast-day, John."

"Very true; I had forgotten that," replied her husband; "people did not think so much of these things when you and I were lads, Jones, did they? our children are better off for teaching than we were."

"I can't say," said Jones, "that I should not have been well off for good learning if I had minded what I was taught, for I had excellent parents, who kept me close to church and school, but I did not think much of what I heard there, I'm afraid. Still I feel the value of it, for it comes back into my mind like an old tune that speaks to one's heart, and I think I could say the Catechism with my youngsters now, though they are not often at fault with it."

"That's more than I could," said Wilkins, "though my poor mother did try to teach it me. I wish she were alive now, to hear me say I wish I had been a better son;" and as he spoke he brushed away a tear with his rough coat-sleeve.

"I'll tell you what it is, Will Jones," continued he, "while I've been working as a mason in Chester, since I was eighteen, you've been happier, and better off, in the old village, and going on in the old ways."

"Could you not have kept to the old ways in town, you see?" asked Jones kindly.

"Well, I wish I had, but I did not," replied the other; "I did as the rest did, worked hard all the week, and idled away Sunday, spending all my earnings, till I married, and then my good woman helped me to save a little every week, and I became something more steady. And now I have left all my Chester friends, I mean to live better if I can. We have a good minister here for one thing."

"Ay, that we have," said Jones; "though he *is* so clever he speaks so plainly that any child may understand what he says, and fond enough the children are of him too; our children came home from the catechising last Sunday, and told us what they had heard, and I am sure it was as good as a sermon, and all about Lent."

"Well, that's a subject I never thought much of

myself, so if you like, I'll walk a little way home with you, and may be you can explain it to me. I don't see how a poor man can attend to these things, he has no time."

"I don't see," said his companion, "that a poor man, who has a soul to save, which is as precious as a rich man's soul, can safely neglect what his Church tells him to do, and live only for this life, and forget that he has a home to seek, in a better world, when time will be over for him."

"Why you speak like a parson, Will Jones, I declare."

"I am trying to tell you what our parson has said to me," said Jones. "I remember when I thought as you do now, and only went to church on Sundays, but since I have put the things of heaven *first*, I do not find that my business goes on the worse for it, besides you know we have evening services, on purpose for us working men. But now I will tell you what I remember about Lent, though the minister will do it far better.

"Ash Wednesday is the first of forty days, which are set apart by the Church, as a time for fasting and prayer, and humbling ourselves on account of sin, and denying ourselves, not only sinful pleasures, but everything which would fill up our hearts, and make them worldly. And the minister said, that though we ought always to humble ourselves before GOD, yet if we had not an appointed time to do it especially, we might neglect it altogether, and he said that the Church had arranged it before Good Friday, that we might come to the commemoration of our SAVIOUR'S sufferings and death, after repenting of our sins, which nailed Him to the Cross, and feeling our need of such an atonement. Forty days, you know, was the time that our LORD JESUS CHRIST fasted and suffered the temptations of Satan, in the wilderness, for our sake."

"I think we ought to confess our sin and pray earnestly for pardon," said Wilkins, "but fasting is not so much for us poor hard-working folks, is it?"

"Why I don't see that there is any question about it," said Jones; "our Church tells us to fast, without making any distinction, and we know that our LORD tells us in the Holy Scriptures, *how* and why we are to fast; not to seek praise of men but to serve GOD Who seeth in secret. Surely even we have enough of the good things of this world to deny ourselves many of them; don't you think we have? though poor we are not often starving."

"Why we have not often such a dish as the salt fish people have on Ash Wednesday, by way of fasting," said Wilkins.

"Those who think nothing seriously on the subject, and just follow an old custom, which was to eat fish in Lent, observing the form, and forgetting the spirit, of fasting, may do so; but depend upon it, they who really mourn for their sin, and desire 'to keep under the body, and bring it into subjection,' will fast very differently."

"How do you fast?" asked Wilkins.

"I never fasted at all, till two or three years ago, I heard a sermon about neglecting it, as a means of grace, and then my wife and I talked it over, and we asked the minister about it when he called, and he told us all, and much more than I have told you. We find the best way is to have no dinner on particular fast days, but tea and bread, and the children have as much of that as they like, and we can take or leave it, as our minds and bodies require. But you know, fasting is only useful when it is a sign of our sorrow for sin as well as a help to be more spiritual-minded; it can never be a good work."

" O no," replied Wilkins, " and if it were, such poor sinners as we are can hope for nothing by our good deeds. I am much obliged to you for all the pains you have taken; I will talk it over before Ash Wednesday with my good woman, for I like to begin as I mean to go on, it makes it easier in a new place too."

" You will find many here who will be friends of the right sort," said Jones.

" I am glad to hear it," replied the other, " and to think we shall have you and your wife as neighbours. We will try to follow your example."

" We will both try to follow a much better," said Jones, " but I think you had better talk to the minister."

" Ay, so I will," said Wilkins, " he was down with us yesterday, and I'm to go to him on Saturday, about little Johnny and Mary, that are to go to school on Sunday; they asked me what Ash Wednesday meant, when they heard the services given out in church, but I could not tell them why it was called so."

" Because ashes sprinkled on the head, as a sign

of mourning, was a custom observed in the Church at
one time, I believe; but when people came to be
more superstitious than religious, it was wisely discontinued, our minister said; but I think with him
that we are mostly worse than superstitious now; we
are more like infidels, and care little for our souls.
The word Lent, means spring, which is the time of
year in which this season returns. But we will say
good night now, or your wife will wonder where you
are," and with a hearty shake of the hand, these old
acquaintances, but new friends, parted.

Good Friday.

COLLECT.

ALMIGHTY GOD, we beseech Thee graciously to behold this Thy family, for which our LORD JESUS CHRIST was contented to be betrayed, and given up into the hands of wicked men, and to suffer death upon the cross, Who now liveth and reigneth with Thee and the HOLY GHOST, ever one GOD, world without end. AMEN.

ALMIGHTY AND EVERLASTING GOD, by Whose SPIRIT the whole body of the Church is governed and sanctified, receive our supplications and prayers, which we offer before Thee for all estates of men in Thy Holy Church, that every member of the same, in his vocation and ministry, may truly and godly serve Thee; through our LORD and SAVIOUR JESUS CHRIST. AMEN.

O MERCIFUL GOD, Who hast made all men, and hatest nothing that Thou hast made, nor desirest the death of a sinner, but rather that he should be converted and live; Have mercy upon all Jews, Turks, Infidels, and Heretics, and take from them all ignorance, hardness of heart, and contempt of Thy Word; and so fetch them home, blessed LORD, to Thy flock, that they may be saved among the remnant of the true Israelites, and be made one fold under one Shepherd, JESUS CHRIST, our LORD, Who liveth and reigneth with Thee and the HOLY SPIRIT, one GOD, world without end. AMEN.

"DEAR grandfather, there is a boy crying 'Hot cross buns,' do have some for breakfast, you know it is Good Friday, and every one eats them to-day; we can have two for a penny, just one each; may I run after him?"

"No, Jem, you know I never give you hot cross buns, and I will tell you why."

But I must first tell my little readers something of Jem and his grandfather. The little lad was left an orphan at the tender age of three years, and from that time he was brought up by his grandfather, Richard Barrow, who was a razor-grinder, and known in the neighbourhood where he lived, a dirty and dull street in London, by the name of honest old Dick, an appellation which he well deserved. By his industry he supported himself and his little grandson. Old Richard was not an ignorant man, some people said he had seen better days, and that misfortune had come upon him, but no one knew if this was so, for honest Dick never spoke of it, and appeared happy and thankful to God Who gave him health and strength to earn his daily bread. Jem was very fond of accompanying his grandfather in his rounds, and knocking at the doors to inquire if there were any knives or scissors to grind; but good old Richard generally sent him to the school, and he was always there on Sundays.

"When I was a little boy, that is many years ago, lad, I asked my mother the same question you have put to me, and she said the Cross was a holy sign, and that it was wrong to put it on feast cakes, and cry them about the streets. Do you think, Jem, that the boy you just heard thought of what he was saying, and the reason why the Cross is so holy?"

"No indeed, grandfather, I am sure he did not, for I saw him snatch a bun from a little boy's basket and kick it in the mud."

"I will tell you, Jem, the origin of these buns. Many years ago, when the feasts of the Church were better kept, and people were more devout than they are now, Christians used to come from great distances to worship GOD in His temple, for there were not so many churches then as there are now, and when they had walked very far, and were weak from fasting, or when they came out of church after a long service, little cakes were sold at the door, and had on them the sign of the Cross, to remind those who ate them of the great sacrifice which CHRIST made for their sins, but now this old custom is abused and it is made a feast instead of a fast. This day is a day of sorrow and yet of rejoicing, of sorrow for our sins, which required so great a sacrifice, even the death of GOD's only begotten SON, and of rejoicing in the hope which we have in Him."

"But, grandfather, why did the Jews nail JESUS our LORD to a cross? was it a very dreadful death?"

"Yes, lad, it was not only the most cruel, but the most shameful death; and don't you think, my boy, that we ought to love our blessed LORD with all our hearts, and regard the Cross as sacred, when He suffered so much to save us from the punishment due to our sins? The Holy Cross is a sign of our faith; do you not remember last Sunday when a baby was baptized, the minister signed his little forehead with the Cross, telling the congregation that it was 'In token that he should not be ashamed to confess the faith of CHRIST Crucified,' &c.? In the Gospel for to-day you will read the account of our Blessed LORD's crucifixion; find it out in your Prayer-Book, Jem, and then it will be ready when you are in church. Do you know the meaning of a type, my boy?"

"O, yes, grandfather; the master at the school told us the other day that it was a figure, or as he said, a shadow of a thing to come; and he told us that the brazen serpent which Moses lifted up in the wilderness was a type of CHRIST; and that Isaac was also another type."

"Yes, Jem, Holy Scripture is full of types; do you remember reading that a cruel soldier pierced the SAVIOUR's side, 'and forthwith came there out blood and water?' This, many think, was a type of the Holy Sacraments of Baptism and the Eucharist, or LORD's Supper. You have already received the Sacrament of Baptism, and it will be a blessed day to your old grandfather if he lives to go with you to your first Communion; but should it please GOD to call me away before that time, you will be a good lad, Jem, and daily pray to our FATHER to keep you in the path of duty."

The little boy began to cry, for he dearly loved his only relation, and the thought of losing him was dreadful to Jemmy; but old Richard told him to dry his tears, for it might be GOD's will to leave his old grandfather alone in the world; "but you know, lad," said he, "we must

'Leave it all in His high hand,
Who doth hearts as streams command.'"

"Do the Jews who are now living keep Lent, grandfather? for the other day I heard Mrs. Wilson say this was a fast time with them, and that they ate some kind of bread, but I can't mind the name."

"No, my boy, they do not believe in our Blessed LORD, but like their forefathers look for a temporal

King in the MESSIAH; this is, however, a holy season with the Jews, for they commemorate the Passover, which is another type of CHRIST. When the Israelites were in bondage in Egypt, and Pharaoh would not let them go to serve GOD as He had commanded them, the Almighty plagued the Egyptians, and as their king still hardened his heart and refused to let the Israelites depart, GOD smote all the first-born among the Egyptians, but commanded his chosen people to slay a lamb without spot or blemish, and sprinkle its blood with a bunch of hyssop, which is a bitter herb, upon the door-posts of their houses, and the LORD told them that when the destroying angel saw the blood sprinkled upon a door he would pass over that house, and the Jews were also to stay indoors all night and solemnly eat the flesh of the lamb with unleavened bread; they were to be prepared for a journey, for GOD would deliver them from the Egyptians.

"The Paschal Lamb, as it is called, was thus a type of CHRIST, of Whom St. John Baptist said, 'Behold the Lamb of GOD Who taketh away the sins of the world.' Isaac was another type of the SAVIOUR, for though GOD did not permit him to die by the hand of his father, Abraham, to prove whose faith He commanded the Patriarch to slay his only son, the child of promise; Isaac carried the wood upon which he was himself to be offered up, as our Blessed LORD bore His own cross; and we also must bear whatever cross it may please GOD to lay upon us in patience and meekness, and thus endeavour to follow the example of our SAVIOUR."

"How can we bear our cross, grandfather? all who love the Lord Jesus cannot be crucified as He was."

"No, Jem, by our crosses I mean those sorrows and afflictions with which it often pleases God to visit His servants in this world, that they may learn to 'set their affections on things above.'"

"Will the Lord Jesus" (said the boy reverently) "give you and me a cross, grandfather?"

"Yes, lad, I have seen sorrow, but God has been very merciful to me, Jem," continued the old man; "I will tell you the story of my life, which is now wellnigh spent.

"I was born in the village of Heyford, where my father kept a general shop, and was what people call well to do in the world; both he and my dear mother were careful, saving people, but were always ready to assist those who required help. I was their only child, and they gave me as good an education as they could afford. When I was twenty-five I married, and within three years from that time, my father and mother died, leaving me in possession of a good property, for one in my rank of life. I had long been anxious to leave the shop, and as soon as I could arrange to do so, I quitted Heyford. Your father was then a year old. I had been told that Liverpool was a great place for business, and thither I went with my wife and child. I had no experience in the world, and knew no one of whom I could ask advice, and my dear simple-hearted wife had no thought of guile; therefore it was not surprising that I fell a victim to the designs of an unprincipled man, who persuaded me to join him in some business which I did not understand, but he promised to instruct me; all my capital was invested, for he was so fair-spoken I trusted him implicitly. He deceived me, my ignorance of business made me an easy dupe, and one morning I was surprised by a number of creditors, claiming large sums. I sent for my partner to settle with them, but he had quitted the town, carrying with him my all, and I was thus a beggar, for my creditors were hard men, and they left us penniless. Bitter and revengeful were my feelings towards the man to whom I owed my misery; had I been alone, I could have better borne my change of circumstances, but my wife and children were dependent upon me for subsistence, and I knew not how to procure it. I had been taught no business, for though I had served in my father's shop, I disliked it, and was seldom to be found there. After applying at several places, I at last obtained employment as a porter to one of the large shops in the town, and received a salary of sixteen shillings a week; this was a great change from our former comfortable home, but my dear wife was so gentle and uncomplaining, and my little boy such a sweet merry little fellow, that I should have been happy but for one feeling, which I cherished as if it had been sacred; it was a deep hatred of my former partner. I brooded over my wrongs and his treachery, and vowed in my heart that I would never forgive him. When I had been in Liverpool six years, I had a dangerous illness, and the doctor thought I could not recover. I longed to see a clergyman, and yet feared to inquire for one, for I knew he would ask me if I were in charity with all men, but my wife went unknown to me, and fetched the clergyman of our parish. I had only seen him at church, for though he had occasionally called at our cottage, I was out all day, and thus never met him. When he entered my room, I was lying still with my eyes closed, and my wife thinking I was asleep, said to the minister, 'he has never been the same man since our misfortunes, sir; I fear there is something heavy on his mind.' He said he would sit by me till I awoke, and she left the room.

"I told him I had heard my wife's observation and that it was true that a heavy weight was on my mind, and then I confessed the whole truth, and how I had nursed my feeling of bitter hatred. He spoke to me kindly, and read the last words of our blessed LORD on the Cross,—' FATHER, forgive them, they know not what they do;' and then he exhorted me to pray to GOD with all my heart for that holy spirit of forgiveness. I told him that I had not said the Lord's Prayer for a long time, because I could not say ' as we forgive them that trespass against us,' but that I had that morning, with the feeling of a dying man, confessed my sin to GOD and prayed for pardon. The good clergyman often came to see me during my sickness, from which, by GOD's blessing, I recovered, and how heartily did I thank Him Who had not cut me off in my sin of murder, for ' whosoever hateth his brother is a murderer.' The kindness of Mr. Barry, that was the clergyman's name, procured for my son a situation in London, and thither we removed, and with some money, which our kind friend raised for us, I purchased my razor-grinder, for as a boy, I had often amused myself with one in our village; it has been my support ever since. You have heard me tell how your father went to sea and found a grave in the ocean, and your poor mother did not long survive him; but it is just church time, so come and say the hymn for to-day, and then we will go." Jem readily obeyed, and in a clear voice repeated the following:

> Whilst on the Cross, Thy latest breath,
> Thou breathest in the pains of death,
> Teach us, O CHRIST, to lift on high
> And fix on Thee our steadfast eye.
>
> By Thy Cross Thy saints are framed,
> By Thy Cross Thy love proclaimed,
> By Thy Cross is healing given,
> By Thy Cross Thou openest heaven.
>
> From Thy Cross, as from a throne,
> Thou shalt rule the world alone,
> Lifted on the accursed tree,
> All men shalt Thou draw to Thee.

Old Richard and his grandson went to church, and there heard from the lips of GOD's appointed minister, of His infinite mercy in sending to us His only-begotten SON to die for a guilty world; and perhaps amongst the whole congregation there were not lifted up to the throne of grace prayers more earnest than those which fell from the lips of the aged man and the young child, who form the subject of this story.

Old Richard is gone to his rest, and Jem, no longer a child, has his cross to bear in this life, but he looks beyond this world to that SAVIOUR Who is gone up on high, and has " received good gifts for men." The pious care of his grandson has placed over the old man's grave a stone, and surrounding the sacred emblem of our faith, are the words:

"BY THY CROSS AND PASSION, GOOD LORD, DELIVER US."

Easter Even;
OR, THE RETROSPECTION.

COLLECT.

GRANT, O LORD, that as we are baptized into the death of Thy blessed SON, our SAVIOUR JESUS CHRIST, so by continually mortifying our corrupt affections we may be buried with Him; and that through the grave, and gate of death, we may pass to our joyful resurrection; for His merits, who died, and was buried, and rose again for us, thy SON JESUS CHRIST our LORD. AMEN.

"Commune with your own heart upon your bed, and be still."—
Psalm iv. 4.

A palmer old and full of age,
Sat and thought upon his youth,
With eyes' tears, and heart's ruth,
Being all with tears ylent,
When he thought on years mispent.
R. GREENE.

MARY MELVILLE was the only child of a rich banker of Linford, a little town in one of the Midland Counties of England. She was a most favoured child of fortune, the idol of her father, the heiress of her little world, there seemed nothing wanting to complete her happiness. What was then the cause of the tears that trickled down her cheeks as she leaned her head against the open casement?—It was Easter Even, and the eve of Mary's birthday.—The moon was high in the heavens, but its brightness was obscured by dark clouds. The gloominess and stillness of the night seemed well to accord with Mary's feelings, as she thought on the nineteen years of her life that had passed so wasted, and so ill-spent.

She remembered the good resolutions she had made at her mother's death, which, not having been strengthened by prayer, had been forgotten when the transient feeling of grief had passed away. One Easter after another had glided by, and now another had come round, and still found her the same thoughtless girl she had been four years before. It was an awful reflection, nineteen years quite lost; and the thought that, perhaps, another year might not be granted her to amend, and that she, like the fig-tree, might be thought unworthy to cumber the ground.

———

Mary had just returned home from church, for in the parish of Linford Easter Even was always kept holy, and Divine Service performed at nine o'clock in the evening. It was the first time that she had ever attended those services in the beautiful old church, made more solemn by the lighted lamps scattered among the "o'ershadowed aisles;" the dim figures of the worshippers around, and most of all, the clergyman's earnest appeal to the people, made an impression upon her, never to be forgotten.

Mr. Courtenay had said in his sermon that, as he hoped all present had throughout Lent fasted with our Blessed Lord, and during the past week had suffered, and been crucified with Him, so did he hope that on the glorious morrow they also might rise with Him. "If so be that we suffer with Him, that we may also be glorified together." *

* Rom. viii. 17.

These words brought no comfort to poor Mary; she had not fasted with her LORD during the holy season of Lent, nor had she been crucified with Him, how could she then hope to be glorified with Him? These and many other thoughts passed through Mary's mind that night, she hid her face in her hands, and wept many repentant tears. At that moment the clouds dispersed, and,—

"The mellow and radiant moonlight
Streamed through the windows, and lighted the room, till the heart of the maiden
Swelled and obeyed its power like the tremulous tides of the ocean." *

Mary looked upon this as an emblem of brighter things, and remembered that "there is more joy over one sinner that repenteth, than over ninety-nine just men."

"One waits on high
To tell our contrite yearnings o'er,
And each adoring sigh."

Her SAVIOUR had suffered for her, had been crucified and buried for her sins, He would then, when risen, make intercession for her at GOD's Right Hand, and with this hope did Mary make a full confession of her sins, hiding nothing from herself, and ending with the beautiful confession of our Church. Midnight came, and still found Mary "watching." That Vigil was never forgotten, and formed one bright spot whereon to rest in the dark retrospect of her former life.

———

Easter Morning proved as bright in its fulfilment as the night before had promised. It was a beautiful

* Longfellow.

sight to see the multitudes of poor and rich flocking from all sides to unite with one voice in psalms of praise and thanksgiving, to "celebrate the appointed time, the solemn day of Praise." * The birds even seemed to rejoice, and united their voices in the loud anthems.

Mary awoke with a lightened heart, her good resolutions were again renewed, and again she prayed for strength to keep them.

She was fully aware that she had often been remiss in all her duties, and felt very anxious to lead a new life, but she was too ignorant of the state of her own heart to know where to begin a correction, as her fallings away after Easter Day too clearly proved to her. The more she thought the more thickly did her sins seem to crowd around her, and she was nearly in despair when she remembered the exhortation she had heard on the preceding Sunday, which counselled all those who could not quiet their consciences "to go to some discreet and learned minister of God's Word, and open their grief to him, that they might receive the benefit of holy comfort and advice."

Mr. Courtenay had such a gentle and kind manner, that not even the youngest of his parishioners were afraid to go to him in any of their troubles. His counsel was ever ready for the perplexed, his comforting words for the sorrowful, his strength for the weak, his prayers for the sick; he was indeed their pastor and their *friend*.

* Psalm lxxxi.

One morning after prayers, Mary sent to ask him whether she might have a few moments' conversation with him, and was accordingly ushered into the vestry.

For some moments her heart beat so, that she could scarcely speak; but Mr. Courtenay's manner soon reassured her, and she was gently led on to confess her feelings on Easter Even, her resolutions that night, which she had vainly endeavoured to keep, and her numerous fallings away ever since.

"Miss Melville," said Mr. Courtenay, "do not be discouraged by all these failings and short-comings, they are the necessary consequences of human frailty, and, I fear, that even yet before you can make any steady progress in the *true* path, many more troubles and disappointments are in store for you. There are few of us who have not suffered in the same way. I should advise you to begin immediately a system of self-examination, without which you will never be able to understand or watch over the state of your soul. 'He that covereth his sins shall not prosper, but whoso confesseth and forsaketh them shall have mercy.' * If you consider the daily omissions of duty, the coldness of your devotions, your many vain thoughts, and unkind motives, you will soon see the absolute necessity of scrutinizing your actions and thoughts every day.

"The less frequent the examination, the more difficult will you find it to remember and to repent of long past sins. How many forgetfulnesses, and negligences, how many follies, and how many actual

* Proverbs xxviii. 13.

sins must be forgotten, and go unconfessed, unrepented, and therefore unforgiven ; for how can we be forgiven our sins unless we repent, or repent unless we know them, or know them unless we think about them. You must not only think it sufficient to remember *what* you have done, said, or thought throughout the day, but also why you did it, whether with a view to God or the world. 'I thought on my ways, and turned my feet unto Thy testimonies,' said the Psalmist ; surely if David was walking in the wrong way before he had weighed his actions, *we* cannot be safe until we have ' thought on our ways.'

"This is the only way, Miss Melville, to lasting conversion," continued Mr. Courtenay. "It is mostly by little steps that we fall into evil ways, and how will you know when you fall out of God's way unless you follow your life step by step ?

"Do not be discouraged at the idea of reversing your whole life, of which, perhaps, you can scarcely remember a day; *do what you can*, and God will supply the rest. Bring back your past life before you, as well as you can ; some sin will surely be remembered. Trace it back to its beginning, and see whether it is conquered or not. Pray the All-seeing God to lay open your heart and to have compassion on your infirmities, and He will strengthen you. Only do not delay; time is gliding by, year by year passes on rapidly, and the 'night cometh when no man can work'

"Your examination should be daily, not weekly or monthly, as then so many faults will not escape your memory. When you awake in the morning set before you the temptations and duties of the day, and form the earnest purpose to give yourself up to God, and act during the day so as to please Him, and at night examine yourself, ' not lightly,' but truly, hiding nothing from yourself."

" I was never so thoroughly aware before," replied Mary, " of the absolute duty of self-examination, though I have often attempted to examine myself, especially before receiving the Holy Communion, but as I have had no method, I have too often neglected it. I should be so much obliged if you would give me a plan to begin on."

" Examine your life and conversation by the rule of God's commandments—there can be no better plan than that: I will write you down a few heads, but do not think I mean that the few I write down will be all you have to do. I only mean them as guides, the rest you must follow up according to your own feelings."

THE EXAMINATION.

Have I ever denied the existence of God, or loved other things more than Him?—Heb. xi. 6.

Have I ever been tempted to forego the love and approbation of God for the friendship of the world?—S. James iv. 4; 1 S. John ii. 15.

Have I always remembered the honour due unto God, and have I kept my tongue from talking lightly of holy things?—Ps. xcviii. 8; 1 Tim. vi. 1.

Have I observed all God's holy ordinances, have I due reverence to His house and ministers?—S. Luke i. 6; Psalm xxvi. 8.

Do I take God's Name in vain by inattention when praying, or by praying for such things as I ought not?—S. James iv. 2, 3.

Do I observe all the fasts and festivals of the Church, and especially the LORD's Day?—Joel i. 14; Acts xiii. 23; S. John v. 1; Isa. lviii. 13.

Do I honour and reverence my parents, obey them in all lawful things?—Ephes. vi. 1; Prov. i. 8; S. Matt. xv. 5.

Do I submit myself to my pastor, listen to his instructions, and seek his counsels in all my difficulties?—Heb. xiii. 17; Hag. ii. 11.

Have I put any restraint upon my temper during the day, and laboured to subdue my passions?—1 S. John iii. 15; S. Matt. v. 22.

Have I imposed on any one, have I repaid all I borrowed, and fulfilled all I promised?—1 Thess. iv 6; Psalm xxxvii. 21.

Do I avoid all lying and deceit, slander and evil reports, and take no pleasure in speaking ill of others?—Prov. xxiv. 28; Ephes. iv. 25; Titus iii. 2; 1 S. Peter ii. 1.

Do I avoid all covetousness and envy of other men's goods, and am I contented with the situation in which GOD has placed me?—Ephes. v. 3; 1 Tim. vi. 6; Phil. iv. 12.

Mary went home with a lightened heart, and strengthened resolutions to make a better use of the many talents GOD had trusted to her care. Her first act was to set apart one place in her room for prayer and meditation, with which no worldly thoughts were connected.

At one end of her room was a pretty oriel window which looked out upon a woody dell, through which glided the river; a little on to the right was seen the grey tower of the Church, and an old ivied ruin which had formerly been a priory, whose dismantled walls and ruined windows told a sad tale of puritanical zeal. This recess Mary chose for her closet.

In it she placed a little table, and a stand of devotional books.

It seemed indeed as you stood at that window and gazed at the lonely view beyond, that it was a holy place, into which no earthly thoughts could enter. The solemn stillness of the church, with its dark overhanging yew trees, the quiet ripple of the river, and the stately ruins of the priory completed the solemnity of the scene.

Here for many days and weeks did Mary kneel, and question herself concerning her soul. Alas! how much worse did she find it than she thought possible. Little weaknesses hardly known, sins long since forgotten, now rose up like phantoms before her.

Days and weeks passed, and still she found many of them uncorrected. How hard it is to conquer the faults of years! We must not despair if temptation after temptation arises, and still we fail; perhaps it is a trial sent from God as a punishment for former neglect.

Christmas came round, and brought a very severe winter. Nothing was heard on all sides but murmuring and distress. The little town of Linford soon became infected with the general discontent, and groups of people might be seen whispering in the street as if something was amiss. For some time Mary took no notice of this, but at length she perceived a great change in her usually kind father, everything in his house appeared changed in his eyes; he either was always finding fault, or sat for hours in moody silence.

In vain did Mary press him to confide to her what troubled him; he would sharply deny having any grievance, and then a moment after, with tears in his eyes, would stroke her head, and call her his poor child.

Poor Mary had no other comfort than in prayer, and she spent hours in her chamber, praying GOD that when trouble came she might be able to bear it, and that she might be a comfort to that parent, who for so many years had only lived for her. She examined her heart, and found how little she had ever thought of the day of adversity, and how she,

> "Unthinking, idle, wild, and young,
> Had laughed, and talked, and danced, and sung,
> And proud of health, of frolic vain,
> Dreamed not of sorrow, care, or pain."

The days were just beginning to lengthen, and the pretty spring flowers were peeping their heads above the ground, the birds seemed doubly to enjoy the mild spring after the severe frosts, and deep snow.

Everything looked bright and beautiful, and Mary felt as if she could hardly take in all the lovely things of GOD's creation. The day was so tempting that she resolved to go for a long walk to a hedgegrove some way off, which was famous for its beautiful wild violets. Mr. Melville was particularly fond of these flowers, and anxious to surprise her father with a bunch in the evening she wandered farther than she intended, and was obliged to hasten home as fast as possible to be ready for evening prayers.

Just as she was about to enter the Lich Gate she

saw her maid (still designated by the familiar name of nurse) running towards her. Mary's heart sank within her, for something unusual must have occurred, she knew, to cause nurse Aly to run, an event scarcely ever known to have taken place even in her younger days.

She was a truly good woman, and had lived with Mary since she was a month old, and for whom she would have borne anything rather than give her child (for so she always called her) unnecessary pain; but she was not very judicious, and upon seeing Mary, exclaimed, without a moment's hesitation, " O, come home this moment, dear Miss Mary, for master's dying! "

For a minute Mary stood perfectly motionless, but the fear of being too late gave her fresh energy, and she darted home like an arrow. At the door she met Mr. Melville's head clerk leaving the house in great agitation. " My father," she cried,——

" Is very ill, Miss Melville, but Dr. Barnes says he must be kept very quiet; you had better not see him yet——"

" O no ! Miss Mary," said nurse Aly, who came up at that moment quite breathless, " you will find master sadly altered."

" O, let me see him, I will be composed, indeed I will," said she, "only let me see him once more."

Dr. Barnes agreed that Mary should see her father on condition that she showed no emotion. He slowly led the way without speaking, but when he reached the bedroom whispered, " Remember, you will scarcely know him, but forget your own feelings for his sake."

Mary's feelings seemed worked up to a supernatural pitch, and without uttering a word, she walked up to Mr. Melville's bedside. One glance at his altered countenance told her her father was lost to her for ever.

Through that long night Mary watched by his bedside, and leant in silent anguish over his changed face, vainly watching for one sign of returning consciousness. Once he said "Mary," but in an instant he relaxed into his former state, from which nothing could arouse him. Before break of day, his body was at rest, and his spirit had returned to GOD Who gave it. The blow was so sudden that for a few days Mary felt quite stupified, but a dreadful feeling of loneliness soon came upon her, and the recollection that she was desolate—alone in the world—alone did I say? No, for she knew there was One Who would never forsake her, Who is "the Father of the fatherless, and a Judge of the widows." *

Mr. Melville had for some time past been engaged in unfortunate railway speculations. A rumour of this got about and caused a great run upon his bank; he was, however, able to ward off the evil day, but another fatal speculation ruined him, and that morning his bank had stopped payment. The anxiety of months soon preyed upon a naturally delicate constitution, and the shock of that morning had brought on a paralytic stroke.

* Psalm lxviii. 5.

After the funeral Mary entered upon the disagreeable duty of examining her father's papers, and found the utter ruin in which he had left his affairs. The little fortune she inherited from her mother was safe, but how could she consider this her own, when her father had brought so many in that little town to starvation? She had health and strength to gain her livelihood, which many of them had not. Her resolution was taken. There should be no slur on her father's memory if she could help it, all she had should be devoted to pay his crediters—and she was penniless!—but Mary was conscious of possessing industry and talent, and had no fears of the future. She wrote an account of her father's death, and the sad change in her worldly prospects, to a kind friend, begging her to procure her a situation as a governess. In a fortnight her fate was decided; on Easter Monday she was to leave her home for ever, to go among strangers.

Easter Eve again came round, the moon again cast her silvery shadows across her room, again did Mary Melville lean out of her open window, and again did she make a retrospection of her former life.—What changes had one short year brought round! The last Easter she stood there envied by many, but with a canker in her heart—this Easter Eve she stood there a poor, neglected orphan, but though few would have believed it, she now felt a happiness before unknown to her; for had not GOD shown her He would accept her endeavours to amend, and that He would receive her as His child?—" For whom the LORD loveth He chasteneth, and scourgeth every son whom He receiveth. No chastening for the present seemeth to be joyous but grievous, nevertheless, afterwards it yieldeth the peaceable fruit of righteousness to them which are exercised thereby."

Easter Day.

COLLECT.

ALMIGHTY GOD, Who through Thine only begotten SON JESUS CHRIST hast overcome death, and opened unto us the gate of everlasting life; We humbly beseech Thee, that, as by Thy special grace preventing us, Thou dost put into our minds good desires, so by thy continual help we may bring the same to good effect; through JESUS CHRIST our LORD, Who liveth and reigneth with Thee and the HOLY GHOST, ever one GOD, world without end. AMEN.

Thou art gone to the grave, but we will not deplore thee,
Though sorrows and darkness encompass the tomb;
The SAVIOUR hath passed through its portals before thee,
And the lamp of His love was thy guide through the gloom.

Thou art gone to the grave, but we will not deplore thee,
Whose GOD was thy Ransom, thy Guardian and Guide;
He gave thee, He took thee, and He will restore thee,
And death has no sting, for the SAVIOUR hath died.

"ONLY a week to Easter Sunday, and then I shall be a chorister-boy, Aunt Mary. I shall be so happy then: I often sit next the boys now, and I am getting on nicely with my singing: the organist says that I shall be admitted. So, Charlie, you will see me wear a white dress and take my place in the cathedral for the first time on Easter Day. You shall come and sit near me, and then, I dare say, by the time you are old enough, there will be a vacancy, and you will be a chorister too."

Charley seemed pleased with this thought, and

proud to think of his brother Frank being one of the boys, whose singing and whose white dress had so long been an object of admiration to them both.

Their Aunt Mary did not like to hear her little nephew speak in so thoughtless a manner as he did, and look forward to Easter Sunday without any thought of the holy event which it commemorates; but as she saw that the boys were full of fun and play at the moment, she made no remark, and waited for a better opportunity to talk to them about it.

Frank and Charlie Woodward lived with their grandmother and their uncle Robert, in a pretty little house near the cathedral of E——, they lived there because their uncle held a situation in the cathedral; and as he knew something of music, he had taught the boys to sing, and encouraged the taste which they had early shown for it. The little boys had no mother living, she had died when Charlie was born, and their father was a soldier, and had been many years in India.

Their grandmother was very fond of them, and if she had a favourite, it was Frank, who with his laughing eyes, and bright healthy face, was a great contrast to his delicate-looking brother; Charlie had a thoughtful look, and a grave, quiet way with him, which made some people think he would not live. They were affectionate children, though, as Aunt Mary always said, when she came from time to time on a visit to her mother, they were a little spoilt, and had too much their own way. The children were very fond of her, and when, one day, soon after Frank had spoken about being made a chorister, she called them into her room, they gladly obeyed, and were soon seated, one on her knee, and the other by her side; for Frank, though a fine boy for his age, was only nine years old, and his little brother was a year younger.

" You are looking forward very much to Easter Sunday, I know, my dears," said their aunt, " but I am afraid you do not think much about what that joyful day brings to our remembrance. I am sure you know what we commemorate then."

" Oh, yes, aunt," replied Frank, " it is the resurrection day of our LORD JESUS CHRIST. I know very well about it, but it is true I have thought of nothing else but about being a chorister; I can't help it, I am so happy. Henry Dickson, that's the best voice now, says that I shall be the second best of the little ones already, though I *am* the youngest," and the little boy began to sing a sacred air in a thoughtless way, as he spoke.

" I like to see you happy, Frank," said Aunt Mary; " I love you dearly, and I loved your dear mother, my sister, before you were born, and that makes me sorry to hear you so thoughtless about holy things: the cathedral is the House of GOD. It has been solemnly consecrated to His service, and He has promised to be present there. I am afraid that my little Frank will go into that sacred place, and take the holy Name of GOD upon his lips, and sing the praises of the Almighty, and all the while his heart will not be praying, but will be full of vain thoughts about which boys sing best, and such things; and if so, he will be turning a great privilege into a sin, and it will be a very awful thing; for GOD has said that He will judge those who draw near to Him with their lips, while their heart is far from Him."

"But the boys will make me laugh, aunt; some of them talk and play while the lessons are being read."

"I know they do," replied Aunt Mary, "and it is very easy to see, from the way in which they put on their surplices, and run shouting through the cloisters, that they forget in Whose service they are permitted to join; but you need not do wrong because others do. If you pray to GOD, He will give you His HOLY SPIRIT, and help you to praise Him with all your heart. There is little Willie Taylor, I do not think he often forgets that he is in the house of GOD."

"No, aunt, the other boys laugh at him because he will not play in the cloisters, and call him names."

"And whom will you be like, Frank? like Willie, or the other boys?"

"I will walk with Willie always, and I will be like him."

"I pray that you may have grace, my child, you must not trust to your own strength, or it will fail you. You will find it hard to keep down your own spirit, and harder still to bear to be laughed at; but when you were baptized, I promised for you, as your godmother, that you should be a faithful soldier of CHRIST. Now a soldier does not run away at the first sight of the enemy, does he?"

"Oh, no, aunt; what would father say to that?"

"You are not too young," continued Aunt Mary, "to begin to fight the good fight of faith, and you must either resist the world, the flesh, and the devil, in whatever form their temptations come, or you must be overcome by them, and be no more a faithful soldier of the LORD JESUS; but if you try to do what is right, the SAVIOUR will give you grace to overcome at last, though you may often have fallen into the enemy's snare. I think that you will have many temptations when you are a chorister-boy, but if you resist them, you will find it a great blessing to have been called so early to take part in the service of GOD. Do you remember the story of little Samuel?"

"Oh, yes," said Charlie, "his mother promised him to GOD at his birth, and she took him to Eli, and he lived in the Temple and ministered."

"GOD, who watched over little Samuel, and called him by his name, looks down now, as He did then, upon the little boys who are privileged to minister in His temple. I shall be very happy to see my dear Frank one of them," continued his aunt, "but I shall be very anxious to know that he prays with his whole heart, and that he tries to forget the people who are in the cathedral, except that they are fellow-worshippers with him, and to raise his mind to think of the holy angels who are there, unseen, and above all, of the presence of GOD Himself."

Easter Sunday, anticipated by the children with so much pleasure, came at length; a bright beautiful day it was, with sunshine that seemed to light up the city with gladness, and to speak to Christians of the rising of the Sun of Righteousness.

Charlie sat with his grandmother and aunt, on a bench opposite to that part of the cathedral where

Frank took his place. Their aunt was pleased to see that they both appeared to remember her words. Charlie did not look up and try to attract his brother's attention, and Frank seemed really to join in the holy service; he knelt that he might say a prayer, as soon as he had reached his seat; and his aunt prayed for him, that 'He Who has perfected praise out of the mouth of babes and sucklings,' would accept his prayer, and hallow his young life. It is not often that anticipated pleasure realizes the bright hopes we form of it, but Frank had begun his day of joy with prayer, and in singleness of heart had asked the blessing of God, and his Easter Day was as happy as he had expected. When the twilight fell on the old cathedral tower, and on the waving trees, just bursting into bud, whose light green contrasted so well with the dark grey stone of the venerable building, he turned from the window where he had been sitting watching it, and recalling one by one the holy strains in which he had lately joined,

"Are you here, Aunt Mary?" he exclaimed, "I thought there was no one in the room."

"So did I, at first," replied his aunt, "I do not often find one of my nephews so quiet as you are now; what have you been thinking of?"

"Of a great many things, aunt," said Frank, going up to her and leaning against her knee. "I have been thinking how true it is about God and heaven; I wish I could think of it oftener: I am always forgetting. Do you think that the prayers twice a day will help me to remember?"

"I am sure they will, if you join in them earnestly, my dear."

"I hope I did to-day," Frank replied, but then he said, " Oh, I forgot, you promised to tell me why the LORD CHRIST is called our Passover. Is it because the Paschal Lamb that the Jews were ordered to kill, is a type of the SAVIOUR?"

" It is, my love, and as the destroying angel passed over those houses upon whose doors the blood of the lamb was sprinkled, so it is the precious blood of CHRIST, applied to our hearts, in faith and holiness, which will save us from our death eternal. This may well be a joyful day to us, for if our LORD had not risen from the grave, the work of our salvation would not have been perfected. The Apostle Paul says, 'If CHRIST be not raised, ye are yet in your sins.' 'But now is CHRIST risen from the dead, and become the first fruits of them that slept.' The sting of death is taken away, and the Christian falls asleep in JESUS, his body slumbers in the ground, and his redeemed soul rests in paradise, until the 'Dead shall be raised incorruptible.' 'Then shall be brought to pass the saying that is written, Death is swallowed up in victory.'"

" I think Easter is the greatest day in all the year, aunt," said Frank, after a few minutes. " How happy the Apostles must have been, and the Virgin Mary! Do you think they knew beforehand how the SAVIOUR would rise from the grave?"

" Our LORD had foretold His rising from the dead upon the third day, and they had believed that the LORD JESUS was the true MESSIAH, and as such the 'Mighty GOD,' the 'Everlasting Father,' Whose kingdom was to have no end; but their faith had been sorely tried; they had witnessed the agonizing death of their Divine Master, they had heard the insulting taunt of the people, 'If Thou be the King of Israel, save Thyself; come down from the cross, and we will believe in Thee.' It is true that our SAVIOUR had told them of his death, saying, ' A little while, and ye shall not see Me, and again a little while, and ye shall see Me, because I go to the FATHER,' 'And now I have told you before it come to pass, that when it is come to pass, ye might believe.' But their beloved Master was no longer with them to speak the words of divine truth, and the HOLY SPIRIT the Comforter, Who was to teach them all things, was not as yet vouchsafed to them; they were now as sheep without a shepherd; a little band of afflicted men in the midst of their enemies. Think what must have been their feelings when the joyful news was heard at last, ' the LORD is risen.'

" Mary Magdalene, and Mary the mother of James, were the first to carry these glad tidings, for they had risen early in the morning of the first day of the week (which from this time became the Christian Sunday, you know), and had taken spices to embalm the holy body; but when they came to the sepulchre, they found that the guard of Roman soldiers placed there by Pilate, were gone away, in fear, and that the stone which covered the tomb had been removed by an angel; they ran and told the eleven disciples, and Peter and John came also, and beheld the empty sepulchre, and they returned to the others to confirm the words which the women had spoken.

" By this time Mary Magdalene was come back, and the women who staid weeping for their LORD'S body, saw two angels sitting in white, the one at the head and the other at the feet; at this sight they trembled, but an angel bid them not to fear, telling them that JESUS, Who was crucified, was also risen, and was not there, and called to mind what JESUS had told them concerning his resurrection the third day; after this our SAVIOUR made Himself known to Mary Magdalene, and from this time to the day of His Ascension, which was a period of forty days, He appeared frequently to His disciples: on the eighth day (our Sunday), when they were assembled for public worship; and to two of them as they journeyed, and talked of His death; afterward He was seen of five hundred of the brethren at once.

"We never read that our LORD made Himself known to any who were not His disciples, after His Resurrection. He had Himself said, 'The world seeth me no more;' but it was on these solemn occasions that our SAVIOUR gave to His Apostles that sacred commission which has ever since remained with their successors, the Priests of the Church; sending them to 'preach to all the world repentance and remission of sins in His Name,' promising 'to be with them always, even to the end of the world.'"

Twelve months had nearly passed away, and the season of Easter was again approaching. The child who had once looked forward to it so eagerly, was a second time preparing for it, but with very different feelings, for a great change had passed over little Frank's life. I will tell you his short story in his aunt's words: writing to his father, she said:

"We are very anxious about Frank: a year ago

he was a remarkably healthy child, and the life of the house; but a severe attack of inflammation, which was caused by a cold last Christmas, has reduced him to a state of so much weakness, that we fear he can never recover. His gentleness and patience in suffering have endeared him doubly to us; for several months before his illness, he appeared to have a growing love for heavenly things: his conscience was more tender, and he was not happy till he had confessed any childish fault, and received forgiveness for it; he was more obedient to us, and more than ever affectionate to Charlie. We shall indeed mourn him long. He took great delight in attending the services of the cathedral, and felt the loss of this privilege more than any other consequence of his illness. We are daily grieving and fearing to lose him, but should we not rather be rejoicing in the mercy which has taught him thus early to love the courts of the Lord's House, and prepared him for brighter joys above? We are sad at the thought of his death, but surely our Saviour has said concerning him, 'Because he hath set his love upon Me, therefore I will deliver him, I will set him on high, because he hath known My Name,' and this should be our comfort."

It was the evening of Easter Monday, and Frank was lying on his little bed alone, for his aunt had just left him. "Is that you, Charlie," he said, "I knew it was nearly time for you to come, tell me, what was the Anthem?"

"It was, 'Concerning them which are asleep, that ye sorrow not even as others which have no hope,' brother," said Charles. Frank turned his face away for a minute, for his eyes filled with tears; they were happy thoughts which caused them, but he was weak now, and could not bear any emotion.

"Charlie, dear," he said, "I think I shall die soon, and then will you remember those words, and be happy about me? I should like to die this Easter, if it is God's will. Don't cry, Charlie, you know we shall meet again. Look there, at my little pot of snowdrops, how fresh they look with their white blossoms. Do you remember what little cousin Eliza said, that she could not understand how the beautiful flower lay hid in the small dark root? so it will be with me; when the resurrection morning comes, I shall rise again, for 'them which sleep in Jesus shall God bring with Him,' and Charlie, dear, you'll be a good boy, and try to love and fear God. I hope you will be a chorister-boy, for I should like you to remember me in the holy cathedral; and still more, because I think it will help you to be good: it makes it easier to try to do right all day when you have prayed with all your heart, 'Vouchsafe, O Lord, to keep us this day without sin,' and you cannot encourage naughty tempers while you are going to say, 'Day by day we magnify Thee,' for that would be a mockery. Will you always think of me when you are singing those words?"

Charlie could not answer for his tears, but he threw himself on the bed by his dear brother, and sobbed, for his grief was great, and Frank stroked his hair and tried to soothe him. When their aunt came in, she was afraid that Frank had excited himself too much, so she led Charlie away, and talked kindly to him in another room. When she returned to Frank, he told her of his great wish about his brother, and how he was sure that the words she had said once to him were true, about its being a great privilege to serve God in this way. " I was often inattentive, I am afraid, aunt," he said, " and sometimes I used to draw in my book, and cut my name in the bench; but I was very sorry afterwards, and I did not do it any more after Mr. Brown, the minor Canon, talked to us about it : I know it was very wrong; I told Mr. Brown about how I used to do it the other day, and he said God had forgiven me for the Lord Jesus' sake.

"I am glad we live so near, it makes me happy to hear the organ, it swells so loud; I can follow the words every morning, ' O come, let us worship and fall down.' It seems to me to be like what we shall sing in Heaven ; and that thought makes me love to join in the service here."

Several months passed away after this, and Frank still lingered on his bed of sickness. One morning in August, the window of his room was open to admit the air, for he was very faint, and sinking fast: he lay with his eyes closed, and his aunt, who sat by him bathing his temples, thought that he could no longer hear the sound of the cathedral music, which was borne on the summer air, but Frank was following with his heart the strain he knew so well. As the Te Deum ended, the music was louder, and he raised himself up, and breathed a parting prayer, saying, "O Lord, let Thy mercy lighten upon me, as my trust is in Thee : O Lord, in Thee have I trusted——" and before the last words of the hymn died on the air, the immortal spirit of the child had fled.

"He that believeth on Him shall not be confounded," said his aunt solemnly, as she gently closed his eyes, and composed the little form for its long sleep.

And Charley lived to become a chorister, and afterwards a Deacon in the Church, and to sustain the duties and trials of a long life, with the hope that had cheered his little brother's early death. When he became a Deacon, his home was far from the city where he had passed his childhood, but he never sees the spring flowers without remembering the snowdrops that his infant hands planted in the green grass by his brother's grave, or the words of the dying boy, which had made them so precious an emblem in his eyes, of the Resurrection and the life to come.

"Blessed are they that do his commandments, that they may have right to the tree of life, and may enter in, through the gates, into the city."

Ascension Day.

COLLECT.

GRANT, we beseech Thee, Almighty GOD, that like as we do believe Thy Only-begotten Son our LORD JESUS CHRIST to have ascended into the heavens, so we may also in heart and mind thither ascend, and with Him continually dwell, Who liveth and reigneth with Thee and the HOLY GHOST, one GOD, world without end. AMEN.

"WHY are you putting out my clean tippet and frock, sister Annie? It will not be Sunday to-morrow."

"I am glad you asked me, Nelly dear. To-morrow will be Ascension Day, one of the greatest days in all the year. You know why we observe Christmas Day, don't you?"

"Oh, yes, because the LORD JESUS was born on that day."

"And if we ought to keep so holy the day when our SAVIOUR was born into the world that He might begin the work of our Redemption, do you not think that the day on which He ascended again to glory, having finished the great work of our Salvation, should be a joyful holy day to us for ever? Don't you remember last Ascension Day how father talked to us about it, and we went to church with him?"

"No, sister, I can't remember so well as you can."

"Very likely not, because you are such a little girl, so I must try and tell you all I know, as you have no better teacher. When you are a little older, I hope you will go to Sunday School, as I used to do."

"I am only waiting to see whether we shall stay long in this town, we shall see what grandmother says in her letter; but Annie, you know, we can never have any dinner if you don't finish your plaiting, and get sixpence for it. Must we go without dinner to-morrow?"

"I hope not, Nelly; see how much I have done already, that is why I have been up so early every morning this week, and why you have called me so often before I came to bed. I do not wish my darling to be hungry, but even if we did lose our dinner, would it not be a little thing to deny ourselves for the sake of the SAVIOUR, Who has done so much for us, and is it not better to let our bodies want food, rather than to neglect our souls, which will live for ever? All the good things which we can have, are the gifts of our SAVIOUR, Who has ascended on high to plead for us with His FATHER, to watch over us while we live, and prepare an everlasting home for us when we die; and shall we forget to thank Him for them? but come now, and hold my straws for me, there's a good girl."

"How fast you get on, sister, you will soon have done."

"Yes, and then we will go together to carry it to Mrs. Tate's, and she will give me a shilling, and we will buy something for supper to-night and for dinner to-morrow." The work was soon completed, and the sisters set out together; little Nelly springing for joy at each step, and holding fast by her sister's hand. It was pleasure enough for her young loving heart to be out in the fresh spring evening, and by her sister's side, for they were all in all to each other in the wide world. Their last surviving parent had died some months before, and his long and severe illness had wasted little by little the small property they possessed. His children, no longer supported by his industry, depended upon the scanty earnings of the elder sister, but yet in her eighteenth year. They rented a small room in the town where their father had died, while on his way to his own village in the North, which he was anxious to reach, in order that he might leave his children with some of their relations. His death, and the expenses following upon it, exhausted their scanty purse, and Annie, who had received a good education, and had had frequent opportunities of cultivating her taste for reading, as her father had been for some years foreman in a bookseller's shop, after writing to her father's relations, had sought and obtained work, which maintained herself and her sister for the present.

It was no wonder that she felt more than a sister's tenderness towards the little one, who had no other protection than herself, or that Nelly gave all the warm love of her heart to her who was at once the only mother she had ever known, and the gentle playfellow and companion of her young sports. Nelly was a simple, light-hearted child, but her early experience in sickness and sorrow, and of the serious wants of

4*

life, had given her a practical wisdom beyond her years, in many things, and Annie really felt, what she often said with a smile to the neighbours, that her sister Nelly was such a wise, useful little woman, that she did not know what she should do without her. Poor as they were, they lived a very happy life. It was pleasure enough to Annie, to work early and late for one so dear; and the little one grew up like a bright hedge flower, sheltered from much of the evil of the world, believing and doing without hesitation whatever her sister said or wished, for Annie's word was law to her, and her sister tried above all things, to draw heavenward the trusting heart that looked to her in all things.

Little Nelly woke with the birds next morning, but she lay quite still, watching her sister, who was yet sleeping; for she knew that Annie had been up late, washing and sewing their clothes, but she slept so much longer than usual, that at last she was awoke by two loving little arms thrown round her neck, and the words, "won't you get up, sister? see, the sun is shining in at the window, and remember we are to have *quite* a holiday, you said."

"Yes, a very happy holy day, I hope; shall we take a country walk, and go out into the fields before it is time for church?"

"Oh, yes, yes," and Nelly clapped her hands for joy. "I will make such nosegays, sister, they will smell sweet by your side, as you work, all the week."

The flowers and leaves had not shaken off their dew in the warm air of a May morning, before the two sisters had reached the green fields, although they had half an hour's brisk walking to bring them there.

Then they were happy indeed, they could not gather fast enough to please Nelly, who was divided between the fields rich with golden cowslips, and the pale, beautiful primroses, which shone like stars in the hedge-rows, and the little violets too, peeping out from their beds of leaves, with here and there a white one, which was esteemed a treasure; they were all gathered in turn, and she was tired out at last, and sat down by her sister's side to tie them up in bunches.

"It is ten o'clock, sister, I hear the clocks of the town quite plain, though it is so far off; we will rest a little while, and then we must walk straight back, not running about after every tall cowslip, Nelly, or we shall not be in good time."

"I will not look for one more," said Nelly, resolutely; "see how many I have got, and how pretty my basket looks!"

"It has been a great pleasure to us to leave the noisy town, and come out into these sweet fields, Nelly.'

"Indeed it has; I should not be happier if I had all the money in the world

"And so it should be with our souls; to-day, Nelly dear, they are living in the world just as we are in the town, to do the work which GOD appoints, but it is not their home, and it should not be their rest. In the prayer that we shall say in church in the Collect for the day, we shall ask GOD to help us, that like as we believe that the LORD JESUS has ascended into the heavens, so we may in heart and mind thither ascend, and with Him continually dwell; that is what we should try to do to-day, and not only to-day, but very often, for Christ has said to us, ' Set your affections on things above, not on things on the earth,' we should look 'not at the things which are seen, but at the things which are not seen, for the things which are seen are temporal; but the things which are not seen are eternal.' Do you understand what I mean, Nelly?"

"I think I do, sister," said the child, putting her hand fondly within her sister's, and looking up attentively.

"Do you remember one day, when you saw how many pretty things the little Jacksons had, and how they had a nice garden, and could dig in it, and money to buy seeds; you wished so much that we were as rich as they were, that you could not forget it all day, and you told me that you could not help thinking of it all church time next day." " Yes, sister." " Well, that was very wrong, you know; that was not being contented with what God gives us; and that was because you were thinking of this life as if it were our home, and wishing only to enjoy it, and that is what we are all tempted to do; and the way not to fall into this sin, is to live by faith, and to raise our hearts to heaven more, which is our true home. Do you think that if you had been alive, and living in Jerusalem at the time when our Blessed Lord was crucified, you would have cared so much about little things? Suppose that you had stood on Mount Calvary, and had seen the Cross raised, and had witnessed the death of the Son of God, and had been there when the sun was darkened, and the veil of the Temple was rent, would you not have thought so much ever afterwards about the love of the Saviour in dying for us, that nothing would have put it out of your heart?"

"I am sure I should," said little Nelly solemnly. "Or suppose again," said Annie, "that you had stood with the Apostles when the Saviour, risen from the tomb, and glorified, was parted from them and carried up into heaven, would you not have gone back to your earthly home, if it was ever so poor and mean, saying to yourself, as the Apostle Paul did, 'none of these things move me;' would you not have felt, I have a glorious home above, whither our Saviour Christ is gone before, whatever may be the life which it is His will I should lead on earth; whether it is long or short, happy or suffering, I shall 'rejoice, even in tribulation,' for the hope that is laid up for me in heaven.

"You would never have cared then, Nelly dear, about whether we were rich or poor; but because we live so many years after our Lord has ascended into glory, it is not the less true, His death was not less for our sake, and now we should ' walk by faith,' that is, we should believe and think of these holy things with all our hearts, till it is as if we saw them with our eyes; that is why the holy days are observed by Christians, that they may never forget the great love of our Master and only Saviour in dying for us, and the innumerable benefits which by His precious blood-shedding He hath obtained for us."

Soon the bells rang out from every church tower,

and the sisters quickened their steps; they had time to leave their flowers, and to fetch their Prayer-Books, and to be quietly seated in church several minutes before the prayers began. Nelly understood every part of the service much better than she would have done if her sister had not talked to her of it beforehand; when the hymn was sung, and a lady who stood near lent them a hymn book, she pointed with her finger to one verse, because, she said afterwards, it was so like what Annie had told her; it was,

"O grant us, Lord, with Thee to die,
With Thee to rise above the sky,
To spurn the things of earth, and love
The eternal treasures stored above."

And when the anthem was chanted, which was, "Lift up your heads, O ye gates, and be ye lift up, ye everlasting doors, and the King of Glory shall come in," you would have thought if you could have seen the child's earnest uplifted eyes, that the glorious vision of the Ascending Saviour was indeed present to her mind.

When the sermon was concluded, Nelly took the Prayer-Book and walked timidly down the aisle with the other people who were leaving the church. It was almost the only time she was ever alone, when Annie stayed to receive the Holy Communion; she did not wander about the churchyard, but remained quietly sitting in the porch, and the good old Sexton who opened the door after the Communion Service was ended, patted her on the head, and seemed pleased to see her learning the collect so busily; she did not talk much as they walked home, though she was so very happy, for she knew that when Annie had received the Holy Communion she was generally silent, as if her thoughts were very solemn.

If you had seen Nelly getting the dinner ready when they reached home (for Annie, who worked hard all the week, was to have a holiday, she said, and Annie gladly entered into all her little sister's pleasant ways), you would have been sure that she was, as her sister said, a useful little girl.

And very merry she was, too; and when she had cleared away everything, for she would do it all herself, she placed the flowers on the table, and brought Annie's Sunday books, and fetched her own little stool and sat down by her.

Annie knew that all this was meant to ask her to tell some Scripture stories, and so she told Nelly about Enoch, who was translated to heaven without dying, and of how all his life he remembered GOD, so that it was said, " Enoch walked with GOD and he was not, for GOD took him;" and of Elijah the Prophet, who was taken to heaven in a chariot and horses of fire; and many other beautiful things; and then she read again to her what they had heard in church, of how the LORD JESUS was parted from the Disciples as He was blessing them, and a cloud received Him out of their sight. And she told her that they should one day see the SAVIOUR reappear seated on the clouds of heaven, and all the holy angels with Him; for that an angel has said, " This same JESUS, which is taken up from you into heaven, shall so come in like manner as ye have seen Him go into heaven."

Then the books were put away, and it was Nelly's

treat to make tea with some of her fresh cowslip flowers, and no tea had ever tasted half so good, she thought. She persuaded her sister to take another walk in the evening, that they might gather more, and put them in a bag to . dry. Time passes quickly when we are happy, and Nelly could scarcely believe that it was so late when Annie said that it was seven o'clock, and that they must be going towards home.

Before she undressed, she answered her sister's questions so correctly, and said her collect and hymn so perfectly, that Annie felt sure that she would never again forget the day of our Lord's Ascension.

Whitsunday.

COLLECT.

O GOD, Who as at this time didst teach the hearts of Thy faithful people, by the sending to them the light of Thy HOLY SPIRIT; Grant us by the same SPIRIT to have a right judgment in all things, and evermore to rejoice in His holy comfort; through the merits of CHRIST JESUS our SAVIOUR, Who liveth and reigneth with Thee, in the unity of the same SPIRIT, one GOD, world without end. AMEN.

    O HOLY GHOST, Who didst descend
        At hallow'd Whitsuntide,
    With us, until the world shall end,
        And with Thy Church abide!
    Thou camest like the wind, with rushing mighty sound,
    And fiery tongues were seen to burn on all around.

    E'en like the wind Thou camest down,
        With footsteps all unseen;
    For only by the fruit 'tis known
        Where'er Thy grace hath been;
    Thy power to cheer and cleanse is seen in awful flame,
    The tongues set forth Thy will, the Gospel to proclaim.

    Thou dwellest with Thy Church below,
        An unseen present GOD;
    And in all Christian souls we know,
        Thy holy feet have trod;
    O Giver of all light, O Giver of all love!
    Fit us to dwell with Thee in Thine own house above.

WHAT a pretty little thing he is, mother! see how he holds my finger in his tiny hand; he will know me some day, and like to come to me. May I nurse him now?"

"Yes, if you will sit quite still, and hold him carefully," said Mrs. Smith, as she placed her infant in the arms of his sister, Emma (for that was the little girl's name) was much pleased to be allowed to take the baby. She had never had a brother or sister before, and she was quite proud of her charge.

"See, father," she said, when he presently entered the room. "How quiet baby is with me; what will his name be?"

"He must have your name, Richard," said Mrs. Smith to her husband. "I am glad we fixed on next Sunday for his christening, Whit-Sunday is a good day for it. I have been thinking about godfather and godmother; I should like my sister Mary to stand for one, and your cousin James would be a good godfather, and I am sure he won't refuse; but who shall we ask for the other?"

"Why, that's an important question, Nancy," said her husband. "You see James and I being both sailors, and out on such long cruises, even if we live, the little lad will have to look to his other godfather most; and if our ship should be lost, James and I should go together, so we must be careful whom we choose. Never look sad at the name of death, my dear, it is no nearer because we think of it. A Christian can never die before his time; we are in the hand of GOD at sea as well as on shore."

"What do you say to Edmund Jones?" said Mrs. Smith.

"I think we could not have any one more able and willing to help us," replied her husband; "Ned Jones is not the man to forget a promise which he makes in the presence of GOD, and if he stands godfather, we shall know that if our child should have the misfortune to lose his parents, he will be taught and looked after; so I will go and ask Ned at once," and with these words, Smith left the cottage.

He had not been gone many minutes, before a neighbour looked in to see the baby. " Well, Mrs. Smith," she said, " I suppose we shall have fine doings at your boy's christening, and your good man home sooner than you expected him this time, it's all as luck would have it."

" I am very thankful to GOD," said Mrs. Smith, " that my husband is at home to be present when baby is baptized. It will be a very happy day, but I do not think that it will be what you would call a fine party. We are going to take our child to church next Sunday."

" I'd wait till Monday, if I were you, and make a day of it; all your friends will have a holiday then, and you might have quite a merry-making."

Mrs. Smith did not like her little girl to hear Holy Baptism spoken of in this manner, but as her neighbour was a good-natured young woman, although very ignorant, she hoped she might be able to say something which would be useful to her, so she took the baby, and sent Emma up stairs.

" You must not be offended with me, Mary," she said to her neighbour, " you know I am much older than you, and you are but newly married; may be you have not thought much about what a holy thing Baptism is, or you would not talk of it so. My husband and I think it would be a great sin to make a christening an occasion for a day of mere idle pleasuring, it would be profaning a Sacrament, so to speak. You would think it very wrong, I know, to go to church and receive the Holy Communion, and then to go by rail and spend the day in the same manner that you passed last Whit-Monday, that you told me of."

"I have never received the Holy Communion since I was a girl," said Mary Grant, colouring; "I left home, and took a place in London soon after I was confirmed, and then I came here when I married; somehow I have not thought about those things since I left school, so much as I ought, but I certainly think it would be very wrong to do as you say; but surely a christening is a different thing."

"There are two Sacraments, you know," said Mrs. Smith, "Baptism and the Supper of our LORD. In the one, the gift of the HOLY SPIRIT is first bestowed, and by the other it is continued, just as natural life, given to an infant, is sustained and nourished by food. We fixed upon Whit-Sunday, because it is the anniversary of the descent of the HOLY GHOST upon the day of Pentecost. It has always seemed such a very sad thing to me," continued Mrs. Smith, "that Whitsuntide should be remembered, as it so often is, only as a holiday, and that so many should forget the reason of our rejoicing at that time. Surely the gift of the HOLY GHOST, the Third Person in the Blessed Trinity, the promised Comforter, Who came as on this day to abide in the Church of CHRIST, should be celebrated in a different manner. You know you told me, Mary, that you were quite uncomfortable at the gardens last year, because there were so many intoxicated and disorderly people. I think we shall not enjoy our holiday less because we shall try to bear in mind the subject of the festival, and to keep the Sabbath day holy first."

"Then you will take your baby to church on Sunday."

"Yes, for the afternoon service, that we may have the prayers of the congregation; the godmother and godfathers will come in to tea with us; we shall have a very happy evening. I wish, though we shall not have any other friends with us, perhaps," added she, "as your husband is away, and you are left alone, you would come to church and make one of us, we should be very glad to see you."

Mary willingly promised to come, and Mrs. Smith was glad to have an opportunity of thus bringing before her young neighbour a remembrance of holy things which she feared she had long neglected.

The following Sunday was truly a happy day in Richard Smith's family. "It is such a pleasure," he said to his wife, "to go to church, though, thank God, we have the same Divine Service on board ship; and to think that our little son should be christened my first Sunday at home."

They had heard a faithful sermon, in the morning he said, the text of which was, 'I believe in the HOLY GHOST,' and he repeated as much as he could recollect to his wife, as she was unable to go both morning and afternoon.

"I am sorry you could not go, Nancy," he said, "and hear it all better than I can tell you; the sermon is to be finished in the afternoon, however, so you will hear the last part of it." Accordingly, in the afternoon they went, with the sponsors, and Mary Grant, who did not often go to church, I am afraid, for she hardly knew where to find places in her prayer-book. There were several parents besides the Smiths, who brought their children to be baptized that day, and a pleasant sight it was to see them sitting together, with the little ones who were waiting to be received into the fold of the good Shepherd,—and if holy angels minister, as we are told they do, on earth, surely they were there, watching with holy joy over the redeemed children who were given back to their mothers' arms, "with JESU's mark impressed, to nurse for JESU's sake."

"My brethren," said the clergyman in his sermon, "we considered this morning the miraculous Descent of GOD the HOLY SPIRIT upon the Apostles, and the wonderful gifts which accompanied His presence, whereby the Gospel was preached in all lands. We have dwelt this afternoon on His presence amongst ourselves, and the manner in which he deigns to visit us, in the Blessed Sacraments, and in the words of CHRIST read and preached by His appointed ministers. We know that in the cleansing water of Baptism the original sin of those little ones who have to-day been made members of CHRIST, has been washed away, we are sure that the gracious gift of the HOLY SPIRIT has been vouchsafed to them, for they are too young to oppose by wilful sin the grace of the Holy Sacrament; but the seed of heavenly grace thus planted in their hearts, will grow up with the poisonous weeds of sin, which still cleaves to their nature.

"It is a solemn responsibility which rests on parents and sponsors, that of nurturing the germ of grace which alone can root out the lust of the flesh, the lust of the world, and the pride of life, and to train the children for whom they have besought the gift of eternal life, that they ' Grieve not the HOLY SPIRIT of GOD whereby they are sealed.' "

"Mother," said Emma, when they had reached home, "I have often seen babies baptized before, but I never cared so much about it, and the words which the Minister said about our SAVIOUR blessing little children, never seemed so beautiful to me as they did to-day."

"I hope," said her mother, "that you will always think in future how very dear the little children that you see brought to be christened are to their parents, just as our little Richard is to us, and then you will pray for them; but above all, we must remember how precious is every soul, since CHRIST has died to save it."

Emma liked very much to see her baby brother's name, and the date of his birth, and of his baptism, written beneath her own in her father's large Bible, and she admired the Prayer Book which her Uncle James, as she called him, who was one of the godfathers, had given to him, and which was to be put away for him till he was old enough to use it. I do not think that it would be easy to find a happier party than the little family group who passed that Sunday evening at Richard Smith's. Mary Grant could not help comparing it in her own mind with other evenings she had spent on similar occasions, where there was more loud laughing and talking, it is true, but none of the real happiness which is to be found only where the fear and love of GOD have a place.

Emma said that she should remember all about it, and tell little Richard, when he could understand it, how he had been nursed by every one there, and how his father had danced him about when he was such a very tiny little thing that she was almost afraid he would be hurt; she hoped he would not be a sailor, she said, and stay away so long on the wide sea, or she should be frightened about him when the wind was stormy, as mother and she were very often about her father.

She had leave to sit up quite late for a treat, and when their friends were gone, her father found in his large Bible that beautiful Psalm which tells us that GOD is every where present, and he made her read to him out of it, " If I take the wings of the morning and dwell in the uttermost parts of the sea, even there shall Thy hand lead me, and Thy right hand shall hold me. Whither shall I go from Thy Spirit?" " The voice of the LORD is upon the waters." " The LORD sitteth King for ever."

Emma had a great treat in store for her the next day. The lady who taught her in the Sunday School, had promised to take her with the rest of her class to pass the afternoon in some cowslip fields, as they had been very attentive at school for some time. The town in which they lived was near the sea, and few flowers grew in the fields where they usually walked, so they were to go a little distance by the railroad, and this was an additional pleasure. You may be sure that the eight little girls were ready in clean frocks and tippets, and with their baskets in their hands at the appointed time and place, where they were to meet Miss Moss, the kind lady who was going with them. Emma walked there with her father, and he thanked Miss Moss for her goodness to his child, and was glad to hear from her that Emma was generally well-behaved in school.

I do not think that there is a pleasanter sight than a field of cowslips in full flower. I am sure that the little girls who lived always in the dusty town thought so, and a very merry run they had, and fine cowslip balls they made with some string, to take home to their little brothers and sisters. When they had filled their baskets, and Miss Moss thought that they were in a quiet mood, and would attend to her words, she sat down with them upon the trunk of a tree, which had lately been felled, and talked to them about the feast of Whit-Sunday.

Many years ago, she told them, when Christianity was first preached, and grown up people as well as children were baptized in large numbers, they used to come to church on this day to receive holy Baptism, because it was the anniversary of the first manifestation of the HOLY SPIRIT, and it was called Whit-Sunday, or White Sunday, from the white dresses worn by them; she talked to them also of the miracles wrought by the Apostles after they had received the gifts of the HOLY GHOST, and then she reminded them that though the power of working wonders, and of speaking languages which they had never learnt, and of perceiving the thoughts of others, was granted to the Apostles alone, for the good of the Church, yet to each of them at their Baptism the HOLY SPIRIT had been given, that their consciences might be enlightened, and that they might be made Christians, not in name only, but in deed and in truth.

She explained to them the great sin of which they would be guilty if they should break the solemn promises then made for them, and reminded them of the awful end of Ananias and Sapphira, who had lied unto the HOLY GHOST.

At this moment they heard the sound of church bells, and after walking for a few minutes they came in sight of a village church; the children asked leave to join in the afternoon service, and Miss Moss gladly gave them permission, as she found that they would have time to reach the train by which they were to return afterwards.

"We are strangers here," said Miss Moss to an old woman who passed near to them; "can you tell me of any place where these little girls may safely leave their baskets and flowers before they enter the church?"

"They are welcome to take them to my cottage," replied the old woman; "it is but a stonethrow from this, and we are in good time, for the first bell has only now sounded, and, if you please, I will step back and show you the way. Wonderful times we live in," said the good old woman, when she heard that the children had come all the way from the town of P—— since the time of morning service that day. "I have lived here near upon seventy years, and was never so far in my life. It will be quite a new world, I say, soon; we old people shall hardly know it; but there is one thing which remains always the same, thank God, and that is His holy Church. When I was a little bit of a thing, ay smaller than you, my dear," she said, placing her hand upon the head of the youngest of the little girls, "I heard the same words sung that we heard yesterday and to-day :

> "'Come, Holy Ghost, Creator, come,
> Inspire these souls of Thine,
> Till every heart which Thou hast made
> Is filled with grace divine.'

"My mother taught them to me when I was but a young thing, and could scarcely understand their meaning, and now I join in them with my aged voice. I could tell you a story," continued the old woman, "that would fill your eyes with tears, only we have no time now, but you will not refuse to listen to a word of advice from one who cannot be much longer in this world.

"Never resist the Holy Spirit; never do what you know to be wrong, or try to put away from you the voice of God which speaks in your heart. I had a son once, he was the only child I ever had, he is far away now, sent from me by his own wickedness, and the last words he said to me were : ' Mother, I never did wrong but something in my heart reproached me all the while, but I would not listen to it.' My poor boy!" said the old woman. "I never see children now but I wish to warn them to escape his fate before their hearts are hardened.".

The children were much impressed by the solemn words of their new acquaintance, and when divine service was over, and they had followed her a second time to her cottage, they did not part from her without many thanks for her kindness, and promises to remember her advice. They had much to tell when they were once more with their fathers and mothers, for neither of them had ever been in a country church before.

"Where are your cowslips, Emma?" said her father, "did you lose them by the way?"

"No, father, I put them in the old woman's jar, for she has no son, and no other child to gather them for her. I only brought this ball home."

Her father kissed her, and said he was glad she had done so, and that he would rather see her a grateful, considerate little girl, than have all the flowers in the world. "And, Emma," he said, "pray to God that you may remember her words; the older you grow the more you will understand the blessedness of those who have not forsaken God and grieved away His Holy Spirit in their childhood and their youth."

Trinity Sunday.

COLLECT.

ALMIGHTY and everlasting GOD, Who hast given unto us Thy servants grace by the confession of a true faith to acknowledge the glory of the eternal Trinity, and in the power of the Divine Majesty to worship the Unity; We beseech Thee, that Thou wouldest keep us steadfast in this faith, and evermore defend us from all adversities, Who livest and reignest, one GOD, world without end. AMEN.

    Praise in the Church's highest strain,
     To GOD the FATHER be;
    And to the LAMB that once was slain,
     And, HOLY GHOST, to Thee!

IT was Sunday morning; the door of King's College Chapel, Cambridge, stood wide open, and people were thronging into it. It was a sight to remember: the glorious June sun shed a golden light on all around.

On every side were to be seen people hastening to the House of GOD: the sound of church bells filled the clear air, collegians in their snow-white dress, and the heads of colleges, in their scarlet robes, passed in all directions towards their respective churches, for it was Trinity Sunday, a high feast day in the Church.

Leaning against the great gate of the College, was a little ragged boy; he looked about him with the air of one to whom the place and the scene were strange: presently he got up and followed the people who were walking towards the Chapel; he waited until those nearest him had passed into the building, and then he entered himself, and stood within the door. There was a burst of holy music, and the little boy held his breath with awe, he gave one glance up the long aisle, and saw the sacred figures painted on the richly coloured windows, and then came the deep tone of the organ again, and he turned quickly away, and sitting down outside, covered his face with his hands.

"Why do you sit there, my boy? why do you not come in to the House of God? it was given to you as much as to any that are within these walls, you know," said a voice by his side, and the child looked up and saw a gentleman looking kindly at him; he stood up, and replied timidly; "Is the great God there then? I thought He was, when I looked in; I'm afraid to go there."

"The great God is everywhere, my child," continued the gentleman, "and He has promised to be especially present in His house of prayer; why are you afraid to go where you feel that He is near?"

"Because I steal sometimes, and tell my mammy lies, and she says the great God will send me to the bad place, but I can't help it, for I am often very hungry."

"And who is mammy?" said the gentleman, gravely.

"She ain't my mother, she's dead: she's father's wife though, but he's dead too, and I've no one belonging to me; I go about with mammy, and Jack, and Tom, that's her sons, but they beat me, and I don't like them, and they steal too."

"Well, my little lad, the bell is stopping, so I cannot talk more now, but after the prayers are over, you shall come with me, and I will try to do you some good, it grieves me that you know so little about the great and good GOD Who made you; come with me now, and when you kneel down in His house, say in your heart, 'O GOD, forgive me for JESUS CHRIST'S sake, and make me Thy child.'" So he took the child's hand and led him to a place near the church door, and then went on a little further himself.

Little Henry, for that was the boy's name, looked about him with wonder for some time, but at last he caught the eye of the gentleman who had brought him there, who was kneeling down not far from him, so he remembered his words, and knelt down and said them as he had been told, though he did not know who the LORD JESUS was: he was thinking whether the gentleman would tell any one he had been stealing, and wishing he had not said so, and whether his mammy would be angry if she knew he had told of Jack and Tom, when the music began again, and every one in the church turned one way, and he heard the words quite plain, "Whosoever will be saved, before all things it is necessary that he hold the Catholic faith."

Then the child felt frightened again, and he thought GOD was surely there, and that he should never be saved, and the tears stood in his large blue eyes, and he knelt down again and said, " O GOD, forgive me, and save me," with all his heart. When the service had ended, and the people were leaving the chapel, the gentleman came up to him, and signed to him to follow, and he took the little boy with him to his own home, and rang the bell for some bread and meat, which Henry ate eagerly. When he had satisfied his hunger, Mr. Barlow called him to him, and talked in a very simple way, such as the child could understand; he told him of God the Father, Who had made the world, of God the Son, Who had redeemed mankind by His death, and of God the Holy Ghost, Who sanctifies, or makes holy those who have been redeemed by God the Son. He taught him that these Three Persons were one God, that this was a great truth, too difficult for us to understand, but which we must believe, and that this Sunday was called Trinity Sunday because it was a day set apart that we might thank God for giving us the knowledge of Himself, and that the word Trinity reminded us of the Three Persons in the Godhead, and the word Unity, that these Three Persons are one God.

Mr. Barlow used a great many more words than I have written down, in the hope to impress upon the child's heart the great doctrine of the eternal Trinity, for it was a sad thought to him that an immortal soul should thus perish for lack of knowledge. He found that no one had ever taught Henry about his soul, or told him of the Saviour, Who died for his sake, and he determined, if possible, that this should not be his last conversation with the little neglected boy.

He asked him where his mammy, as he called her, lived, and having written down the name of the place where she was lodging, he let the child go, promising to see him again the next day.

Accordingly, early on the following morning, he

set off in the direction in which she was to be found, and after a long walk he reached the object of his search. Henry's step-mother and her two sons carried on the trade of travelling tinkers, as they said, or more truly as it appeared to Mr. Barlow, they lived by begging, and were seldom long in one place.

"This is not your own child, I think," he said, putting his hand on Henry's head.

"Not he, sir, his mother was a gipsy woman, and the child takes after her; he is a sore trouble to me."

"Will you give him to me, then?" said Mr. Barlow, "and I will see what I can do for him."

"It's joking you are, sir," replied the woman, "sure an the like of you will not be after troubling himself with such a beggar brat."

But Mr. Barlow proved that he was in earnest, and the woman was only too glad to be freed from the burden of a child, too young to earn its own living. Little Henry was too much astonished to speak, and could hardly believe that he was really to go away with the gentleman, who continued for some time talking with his mammy.

Henry heard him ask whether he had ever been baptized, and heard her say yes, that she knew he had, for she had heard her husband say that he had persuaded the child's mother to take it to the church, though she had not been brought up to any Christian ways.

Then Mr. Barlow gave the woman a present, and told Henry to wish her good-bye. He was glad to see the little boy shed tears at parting, though his mammy had not been kind to him, for it showed that his heart was not a hard one. It is difficult to say who was happier, as they walked through the streets together, Henry, who was lost in thought as to what was to be done next, and where he was to live, or Mr. Barlow, who was thinking anxiously how he should best provide for the temporal and eternal interests of the child he had adopted, for he resolved, that while he lived, he would consider Henry his charge. He stopped at last before the door of a small house, in a quiet street: his knock was answered by a clean looking woman, who curtsied, and seemed glad to see him.

"Well, Mrs. Morgan," he began, "I have brought you something to do, but I know you will not be backward to assist in a good work." Mrs. Morgan said she should be very happy to do anything in her power, but she looked at the ragged child in some astonishment as to what *was* to be done.

"Well, then," said Mr. Barlow, taking the chair offered him, "this is a little boy who is going to be my child in future, he has no father or mother living, and I am going to take charge of him. Now, I have no home to which I can take him at present, for he is too young to be left to himself, so I thought I would ask you to take care of him for me, for a time, and let him sleep in one of your snug little rooms, and provide him with some suitable clothes, for you will know more about such things than I do. I know you will be very kind to him, and I hope that he will give you no trouble. I am going to see about a school where he can go for some hours every day; I think I know of one where I shall place him altogether in time, but he must not go quite among strangers, and into all sorts of temptation, till he knows something more of many things, of which, as yet, he is quite ignorant."

Mrs. Morgan looked very pleased when she heard all this, and Henry liked her at once; he wished that he were going to stay there always, for the room looked so pleasant, with fresh flowers in the window, and a cat, with two pretty kittens, basking in the sun. Henry began to play with the cat, while Mr. Barlow talked in a lower voice to Mrs. Morgan, and he thought that he saw him give her gold, and he coloured red with pleasure, for he guessed that it had something to do with him. And he was right; that very afternoon he was washed, and dressed in a new suit of clothes, and Mrs. Morgan was almost as much pleased as himself, and declared he looked so different that the good gentleman would not know him.

Henry's life passed very happily while he remained in Mrs. Morgan's cottage, and she grew so much attached to him, that she always said she should miss him very much whenever he went away. He used to play with the baby, too, and was quite a good nurse, she said. He went daily to a good school in the neighbourhood, but the first thing that he did after breakfast every morning, was to walk to Mr. Barlow's house, and that gentleman always devoted an hour to teaching him. On one of these occasions, Mr. Barlow called the child near to him, and said, " I am going to take you to a school to-day, Henry, where you will learn to read, I hope, very quickly. You must not be ashamed because other boys of eight years old can read already; it is no disgrace, because you have never been taught; but I must not wait till you can read, to teach you what is in this holy book; young as you are, you are not too young to die; you remember the words you heard in church: 'Whosoever will be saved, before all things it is necessary that he hold the Catholic faith.'

"This book, the Bible, tells us all that will save our souls, and I will try and explain it to you, and teach you something about the great GOD Who caused it to be written for us."

Then Mr. Barlow read from the first chapter of Genesis, how GOD created the world, and said to GOD the SON, "Let us make man in our image," and of the Spirit of GOD, Who "moved upon the face of the waters." Every day added thus to Henry's knowledge of Divine things, and he learnt how our first parents had sinned, and brought death into the world; and how GOD had given a gracious promise that "the seed of the woman should bruise the serpent's head," that is, that one, born of a woman, should destroy the power of Satan; and he learnt how all the history of the Jewish people was to prepare the world to expect the SAVIOUR Who was promised.

And then he heard the wonderful story of the lowly Babe, born of the Virgin Mary, and how He was indeed the Eternal SON of GOD, One with His FATHER before the world began; and Mr. Barlow read to him how once more, when the second Adam, the LORD from Heaven, Who was to restore the creation that sin had ruined, was baptized, the Three Persons in the Blessed

Trinity were again manifested, for the HOLY SPIRIT was seen descending in the form of a dove upon the Son of Man, and a voice was heard from heaven, saying: " This is My beloved Son, in Whom I am well pleased."

While Henry was thus receiving the best instruction from his kind friend, he was also making steady progress in school, and improving very much under the judicious training of Mrs. Morgan.

It was not to be expected that, brought up as he had been, there would not be much to unlearn as well as to learn, but treated as he now was, with equal wisdom and gentleness, he soon became a different child. He could say his Catechism perfectly before many months, for Mrs. Morgan taught it him as she sat knitting in the evening, before her husband came home from work; and she used to hear him read over his lessons for school; he had no time to be idle, and all his spare minutes were spent in carpentering, for Mr. Morgan had lent him some tools, to keep the little lad out of mischief, he said. He soon lost all fear of his friend and benefactor, and he was very glad when he arrived early, or when Mr. Barlow was late at his breakfast, for then he could look round the room and admire the books and pictures, and ask any questions he liked.

" Who is that, sir ?" he said, one day, pointing to a picture of a little boy which was hung over the chimney-piece.

" This picture is the likeness of my son," said Mr. Barlow.

" And that is his dog that he is patting, I suppose Where is your little boy now, sir ?"

"He is grown up now, and is gone far away over the seas, to teach the Gospel to poor heathen, who know nothing about God; do you know that it was the thought of my own boy that made me first speak to you, Henry; for you have eyes very like what his were when he was your age, and you reminded me of him, and of how he has gone far away to teach his fellow-creatures the way to heaven."

"I was like a heathen then," said Henry, "I knew nothing about God."

Mr. Barlow put his hand on the boy's head, and he said, "I shall, perhaps, never see my son again in this world, but we shall all meet together at last, I trust. I have written to him about you, and when he writes, I am sure he will send you a message."

Henry saw that the eyes of his adopted father were filled with tears, so he said nothing more then, but after that, he was very fond of looking at the picture, and thinking of the little boy who had grown up so good, and who loved God so much, as to go away alone to preach in a strange country, as the holy Apostles had done.

One day, Mr. Barlow said to him, "Do you know that a year has passed away since you came to be my child? to-morrow will be Trinity Sunday again; I think you will understand more about it than you did then, though it will always be a subject which the wisest of men must believe without being able to comprehend, for it is far above our thoughts. You learnt on Christmas Day, how God 'so loved the world that He gave His only begotten Son, that whosoever believeth in Him might not perish, but have everlasting life.' And on Good Friday, you remember, we thought of the love of that SAVIOUR in dying for us.

"Last Sunday, Whit-Sunday, reminded us of the Gift of the HOLY SPIRIT, and to-morrow we shall adore the Three Persons in the ever Blessed Trinity, GOD the FATHER, the SON, and the HOLY GHOST, as Three distinct Persons, yet one GOD. And though we acknowledge many times whenever we meet for public worship, the Majesty of the Trinity, yet our Church has wisely appointed one especial day for the consideration of this article of our faith, for there have been in all ages, men who, in the ignorance and pride of their hearts, have refused to believe because they could not understand it.

"Can you tell me in what parts of Divine service we especially honour the Holy Trinity?"

"In the Doxology."

"Yes, and in the Te Deum, and at other times when we say, 'Holy, Holy, Holy, LORD GOD Almighty,' the word Holy is thus repeated in threefold worship of the Trinity. Do you remember when Mrs. Morgan's baby was baptized, in whose name was it signed with the cross?"

"In the Name of GOD the FATHER, the SON, and the Holy GHOST."

"Yes," said Mr. Barlow, "for thus it was commanded by our LORD, and we must believe and obey what He has taught us, though like children, we can scarcely know the meaning of the glorious words we say. Our SAVIOUR has taught us this, for when He was on earth He took a child and placed it in the midst of His disciples, and said that those who would enter into the kingdom of heaven, must be like a little child, that is, must believe with a simple trusting heart.

"It is by the gift of the HOLY GHOST that we are thus enabled to look up to GOD as our FATHER, through the merits of GOD the SON, our SAVIOUR. Our LORD tells us, 'When the Comforter is come, even the HOLY GHOST, Whom the FATHER will send in My Name, He shall teach you all things.' 'Even the Spirit of Adoption, whereby we cry, Abba, FATHER.' Was this great gift ever bestowed upon you, Henry?"

"Was it at my baptism?" replied the child.

"It was undoubtedly, and when afterwards, the seed of heavenly grace was well nigh choked, through ignorance and sin, was it not the watchful care of your heavenly FATHER which brought you to the door of His house, and placed you where you might learn about the glorious inheritance which was promised to you when you were made a member of CHRIST in holy Baptism?"

Year after year, as each sacred season came round, did Mr. Barlow strive to impress its teaching upon the boy's mind, that he might grow in grace and in the knowledge of heavenly things, and his labours were abundantly blessed: he lived to see the child of so much care and love bringing forth the fruits of righteousness, and proving his faith by his works. He lived to see him kneel at the holy altar, admitted to share the highest privilege, even to partake of the most holy Sacrament of CHRIST's body and blood, in that same church at whose gate he had once lingered a homeless outcast, and to bless GOD that he had been permitted to be the means of restoring this wandering lamb to the fold of the Good Shepherd, and Henry became in time, himself a teacher.

He obtained a situation as school-master, through Mr. Barlow's recommendation, and he often says that he could not have chosen any occupation which he should have liked so well, for he remembers his own early days, and he delights to impart to others the blessings so richly bestowed on himself; he is happy in the love and respect of his scholars, and unwearied in his exertions for their good.

One Sunday evening, Mr. Barlow, grown aged now, was sitting in his arm chair waiting, for Henry always passed Sunday evening with him. When he entered the room, he said, " Why, Henry, you are late, I have been looking for you this half hour."

" I am," replied the young man, seating himself by the side of his venerable friend, and looking at him with affection, said, " You know what day it is, sir, Trinity Sunday, and I have been explaining to my boys how we are indebted to that champion of the faith, St. Athanasius, and other fathers and confessors in the Church, for the pure truth which the Creeds have handed down to us; and that led me on, or rather, led me back, I should say, to this day eighteen years ago, and I told them the history of that Trinity Sunday when I first saw you, to whom I owe everything."

" To GOD be all the praise, my son; I remember well with what deep pleasure I first heard your childish voice singing of His glory; may I hear it again in that day when ' a new song shall be sung, as the voice of many waters, and of a great thunder,' and when 'those redeemed from the earth,' shall worship, saying :

"'We give Thee thanks, O LORD GOD Almighty, Which art, and wast, and art to come; because Thou hast taken to Thee Thy great power, and hast reigned. For the kingdoms of this world are become the kingdoms of our LORD and of His CHRIST; and He shall reign for ever and ever. AMEN.'"

S. Andrew's Day.

COLLECT.

ALMIGHTY GOD, Who didst give such grace unto Thy holy Apostle Saint Andrew, that he readily obeyed the calling of Thy SON, JESUS CHRIST, and followed Him without delay; grant unto us all, that we, being called by Thy Holy Word, may forthwith give up ourselves obediently to fulfil Thy holy commandments; through the same JESUS CHRIST our LORD. AMEN.

"COME here, Charlie," said Mr. Spencer to his nephew, a child of eight years old.

"Down, Fido, down," said little Charles, for he was playing with his dog when Mr. Spencer called him; "Will you tell me a story, uncle, and may I call Edwin to hear it too?"

"I do not know whether you will think what I am going to talk about a story," replied Mr. Spencer, "and I am not sure that Edwin is old enough to understand what I am going to say, but you may call him if you like."

Accordingly the two little boys were soon seated on their uncle's knee. They were children of a brother of Mr. Spencer, who lived in India, and they had lately come over to England in a large ship. Mr. and Mrs. Spencer had no children of their own, but they were very fond of their little nephews, and Charles and

Edwin were quite at home already, although they had not been many months in England.

"Now, if you will listen attentively, Charlie, and if Edwin will try to understand what I say, I will talk to you about many holy things," said Mr. Spencer. "To-morrow will be a Saint's day, a Holy-day of the Church, and that is why I wish to talk to you about it," said Mr. Spencer. "After the death of our Lord Jesus Christ, the Christian Church, or all those who became followers of the Saviour, and received the truth which was taught by His Apostles, used to meet together not only every Sunday for public worship, but every day.

"Christians, wherever they are, will be glad to embrace every opportunity for the worship of God, whether they lived eighteen hundred years ago or now. The early Christians, as we call those who lived soon after the times of our Saviour, met together to praise and pray at the peril of their lives from Jews and heathen persecutors; and we, who have no such trials, may well be careful lest we should prove ourselves to be less grateful for our privileges, and less frequent in our attendance upon the appointed means of grace than they were. But besides the weekly observance of the Lord's Day, which was called so, you know, because the Christian Sabbath was changed from the last day of the week to the first, which was the day of our Lord's resurrection; and besides the daily meetings for public prayer, it was the custom of Christians to celebrate many holy days once a year, just as we do now. Can you tell me some of them?"

"Christmas Day."

"Yes, that great day of rejoicing, what event does it commemorate?"

"It is the birth-day of our LORD JESUS CHRIST," said Charles.

"Can you think of any other great days?" asked their uncle.

"Good Friday, the day when JESUS was crucified for us," said little Edwin.

"And Easter, when He rose from the dead; and the day of His Ascension," said Charles.

"Quite right, my children," continued Mr. Spencer, "and besides these great days and others which relate to circumstances in the life of our REDEEMER, the early Christians kept days in particular remembrance of Saints, or holy people who, through the grace of GOD, had lived holy lives, and often died as martyrs by violent and cruel deaths, rather than deny the faith of CHRIST, and cease to preach and teach the truth which was committed to their charge. By degrees, these days became very numerous, and the Church now observes them all in one day, called All Saints' Day, when we meet to praise GOD for all His servants who have departed this life in His faith and fear. But the days which were observed in remembrance of the Apostles, of the Virgin Mary, the first Martyr, S. Stephen, with one or two other holy days, of which I will talk to you another time, are still kept by our Church, and it is our duty to observe them in the way she appoints. To-morrow is the day set apart in remembrance of S. Andrew the Apostle; we shall go to church and hear how he became a disciple of our LORD JESUS CHRIST, followed Him during His ministry on earth, and was one of the twelve who received the especial gift of the HOLY GHOST after our LORD's Ascension into Heaven. We ought to think of these holy and favoured servants of GOD, that we may imitate their examples and follow them as they followed CHRIST, holding fast the faith which they delivered to us, and which they received from CHRIST Himself. You will hear about S. Andrew in the chapters which will be read in Church," said Mr. Spencer; "but now, if you like, I will tell you something about him.

"To-morrow will be the anniversary of the day of his martyrdom; we read that he was put to death for being a Christian and teaching the Gospel, or good news of salvation, by being fastened with cords to a cross. When he saw the cruel instrument of torture on which he was to suffer, he spoke of it as a blessed means by which he should be taken to his LORD and Master JESUS, Who had hung before on such a cross that he might save him and all mankind. His death was most painful and lingering, for, being fastened by cords, and not with nails, he lived two days in dreadful suffering, but while his friends were unceasing in their efforts to procure his release, he prayed only that he might be permitted to depart, and be with CHRIST; and he continued with his latest breath to teach the people who flocked around him. S. Andrew was the brother of S. Peter, and, as we read in the Gospel for the day, when JESUS called them, 'they straightway left their nets and followed Him.' So the LORD JESUS CHRIST still calls us all to follow Him.' He does not, it is true, require many of us to leave our families and friends for His sake, and become preachers of the truth, as the Apostles were called to be, though this is still the duty of many Christians who can go into far countries and heathen lands to spread abroad the knowledge of the Gospel; but to each of us, to every Christian child, the LORD JESUS CHRIST says still, 'Follow Me; leave off loving and caring for any thing more than Me; remember that at your baptism your infant feet were placed upon the narrow road that leadeth unto life, do not wander away into the paths of sin; seek first the kingdom of GOD and His righteousness.' And do we follow JESUS? are my little Charles and Edwin trying to listen to the words of their SAVIOUR, and to say like Samuel, when he was called of GOD, 'Speak, LORD, for Thy servant heareth?' When the LORD JESUS was on earth He spoke by a parable, and called His people sheep and Himself a Shepherd, and He said of this Shepherd, 'the sheep follow Him, for they know His voice,' and then, looking forward to the time when we, who now live, should be upon the earth, He said, 'And other sheep I have, them also I must bring, and there shall be one fold and one Shepherd.' When the man out of whom JESUS had cast the evil spirit wished to leave his country and go with the SAVIOUR, JESUS showed him another way in which he was to glorify Him, and said to him, 'Return to thine own house, and show how great things GOD hath done for thee;' and so it is that in our daily lives we must follow JESUS by thinking before we speak, 'Will what I am going to say grieve the HOLY SPIRIT?' by lifting up our hearts, not only morning and evening, and in the house of GOD, but often during the day for grace to be gentle, and truthful, and self-denying, and humble, and loving, not to do our own wills, but the will of GOD, for CHRIST hath suffered for us, leaving us an example that we should follow His steps; and when we think of holy men like S. Andrew, who have gone before us, and been enabled, by the grace of GOD, to bear and to suffer, and to work as Christians, it should give us fresh courage to press forward, and to strive to do our duty in that state of life to which it has pleased GOD to call us; whether we are little children or grown up people, there are two paths before each of us, the path of pleasure and of ease which leads to destruction; and the path of holiness and difficulty which leads us to GOD. One of these two paths we must choose; if we follow JESUS, we know we shall be able to arrive at the blessed end of our journey at last, for He has said, 'My grace is sufficient for thee.' Will my little boys think of these two roads when they are tempted to do what is wrong, and their hearts say, let us do what is pleasant? There is a town in Germany where the watchmen used to sing verses when the clock struck the hours during the night; when it was two o'clock, they used to sing,

> 'Hark, ye neighbours, hear me tell,
> Two hath tolled on the belfry bell.
> Two ways before mankind are free;
> Neighbour, choose the best for thee.'

"Perhaps, whenever the watchman sang that verse, it reminded some one to choose that one and only way which was safe at last. The Bible tells us, 'there is a way which seemeth right unto a man, but the end thereof is death.' May you, my children, be kept in the narrow road which leads to glory. But now I have talked enough for one day, and Edwin looks tired; you, Charley, shall go to Church with me to-morrow, and you shall tell me to-morrow evening what you remember about S. Andrew."

6

S. Thomas's Day.

COLLECT.

ALMIGHTY and everlasting GOD, Who for the greater confirmation of the faith didst suffer Thy holy Apostle Thomas to be doubtful in Thy SON's resurrection; Grant us so perfectly, and without all doubt, to believe in Thy SON JESUS CHRIST, that our faith in Thy sight may never be reproved. Hear us, O LORD, through the same JESUS CHRIST, to Whom with Thee and the HOLY GHOST, be all honour and glory, now and for evermore. AMEN.

A SAINT'S Day in the country is indeed a happy festival, when the sound of the village bells is carried far on the clear bright air, and the flag with the golden letters inscribed on it, "All glory to GOD," waves from the church tower against the blue sky, and the villagers come out in their holiday dress, all walking one way, to the old grey church. Happy children are walking beside their parents, or winding two and two from the school, across the church-yard, that they may take their places early. Here is an old man led by his little grandson, there a widow with her little girl; she is going early that she may have time to visit her husband's grave, and tell her child about her dear father, who is dead and is buried there. The little girl is asking her mother now what day it is, and the widow tells her that just as she likes to think of how GOD helped her father to be a good man, and to pray that, through the Lord Jesus Christ, she may be saved too and see him again in heaven; so we ought to go to church on the appointed saints' days to think of the holy men who lived long ago, and who, by God's grace, were enabled to spread abroad the knowledge of His Gospel, that we too may come to the same blessed place where they rest now.

I remember many such peaceful scenes as these, but the story that I am going to tell you now is about a little boy who lived and died in busy, working London. The saints' days are blessed there too, for they cheer with their hours of sacred rest those who are toiling for their daily bread in that mighty city; reminding us from time to time that "there remaineth a rest for the people of God."

In the corner of a crowded street in London, two little boys stood trying, on a very cold winter's day, to warm their poor frozen hands by holding them in turns to their mouths; each held on his head a tray filled with white plaster images or ornaments. The elder boy, who was called Ned by his companion, and who seemed about twelve years old, carried heads and figures, while the tray of the younger of the two boys was filled with little houses, castles, and churches, with windows of coloured glass; the name of this boy was David Brown, he was a small thin child about ten years old, with blue eyes and light hair, but his dress was so untidy as well as old, that you would feel sure, when you looked at him, that little David had no mother to take pleasure in keeping him clean and comfortable; and this was indeed true, for both the boys were orphans, and lived with a master who gave them their food and a few pence a week for selling his wares; they might perhaps have had a worse master, for the man with whom they lived was not by nature hard-hearted, and treated them much the same as he did his own two boys, who lived by the same trade, but he had no fear or thought of GOD, and hard times often made him cruel and unjust, so that in the miserable garret where they lived together there was no peace or comfort, but the four boys constantly quarrelled and fought with each other, and all lived alike in fear of the master himself, who would be very violent if either of the boys returned at night without having sold anything.

The two boys were standing, as I have told you, at the corner of a street, when a gentleman who passed, happening to look for a moment at one of the figures on the tray of the older boy, was followed by him down the street, and though the gentleman refused to buy any, the boy still followed him, assuring him that they were very cheap. Little David stood still meanwhile, watching his companion's movements, and did not observe that some men were carrying large pieces of timber past him; he turned suddenly round at last, and struck the end of his tray against the wood, so that in a moment the pavement was covered with the broken fragments of his castles and houses. The poor child cried bitterly, and with such evident fear of his master's anger, that a gentleman who was passing stopped to speak to him, and asked him many questions; he promised to go with David to his master in the course of the day, and to pay for some of his broken images, and in the mean time he told the little boy that he might follow him, for he said he was going to visit his school, and then to church. So David walked along by the side of his new friend, he felt very strange, and hardly knew how to behave, for he seldom spoke to any one but boys like himself, or to purchasers in the streets, but he had not much time to think, for the streets were crowded, and he was afraid of losing sight of his benefactor. The Clergyman stopped at the door of what David thought a very handsome house, and he was surprised when he followed him into a long room, to see a number of boys of all ages, who rose as the Clergyman entered, and bowed, and seemed very glad to see him. Many of these boys were scarcely better clothed than David, but they were all clean and neat, and he felt ashamed, while he looked at them, of his own appearance; the Clergyman talked for a few minutes to some one whom David rightly guessed to be the schoolmaster, and then he turned to the little boy and told him that if he liked to put down his tray, he might sit with the other boys till it was time to go to church; so David sat down by the side of a little boy, who made room for him in a kind manner, and listened to the Clergyman, who began to teach the boys. Poor David! he was quite ignorant of the great and glorious truths of Scripture, and he was glad that no one asked him any questions, but he thought how much he should like to come there and learn.

The Clergyman asked what day it was, and one of the boys answered S. Thomas's Day, and he wondered what it meant, and asked the little boy who sat next him, in a low voice, who S. Thomas was, and whether the school belonged to him. The other boy laughed, and the master noticed that they were talking, and the boy told what David had said, so that he felt very much ashamed, but the Clergyman told him not to be afraid to ask questions about good things, though he must not talk to the boys in school time; but he said that he would talk about S. Thomas, that David might have his questions answered. So he began by asking one of the youngest children who S. Thomas was, and the child answered, one of the twelve Apostles of our LORD JESUS CHRIST, and at the mention of that great Name, it seemed to come to David as in a dream, that once, when he was a very little child, his mother, who had long since been dead, used to make him join his hands together night and morning, and say some words which he had forgotten, but now he remembered that they ended with "through our LORD JESUS CHRIST." David was so busy with these thoughts, that he did not hear the Clergyman's next question, and when he listened again, one of the boys was saying that the word Apostle meant one who was sent, and that the word Disciple meant one who was a learner, and then another answered a question, and another, and another, and David heard how GOD had made the world fair and beautiful, and of how sin came into the world and death, and then of the SAVIOUR, the LORD JESUS CHRIST, Who was made man, and lived a life of perfect holiness, and obeyed the law of GOD which man had broken, and suffered death for our sins that He might be our REDEEMER, for to redeem means to bring back a thing, and the LORD JESUS CHRIST gave up His own precious life to redeem us from everlasting misery, and suffered the punishment of our sins that we might obtain eternal life, for the sake of His righteousness. He heard, too, of how our LORD chose twelve from among His Disciples, and sent them into all lands to preach the Gospel, or glad tidings of Salvation to all people, so that they were the first ministers in the Church of CHRIST. Then the Clergyman asked if any of the boys could tell him what wonderful act of condescension our LORD showed to S. Thomas after he was risen from the dead, and David listened to the wonderful story, and heard how that Thomas had not been able to believe when the other Disciples said that they had seen their LORD and Master, Who was risen from the grave; and of how, when the doors were shut, where the Disciples were assembled together for fear of the Jews, the LORD JESUS Himself drew near, and said, "Peace be unto you;" and of how He permitted S. Thomas to satisfy himself that it was the very same body which had been crucified in which He stood before them, and desired him to place his fingers in the print of the nails, and in the wound made by the spear of the Roman soldier, for the LORD JESUS, Who by His almighty power is present in every place, had heard what S. Thomas had said, when he doubted of His resurrection; then S. Thomas worshipped Him saying, "My LORD and my GOD." The Clergyman asked the boys if they knew why the Church had appointed a day to be observed in remembrance of S. Thomas and the other Apostles, and the boys answered, that we may keep the faith that they taught; and many more things were asked and answered, and then the minister went away, and the boys repeated some lessons, and then they walked out of the school, two and two, and David followed them, walking with the master, who was a kind man, and seated the little boy next himself at church. But the church, O what a beautiful place it was! the sun was streaming in through the coloured windows, and lighting up the holy words that were written above the pillars, and the organ was beginning to sound. It seemed to little David as if it were a beautiful dream, and yet as if he had seen it before; he knew that if he had, it must have been long, long ago, while his poor mother lived, for ever since then he had spent his Sundays in playing and idling about the streets, but now he thought he could remember having been to a church like this with his mother, and something that she had told him of his having been there when he was a baby, and of having his name given him, seemed to come back into his head, but he could not remember distinctly, and he wondered he had never thought about it before; but now the service began, David could not read, and when the master lent him a book he blushed very red, and laid it down again, but he knelt when the others did, and stood up and sat down at the right places, for he watched what the boys all did, and it seemed to come easy to him too, and when the people all said, "I believe in GOD the FATHER Almighty," he was quite, quite sure that he had done that before, and he said "I believe," too, though he scarcely knew what it meant. David saw that the Clergyman who said the prayers was the same who had brought him to the school, and presently he preached a sermon, the text was this, "Now, therefore, ye are no more strangers and foreigners, but fellow-citizens with the saints and of the household of GOD, and are built upon the foundation of the Apostles and Prophets, JESUS CHRIST Himself being the chief Corner-stone; in Whom all the building fitly framed together, groweth unto an holy temple in the LORD, in Whom ye also are builded together for an habitation of GOD, through the SPIRIT."

David understood some of the sermon, though he was not accustomed to hear of holy things, for the Minister used very plain words, and explained the text very clearly; he could scarcely believe at first what the Minister said, that those beautiful words were said to him as well as to every other person in the church, and to every person in the whole world, however poor they might be, who had been baptized in the Name of the LORD JESUS: he could not understand all that he heard, but he learnt enough to know that if he prayed to GOD with his whole heart, and tried to keep His commandments, through the LORD JESUS CHRIST, that GOD would send His HOLY SPIRIT to help him, the same blessed Spirit who had been given to him at his baptism, and that when he died, he would be received into that holy happy place where S. Thomas and all the Saints of GOD were resting now; and that all his sins would be forgiven him, for the sake of the LORD JESUS CHRIST. This was some of what the Minister said, but, as I have told you, it was all new to little David, and by the time he had walked with the Minister to his house, and had had some dinner there, it had almost all gone out of his head, and the Minister was grieved to find that the poor little boy, though born in a Christian country, and baptized in the SAVIOUR's Name, had been suffered to grow up in ignorance of all that could save his soul. He talked very kindly to David, and then he took him to where his master lived, and gave the man some money, as he had promised, towards paying for the broken images; he asked the man to allow David to come to school, and it was settled that he might come on Sundays, though he could not be spared in the week, his master said: but when the Clergyman said there was an evening school on purpose for those who were busy all day, the master gave him leave to go, and David was very happy when he was told that he might go that very evening to the Minister's house, that he might show him the way to the evening school; he wanted to persuade Ned, his companion, and the other boys to go with him, as the Clergyman said they might, but they would not listen to him.

After this the Clergyman saw David always in his place in school and at church, and he gave him some clothes which were always neat and cleanly kept, and promised him a Bible and Prayer-book as soon as he could read; he saw him sometimes too in the streets with the row of little lighted houses on his head, in the dark winter afternoons, and he hoped that, through GOD's grace, there was now a light in the little boy's soul which would never go out, but which would shine more and more unto the perfect day of heavenly light.

It was more than a year from the time when the Clergyman first met David in the streets, when one day as he was leaving the church, a boy came up to him, and said eagerly, " O, sir, please to come and see David, he is dying, and he wants you."

It seemed, on inquiry, that the poor little boy had been severely hurt by a carriage which had run over him while he was crossing the street in a fog and in slippery weather the day before. The Clergyman lost no time in following the boy, who was no other than Ned, David's old companion; when they reached the room where the little boy was lying, the Clergyman saw at once that he was very ill, he was very much bruised and injured, and he had a great deal of fever.

When he saw who was by his side, he cried out eagerly, " O, sir, how shall I be saved? I have been so wicked and sinful, I shall die, and go to the bad place!"

" That's how he has been taking on all night, sir," said the other boy, " and I tell him he need not be so fearful, for he has been as good as a parson this long while, always a saying of his prayers, and reading his books, and begging of us to come to church, and he don't swear now, nor fight, nor cheat the master; I can't bear to hear him take on so about dying." And poor Ned burst into tears, for he had learnt to love the gentle little boy who was now dying, and he wished that he had been kinder to him, and had not mocked him, and called him saint and parson, and other good names in ridicule.

Then the Clergyman sat down by the little suf

fering boy, and talked very solemnly to him, and Ned stood in the other corner of the room, and he heard David telling how wicked he had been, and of many, many naughty things he had done all his life, and since he had known how sinful they were; and he heard the Clergyman say, " My little boy, we are all sinful creatures, we all do wicked things, and we think evil thoughts continually. It is true that you have done nothing that can deserve heaven, but on the contrary, if you were judged by your works you must go to hell, but you know Who it is that has died to save you, and if you put your trust in Him you will be saved and forgiven for His sake.

Then little David looked up and smiled, and the words that he said in church came into his mind, for he exclaimed earnestly, " O LORD, in Thee have I trusted." Then the Minister talked to him of the love of GOD that had watched over him since his baptism, and of how the HOLY SPIRIT had striven with the evil nature that was within him, and that every time he had resisted sin he had, through GOD's grace, obtained a victory, and proved that his faith in the LORD JESUS CHRIST was a true faith, the gift of the HOLY SPIRIT; and then he prayed by the little boy's side, and blessed him, and promised to come and see him the next day. David was very happy after his kind friend had left him, and he told Ned that he was not afraid to die now, for that he believed that his sins were all forgiven him for the sake of the SAVIOUR. Towards the night he became wandering in his head, and though he took some medicine that a good doctor brought him, he became worse very fast, he talked aloud as if he were dreaming, but his dreams were very happy ones, sometimes he thought he was in church, and he would sing and seem to join in the service, and then again he would talk about his mother, whom he had not seen for so long.

When the Clergyman came the next day he saw that little David had not long to live in this world, but he rejoiced to think that the child would soon be taken where sin and sorrow would never reach him more. He told David what he thought, very gently, for the little boy was very weak, and when he told him, the tears ran down the child's cheeks, not because he was unhappy, or afraid to die, but because he felt what a solemn thing it was to go into the presence of God. "Oh, sir, will you pray with me; will you pray that I may be forgiven, for JESUS' sake?" and the little boy bowed his head and joined his hands in prayer, and the Minister prayed often by him, for little David lived nearly a week after this; he was never afraid of death, and at last he longed to go, and used to ask the doctor how much longer he thought he should live. He became gradually weaker and weaker, but as long as he could speak he used to say kind and gentle words to his companions, thanking them again and again for all they did for him, and begging them after he was dead to go to church, and to go to the Minister, and the school, for his sake.

One morning when the Clergyman opened the door of the room where he had visited the little boy so often, he found that he was dead; he had died about half an hour before, and his hands were folded as if his last thought had been a prayer, and so it was, for the Clergyman heard that after a severe fit of pain, the little boy had raised himself in the bed, and said, "LORD JESUS, receive my spirit," and even as he spoke his spirit had fled.

Happy little David! who could weep that his young spirit had been early taken to the blessed world he had learned to love; that He, Who when He was on earth, had uttered those gracious words, "Suffer the little children to come unto Me, for of such is the kingdom of heaven," had gathered this little lamb safely to the blessed fold above?

A few days after this a funeral passed through the streets to the church where little David had first been taken by the Clergyman. The little boy's remains were followed by the companions whom he had so often warned while he lived, and whose hearts seemed touched by his death, and the remembrance of his piety.

His life on earth had been short, but the good that he had tried to do in the Name of the LORD JESUS did not fall to the ground. After his funeral, the three boys who had neglected his advice while he lived, became regular attendants upon the church and school, and some months afterwards the Minister observed with pleasure that David's old master accompanied his sons to church; he no longer avoided the Minister when he visited him, and became, through the grace of GOD, an altered character.

Thus it is that little David, like one of old, "being dead, yet speaketh." You will easily believe that the Clergyman who first met the little boy on S. Thomas's Day, never fails to remember him, and to thank GOD on that day, that he may think of him with humble confidence as among the company of just men made perfect.

> "Both need the same protecting grace,
> To keep them undefiled,
> And both shall in Thy presence stand,
> Thy martyr and Thy child."

S. Stephen's Day.

COLLECT.

GRANT, O LORD, that, in all our sufferings here upon earth for the testimony of Thy truth, we may steadfastly look up to heaven, and by faith behold the glory that shall be revealed; and being filled with the HOLY GHOST, may learn to love and bless our persecutors, by the example of Thy first Martyr, Saint Stephen, who prayed for his murderers to Thee, O blessed JESUS, Who standest at the right hand of GOD, to succour all those who suffer for Thee, our only Mediator and Advocate. AMEN.

LITTLE Stephen Harris was the son of a fisherman, who lived on the eastern coast of England; his parents were poor, and their house, which was very small, and built chiefly of pieces of old ships, looked more like a boat than a cottage, but every thing inside it looked clean and pleasant, for Stephen's father had a good wife who loved to make her husband comfortable, and when he came back cold and tired, after two or three days' fishing on the rough seas, he always found a blazing fire and a hot supper waiting for him, and his clothes neatly mended; and what he valued still more, a loving welcome from his wife and little boy. Many of Harris's neighbours were richer than he was, and returned home to find better food and clothes than he did, but in all the hamlet there were no happier faces to be seen than in John Harris's cottage, when he had returned in safety to his family, and was sitting by the fire with his little boy on his knee, or netting busily at his feet, listening to stories of the stormy sea, while his wife sat darning stockings at his side; and opposite the fisherman, in the warmest corner, sat his aged mother, who always lived with them, now that she was too old to take care of herself. She had been a good mother to John Harris, and when he was a child she had often worked up to a late hour in the night, because she had spent the evenings in teaching her boy to read the Bible, and learn the Catechism, after he came home from his work, and she had her reward now in her son's love and duty.

Often, when he had read a chapter before they went to bed, he used to say, taking her hand in his, "God gave me a good mother, that was the first blessing of my life;" and little Stephen would think how truly he might say the same, and how, when he grew to be a man, he would be like his father, and work for his mother; and he would climb on her knee and kiss her heartily, and then his grandmother would pat his rosy cheek and say, "That is right, my boy, you can never love her too well; take after your father, and she will never have a heavy heart."

So it was, that though trouble and poverty often came into Harris's little dwelling, it was all made lighter by love; they worked hard for a living, but they were never without necessary food and clothing, for they lived in the fear of God, and His blessing was on the work of their hands.

Stephen was about nine years old at this time, he was a pretty little fellow, with an honest, healthy face and curling hair; he was small for his age, and always went by the name of "Little Stephen." He was a favourite with his companions because he was good natured, though a few naughty boys used to tease him because he would not join in their games on Sunday, or use bad words, and this was a trial to little Stephen, for he was a timid child, and of a gentle spirit.

One cold winter evening he went to bed very happy, for the next day was his birth-day, and he was to wear a new worsted comforter that his mother had knitted for him; he was so happy that he could not sleep, and after he was in bed he called out to his mother, " I shall go to church with father to-morrow, shan't I, mother ? "

" Yes," answered his mother, " and I think I can go too, if I can get neighbour Thompson to sit with your grandmother till I come back."

Little Stephen was very glad to hear this, for his father and mother used to take it by turns to stay with his grandmother, and he was very happy when he went out with them both. Presently he spoke again.

" Why was I called Stephen ? was I born on S. Stephen's Day, mother ? "

" Yes, you were born on S. Stephen's Day, and your grandfather's name was Stephen, so we had two reasons for giving you that name," said his mother.

The little boy knew the history of S. Stephen, for he had often read to his mother the account of the life and death of this holy man, which we read in the Acts of the Apostles; how, being full of faith and of the Holy Ghost, he had worked miracles, and done great wonders among the people, until he was falsely accused and brought before the council, when after boldly declaring to them the truth, his enemies put him to a cruel death, by throwing stones at him till he died; and how God had permitted Stephen, the first of the Christian Martyrs, to see in a glorious vision, before he died, heaven opened, and Jesus standing at the right hand of God; and had given him grace to die as his Divine Master had done, praying for his murderers. Little Stephen said to his mother when she told him that they should go to church on S. Stephen's Day, that they might learn to imitate his example, "Mother, I cannot be like S. Stephen, for I have no enemies."

His mother said she would talk to him about that another time.

The next morning he was to set off early with his father and mother, for the church was a good way off, at the top of a hill, so that they walked nearly a quarter of a mile before they even heard the bell. Before they went, Stephen ran down to the beach to help his father to bring up some nets, which were lying too near the sea, and they saw that there was a large net just brought in, and so many fish were taken, that the children who helped to bring the net to shore were allowed to have some of them. The boys called Stephen to come and have his share, but he said he was going to church; upon this several of them laughed at him, and called him names, and one great boy in particular threw water at him, and tried to provoke him to fight. I do not know how it might have ended, if his father had not come up just then and taken him by the hand. While they were walking to church, Stephen told his mother about the boys, and how one of them, Luke Jones, had ill-treated him, and tried to tear his new comforter. And she said how he could now try to be like S. Stephen; and she told his father how Stephen had thought he could have no enemies to forgive. His father explained to him how, if he forgave Luke and all the rest of the boys, with his whole heart, and played good-naturedly with them, and when they laughed at him for going to church, only said he wished they would come too, and if he remembered to pray for them, he would be following the example of S. Stephen, and what was still more, he would be walking in the steps of the LORD JESUS CHRIST, and obeying His commandments.

Stephen listened attentively to his father, and walked thoughtfully by his side; when they reached the church the bells had not ceased ringing, so they sat down to rest outside the churchyard. Stephen opened his Prayer-Book, which had been given him at the Sunday School, and read the collect for the day very carefully; he knew he should be questioned about it at school on Sunday. When the Rector came in sight, Stephen shut the book and rose up, for he knew it was time to go in to church, and he took off his cap and made a respectful bow to the Minister, as he saw his father do, and all the men who were waiting near the church. The Clergyman spoke kindly to several of them, and amongst the rest to John Harris and his wife, who were very old parishioners of his. Stephen did not sit with his parents in church, as he was one of those boys who had been chosen by the Rector, on account of their steady behaviour, and because they had good voices, to assist in singing the praises of GOD in the church. Stephen knew that this was a great honour and privilege, and he not only took great pains to learn how to sing from his master, who came once a week to teach the boys, but he tried to think always of the holy words he was singing, and to remember that he was addressing the great GOD, and joining in a solemn act of worship; he listened attentively to the sermon, in which the Clergyman spoke often about S. Stephen, and in which he exhorted the people to follow his holy example, and live not only in peace with all men, but in Christian forgiveness of those who had in any way injured them; and to remember that the glorious vision of heaven which S. Stephen had been permitted to behold, even while on earth, would most surely be the portion of every Christian who lived, through grace, here in a state of preparation for glory hereafter.

When the service was ended, Stephen joined his parents, and a very happy walk home he had with them, and a merry dinner, for his mother made him a plum pudding, and gave him leave to bring two little neighbours to share it with him. And he was still happier that evening, before he went to bed, when he said to his mother, "I have tried to forgive Luke and the other boys with all my heart, mother; I have been playing with them, and I helped Luke to mend his nets."

Thus Stephen tried to forgive as he wished to be

forgiven; when he repeated the LORD's Prayer that night, he thought he never could have said it if he had not quite forgiven those who had been unkind to him.

I never heard whether Luke continued to treat him badly, but I think it is most likely that little Stephen found how true was the proverb of the wise man " A soft answer turneth away wrath."

S. John Evangelist's Day.

COLLECT.

MERCIFUL LORD, we beseech Thee to cast Thy bright beams of light upon Thy Church, that it being instructed by the doctrine of Thy blessed Apostle and Evangelist Saint John, may so walk in the light of Thy truth, that it may at length attain to everlasting life; through JESUS CHRIST our LORD. AMEN.

IT is a Saint's Day! The day which we observe in remembrance of S. John the Evangelist, in order that we may learn and obey the blessed truths which he taught us by his example, and in his inspired writings. Eighteen hundred years ago, the HOLY GHOST, speaking through the agency of this favoured Disciple of our LORD JESUS CHRIST said, "Love not the world, neither the things that are in the world; if any man love the world, the love of the FATHER is not in him."—1 S. John ii. 15.

"My little children, let us not love in word, neither in tongue, but in deed and in truth."—1 S. John iii. 18.

Love to GOD and love to man, were the holy lessons which this disciple, "whom JESUS loved," most desired to teach, and, indeed, every Christian grace may be included in these two precepts, "for love is the fulfilling of the law."

S. John is supposed to have been very young when he first became a Disciple of our LORD JESUS CHRIST; with S. Peter and S. James he witnessed the transfiguration, and most of the remarkable miracles of our LORD.

Admitted to such close communion with his Divine Master, his heart was doubtless daily growing in holy love. Standing alone of all the Disciples at the foot of the Cross, he was chosen by the dying SAVIOUR to fill the place of a son to his afflicted mother, the blessed Virgin Mary; after this he lived a long life of toil in the service of his REDEEMER; he wrote one of the four Gospels, on which account he is called the Evangelist, and the three Epistles which bear his name. He was persecuted, like his brethren the Apostles, and exposed to cruel sufferings for the faith of CHRIST; but he did not die under any of these tortures, but was once miraculously preserved from death when thrown into boiling oil. After having been banished to the desert Isle of Patmos, he was permitted to see the visions of glory which he was directed by the HOLY SPIRIT to reveal to the Christian Church, on which account they are called the Apocalypse, or Revelation of S. John. It is said that when he was grown so old that he could not walk, being nearly a hundred years old, he used to be carried into the midst of the assemblies of the Christians, and exhort them to *love* one another. What then should we do to whom these words of the Apostle are read, and who have the example of his life of love? should we hear them, admire them, and then carry away no remembrance of them? The Apostle drew all his love from the Fountain of the Love of GOD. That Fountain is still open to all His children. Nay, if we do not pray and strive to obtain this fruit of the indwelling of the HOLY SPIRIT in our hearts, we are not, we cannot be Christians indeed. " If a man love Me," said the SAVIOUR, " he will keep My words; he that loveth not knoweth not GOD, for GOD is love."

Let us then examine our hearts and our lives, by the light of GOD's Word; we must not rest contented with a low degree of this Christian grace, for we know Who has said, " This is My commandment, that ye love one another as I have loved you."

S. John in his Epistle addresses little children, and little children were the objects of our LORD's love and care, to teach us that if we would love GOD when grown up, we must take the greatest pains to keep His love in our hearts while we are young children.

Let us dwell to-day, as much as is in our power, on the thought of heavenly love. When we enter into the house of GOD, let it be our earnest prayer, " that the love of GOD may be shed abroad in our hearts " by the HOLY SPIRIT, and when we return to our homes and our duties, let our friends and relations see the truth of these words :

"The heart with love to GOD inspired,
With love to man will glow."

But what is that love of the world which is so opposite to the love of GOD that they cannot be found together ? Let us be careful to find out what this means, for if we are cherishing this sinful affection, we do but mock GOD when we ask Him to give us "the love of the FATHER." If we compare Scripture with Scripture, we shall find that it is to love any thing more than GOD; it is to love sinfully or too much those things even which are given to us to love. We are commanded to love and honour our parents, yet we read, " He that loveth father or mother more than Me, is not worthy of Me."

It is to have our hearts so taken up with the love of the creature, as to forget the Creator. We all know what it is to fix our hearts so much on some one loved being, that every thought is centred on them; our prayers are almost all for them; we live and strive for them; we think of heaven as of being for ever with them; but, for the most part, we are chained to earth through love and care for them. We have forgotten those solemn words of the Apostle S. John, "Little children, keep yourselves from idols." Then, through the mercy of GOD, perhaps this earthly tie is broken, this idolized being taken from us; and happy indeed are we if this object of our love has been a child of GOD; if, when our hearts are bowed down by sorrow, and our eyes filled with tears, we can yet say, "I shall go to them;" and as we walk through our now desolate paths, we can lift up our hearts to the GOD we had forgotten in our happiness, and acknowledging the mercy which recalled us when we were wandering, can say, "We love Him because He first loved us." Or perhaps the riches of this life have been our world; perhaps pride, or the love of power, or vanity, or the opinion of our fellow men; or perhaps we have time and talents bestowed on us and the treasures of the intellect, or the enjoyment of taste and beauty have filled up every avenue of our heart, and left no room for GOD there. It has been truly said by one of our poets,

> "Whatever passes as a cloud between
> The mental eyes of faith and things unseen,
> Causing that brighter world to disappear,
> Or seem less lovely, or its hopes less dear;
> That is our world, our idol, though it bear
> Affection's impress, or devotion's air."

The great enemy of our souls will allow us even to fill our hearts with religious works; with occupations whose end is to teach the way of salvation to our fellow men, if only he can keep out of sight the state of our own souls, and our own need of pardon, of repentance, and holiness of life, if he can satisfy us with the external things which belong to the service of GOD, and keep the eye of our faith from fixing on the SAVIOUR. This is the great object of the evil one, and following his temptations, the greater part of the world are this day "lovers of pleasure, more than lovers of GOD."

The world of nature is a beautiful one, though fallen from its first perfection. Above us and around us the love and care of GOD for His creatures is manifest, yet the great mass of mankind rise day after day to their work and to their enjoyment, forgetful of the hand which gives and continues to them these mercies.

> "New every morning is the love,
> Our wakening and uprising prove,
> Through sleep and darkness safely brought,
> Restored to life, and power, and thought."

Yet this life, and power, and thought are spent in the pursuit of things of this life, or desecrated to the service of Satan, while for eighteen hundred years the solemn warning of the Apostle we this day remember, has been sounding in the ears of the Christian Church. Whole generations have heard the words and acknowledged their truth, yet the many have slighted the warning, and the few only have sought to wean their hearts from earth, and to fix them on the things which belong to their peace before they are hid from their eyes. If a man love Me, says our Divine Master, he will keep My words, and My FATHER will love him, and We will come unto him and make Our abode with him. He who has recorded these words was lying on JESUS' breast when they were spoken, and surely he is a bright example of one who above all others loved GOD and was honoured by Him.

LORD of all power and might, Who art the Author of all good things, graft in our hearts the love of Thy Name, increase in us true religion, nourish us with all goodness, and of Thy great mercy keep us in the same; through JESUS CHRIST our LORD. AMEN.

The Innocents' Day.

COLLECT.

O ALMIGHTY GOD, Who out of the mouths of babes and sucklings hast ordained strength, and madest infants to glorify Thee by their deaths; Mortify and kill all vices in us, and so strengthen us by Thy grace, that by the innocency of our lives, and constancy of our faith even unto death, we may glorify Thy holy Name; through JESUS CHRIST our LORD. AMEN.

  Say, ye celestial guards, who wait
  In Bethlehem, round the Saviour's palace gate,
  Say, who are these on golden wings
  That hover o'er the new-born King of kings,
  Their palms and garlands telling plain
  That they are of the glorious martyr train.

  Ask, and some angel will reply,
  "These, like yourselves, were born to sin and die,
  But ere the poison root was grown,
  GOD set His seal, and mark'd them for His own."

"OF all the pleasures to which I looked forward when you invited me to visit Wells, Uncle Robert, the thought of the frequent opportunity of going to church was the greatest, and at this season of the year especially. And now, as it happens, I was only once in church on Christmas Day, and have not attended the morning service on S. Stephen's or S. John's day, and I shall not be able to go to-day, either, for Sarah Wilson is still very ill, and I have promised to go and sit with her."

"You do not regret having denied yourself, and attended to the wants of poor Sarah, do you, my dear? Remember that not those only who 'hear the word' are 'blessed,' but 'they who keep it.' No opportunity of usefulness happens by chance, if indeed a Christian may speak of chance at all."

"O no, indeed I do not, uncle, I am very thankful that I have been able to be of any use to poor Sarah. I did not mean that."

"No, I am sure she does not," said her aunt, who just then entered the room, "she did not mind losing several hours of our cheerful evening on Christmas Day, and she had no dinner yesterday, but I know she gives up her greatest treat in staying from church; but we must not make you think too much of your good actions, Susan."

"God forbid, aunt, even if I had any to boast of, that I should do so. I did not mean to seem complaining, but you know a Saint's Day service is a great privilege to me, and when I saw you and Uncle Robert getting ready for church, and the children all passing the door on their way this morning, I am afraid I felt rather fretful when I remembered that I had promised Sarah to go to her, and went out of the beautiful sunshine into her dark room just as the bells were stopping."

"You see, my dear, how much of self and earthly gratification lingers about our best feelings and actions, even our prayers and our charity; we carry the world into all, more or less, and this should lead us to fly more earnestly to the Cross of Christ for forgiveness for every hour's sins and short-comings."

There was a pause for some moments, and then Susan's uncle continued:

"I remember once having heard a little story told of a saint of old, which is something to the point of our conversation. The circumstance is related as having really occurred, but doubtless in the times in which it was written it was a sort of parable, or story told to convey a holy truth by some pious father of the Church, and the simple country people have handed it down as a fact.

"It is related of S. Elizabeth, that though she was constant at her prayers, she never neglected on this account any of her numerous duties, and that on one occasion when she was interrupted many times in her devotion by some domestic calls, she found on her return to them that an angel had written, in letters of gold, the words of the prayer she had commenced when she was called away."

"That is a beautiful legend, uncle, and I see your meaning. I shall often think of it at home, when I am disposed to regret too much that our farm is so far from the church, and that it is so often my duty to stay and help my mother with the children."

When Susan had said this, she put on her bonnet and walked to her poor friend's cottage.

Sarah Wilson had been very ill, and was still in a precarious state, and as she was too poor to have the constant services of a nurse, Susan's kindness in staying with her and mixing her medicines, had been of the greatest use to her. When she entered the house she found that Sarah had been in great pain, and that the doctor had given her a sleeping-draught, and ordered her to be kept quiet for several hours. Susan's first thought was, that as she was not wanted by the poor sufferer she could go to church; but as she stood in the passage, she heard the sound of many little feet, and noisy voices in the room next to that in which the invalid was trying to sleep, so she decided to stay and keep the children quiet. Two sturdy little boys left off playing leap-frog, as she entered the room, and two girls, one younger and one older than their brothers, ran towards her, for she had already made acquaintance with them in their mother's room.

"We must not make a noise," said Susan, kindly, as she sat down and took the youngest child, a girl of about three years old, in her lap. "Poor mother is very ill, you know, and she is trying to sleep."

"I have told them so very often," said Lucy, the eldest of the party, a girl of nine years old, "but they always forget it, and make the same noise again in a minute; and Minnie has been crying because Ned knocked her down, and that always vexes mother."

"But Minnie will be very quiet now," said Susan, as she smiled at the little one on her knee; "and Ned will not be rough any more—that's right, give a kiss and make up," she continued, as the child put up her face to her brother, and dried her eyes. "Now if I stay an hour with you will you be very quiet, and listen to a story which I will tell you?"

"Oh yes! O yes, please, do stay; we will all be *so* quiet."

And the children were seated on the ground in less than a moment.

"I wonder," she began, "if any of you can tell me what day it is."

No one answered till Edward said, "Christmas Day was three days ago."

"Yes," said Susan, "but the three festivals which follow Christmas Day are very particular days. The first is observed in memory of S. Stephen, the next of S. John, and the third, to-day, is the Feast of the Holy Innocents. You remember about S. Stephen, do you not?"

"O yes," replied Lucy, "he was the first martyr, and he was stoned to death."

"Yes, and so the Church has appointed his day next to that on which the SAVIOUR was born. S. Stephen was a martyr in will and in deed, that means that he suffered death for CHRIST's sake willingly; and S. John, the next in order, was willing to suffer death for his Master, too, and he did endure cruel tortures, for he was put into a cauldron of boiling oil on account of the truth which he preached, but he was not permitted to die by the hand of his persecutors; he was a martyr in will, though not in deed; and the little Innocents, of whom I am going to tell you, were too young to know anything about the SAVIOUR, on whose account they were killed, so they were martyrs in deed only. Perhaps you will think this rather difficult, but I tell it you because I hope you will remember the three days that come after Christmas Day another year, and think about the three kinds of martyrs. If you had been at church this morning you would have sung, 'The noble army of martyrs praise Thee. The holy Church throughout all the world doth acknowledge Thee.' Now I want to explain to you how the Holy Innocents are a part of that noble army, and I must choose easy words, for I want even little Minnie to understand what I say.

"At the time when our LORD JESUS was born, Herod, who was king of the Jews, and who was a very wicked man, had heard that there was a wonderful Child born in Bethlehem, for wise men had come from the east, who had seen a star, and who believed that the star was a sign given by GOD of the birth of the SAVIOUR of the world, so they came to Judea, saying, 'Where is He that is born King of the Jews? for we have seen His star in the east, and are come to worship Him.' Now Herod knew that it was written in the Word of GOD by the Prophets that a Governor, Who should rule the people of Israel, should come out of Bethlehem. And as he was a wicked man, it is not likely that he studied GOD's Word to learn about the SAVIOUR who was promised, and Who was to be of the house of David."

"I know who David was," said little Charlie, "he killed great Goliath with a sling and a stone, when he was only a youth, because GOD helped him, and he was a king afterwards."

Lucy told Charlie to be quiet, but Susan said she was glad he remembered the story of the good king David, "but Herod, you know," she continued, "was a wicked king, he did not care about the promised Messiah, and he only feared that another king would take his place and power from him."

"Did the LORD JESUS drive away the wicked Herod?" said little Minnie.

"No, the SAVIOUR said afterwards, 'My kingdom is not of this world.' But Herod came to a dreadful end, even in this life," said Susan. "And now, I wonder if any of you can tell me what he did that was so very wicked and cruel?"

"When he heard that the King of the Jews was born in Bethlehem, he sent and destroyed all the children that were not more than two years old," said Lucy.

"Indeed he did, but he did not succeed in killing the SAVIOUR then, you know, for an angel had appeared to Joseph in a dream, telling him to take the young Child and His mother, and flee into Egypt, so the blessed Virgin and the holy Child were far away when the cruel order was given. Can you think what a dreadful thing it was for the poor mothers when their little children were taken from them and put to death before their eyes? The Prophet Jeremiah had foretold what they would feel, saying, 'A voice was heard in Ramah, lamentation and bitter weeping, Rachel weeping for her children, refusing to be comforted for her children, because they were not.' Rachel meaning the Jewish nation.

"But O, what happy little children they were that were thus permitted to die for their King, as the verse says:

> 'Happiest those who died for Thee,
> That Thou mightst live for them
> A sadder death to see.'

"The painful death was soon over, and then we are sure that they were carried by angels into Paradise, that blessed place where happy souls wait until after the judgment day, when GOD will create a new heaven and a new earth for them. If they had lived perhaps they might have been of the number of those who refused to believe on the Lord Jesus, but they died before they could commit sin; that is why they are called the Innocents.

"Will you try to remember what I have been telling you about them? you know that the Saviour loves little children, and when he was on earth, and His disciples rebuked those that brought them to Him, He was displeased that they should think it a trouble, and try to keep them from Him, and said, 'Suffer little children to come unto Me, and forbid them not,' and He took them in His arms and blessed them. And now that He is in heaven, He looks down on every child with the same tender care, and He has commanded that they should be brought to Him in holy Baptism, that they may be made His children, and enter the kingdom of heaven. It is, then, as if He took them in His arms and blessed them, and He sends His angels to watch over them, for you know He said of children, 'I say unto you that their angels do always behold the face of My Father Which is in heaven.' Will you try and remember these beautiful things, and be gentle and teachable as little children should be whom the Lord has blessed."

"But we can never be martyrs like the holy Innocents," said Edward.

"You will not be put to death for being Christians, as many, even children, have been," said Susan, "because you are born in a Christian land, but you may bear something that is hard for Christ's sake, and then you will be like them. I will tell you a story to show you what I mean.

"I knew a little boy once, his name was the same as yours, Charlie, who was sent away from home to a large school when he was about ten years old. He saw a great many naughty things done by the boys who were at school with him, but he tried to do what was right, and prayed for grace to help him every day.

"Well, one day when he was playing with his companions, they saw some ripe apples hanging on the bough of a tree which grew close to their play-ground wall, and the boys cried out, 'Apples, ripe apples, who will get them? Charlie Adams shall; he is a good climber, he is a capital fellow.' Now Charlie liked to be spoken of in this way, he was proud of his climbing, and he knew that he could easily reach the apples without being seen by their owner, but he knew, too, that God would see him, so he said, 'I cannot take the apples, it would be stealing.' Then the boys laughed at him, and called him coward, and the blood rushed to Charlie's face, but he did not speak angry words, he kept them down, and he only said, 'I am not a coward, but I am afraid to do what is wrong.' Now his companions knew that he was a brave boy; he had borne a whipping from a great boy, only a week before, because he would not tell a lie, and they knew also that the mocking which Charlie bore so bravely, was worse to him than any punishment; but still they went on teasing him, calling him Master Timorous, and good little boy, in ridicule; and they refused to play with him, and pelted him away from the play-ground, and bade him be a tell-tale next, and go and tell the school-master."

"What a shame," cried Edward, "I wish I had been there! What did Charlie do?"

"He walked quietly away, and when, soon after, his mother sent him a hamper full of apples and cake, he divided it with his school-fellows, and they soon learnt to love and respect him, and to find out that 'a good boy is never a coward.'

"Now do you not think that Charlie had something of the spirit which could bear persecution for righteousness' sake?"

"O yes, what a pretty story! do tell us another," cried the children at once.

"Well, I will tell you one more. There was once a little girl and a boy, who were orphans, and who went after their parents' death to live with an uncle and aunt: the girl had a gentle loving heart, her name was Sophy; but her brother George, who was two years older, was of a rough, selfish temper, and he was often very unkind to his little sister. While their mother lived Sophy had been almost always with her, but now they were left very much to themselves, and George used to order Sophy about, and take her books and playthings from her, and if she refused to do anything he wished, he used to strike her and call her names. One day he asked Sophy to go with him and carry his fishing line, for he wanted to fish, but Sophy had work to do for her aunt, and she said she could not go, so George gave her a hard blow which made her head ache sadly. Sophy knew that if she complained of his bad conduct he would be punished, but she said to herself, 'He is my brother, I will not tell of him, I will try to love him all the same, and at last, perhaps he will love me and be good.' Often and often did the little girl suffer from her brother's temper, but she bore it all without a murmur; till at last George's heart was touched by her gentleness and patience, and he became a kind brother, and a good boy.

"May we not say that little Sophy had a martyr's spirit; and do you not think that even the youngest child may bear something for CHRIST's sake?"

It was now time for the children to have their dinner, and Susan left them with the promise that she would come again in the afternoon, and that if their poor mother was still sleeping quietly, she would take them to church. The children on their part assured her that they would be very quiet in the meanwhile.

They looked as neat as Lucy could make them, and were waiting quietly with their Prayer-Books in their hands when their kind friend came for them. They behaved very well, and were attentive during the service, even the little one, who could not understand many words, knew that she was in the house of GOD, and listened quietly to the beautiful music. When they returned home their mother was awake and feeling better, and Susan said that they might each go to her for a minute, and give her one kiss. Little Minnie was lifted upon her mother's bed, and as she put her arms round her neck she said, "It is

Holy Innocents' Day, mother, and I have been to church for the first time."

Her mother kissed her, and asked what her little hymn-book said about it.

"I must try to be attentive,
  When each prayer is said again,
I can always say, 'Our FATHER,'
I can always say, 'Amen.'

"I can always be as quiet
  As a Christian child should be,
At the holy name of JESUS
Bow my head and bend my knee."

Feast of the Circumcision.

COLLECT.

ALMIGHTY GOD, Who madest Thy blessed SON to be circumcised, and obedient to the law for man; Grant us the true Circumcision of the Spirit; that our hearts and all our members, being mortified from all worldly and carnal lusts, we may in all things obey Thy blessed will; through the same Thy SON JESUS CHRIST our LORD. AMEN.

THE valley of Moorhead is as pleasant a place as you can wish to see. The spire of its small, but beautiful church points up into the fresh blue sky, and its shadow falls on the downy hill side on which it is built; neat-looking cottages are scattered here and there in every sheltered corner, lying like nests among the high hills of Cumberland. A few years ago there was no church at Moorhead, it was only a scattered hamlet, sprung up in the neighbourhood of a populous town, and its inhabitants had many miles to walk to the nearest church; this was a great misfortune to them, for not only the aged people and children were thus deprived of the means of grace, but when an infant was born, it sometimes died before it could be baptized, and when any of the little community died they were carried far away, and that too at no little cost, to be buried where those who loved them could never see their graves. It was very different now that GOD had put it into the heart of a good man to build a church for the benefit of Moorhead. There was a Clergyman who lived close to the church, in a little grey house, on one side of the churchyard; you never saw a churchyard which looked more like a place of holy rest for Christian bodies. And there was a school-house, too; I must not forget to describe the school-house, for it is about the children who were taught there, and what they learnt one New-Year's Day, that I am going to tell you.

The school stood about a quarter of a mile from the church, for the cottages were scattered thickly in that direction, and many of them were still further off, so that it was in a central situation, and every child in the Moor cottages could easily walk to it. Miss Norton, the Clergyman's sister, had built the school-house, and she engaged a master and a mistress to teach the children; there were about thirty boys, and as many, or more, girls in the Sunday School; but on week days the elder boys could not attend, for they went to work with their fathers, and many of the elder girls were busy at home too, but then they had an evening class twice a week. Miss Norton taught some of the children herself every day; the Minister, too, catechised them very often, and sometimes Miss Norton would give the master and mistress a holiday, and teach all the children together. They were very glad when she did this, for it was a great pleasure to them to hear the beautiful stories which she read to them, and besides, it was generally on some festival when they were to have a great treat. You may be sure that they were always attentive then, and the little boys were never rude or noisy when they were allowed to come into the girls' school-room, and answer Miss Norton's questions with their sisters. If you had been at Moorhead on the 1st of January, 1850, you might have seen the children walking in little groups towards the school. It was a bright winter's day; the clouds were chasing each other quickly across the blue sky, for the wind was fresh, but the sun had great power, too, and every now and then it would shine out so brightly when the clouds were passed, that the snow melted from off the cottage roofs.

As the children went merrily on their way, they saw at a little distance before them their kind friend and teacher, Miss Norton, and they hurried on, that they might repeat their New-Year's wishes, and offer her the little bunches of everlasting and winter flowers that they had gathered for her. And now they had all reached the room, and had taken their places; there were no books taken out of the bags to-day but the Bibles and Prayer-Books, for they knew that Miss Norton was not going to hear their usual lessons, but to talk to them respecting the Feast of the Circumcision, and the commencement of another year.

"This must be a very holy, and a solemn day, my dear children," she said, "for two reasons. Another year has passed away; we cannot recall one hour of it. It has brought us opportunities of grace, time in which to serve God, 'and to work out our salvation,' and it will appear against us in judgment if we have neglected the means of grace, and sinned away our opportunities of doing good, and squandered the precious hours in mere earthly pleasure. We are all one year nearer to our death, and the new year which begins to-day, may be the last which we shall live to see. There are many fresh graves in the churchyard since we last kept this day; there are little graves as well as long ones; many children who were strong and well a year ago, as well as older people, have died in the course of the last twelve months, and we do not know which of us will be called next, so that it is a solemn thing to enter upon a new year, and we should do it with earnest prayer for grace to lead a Christian life, that 'living or dying we may be the Lord's,' as you heard last Sunday afternoon in church.

"We should say with David, 'So teach us to number our days that we may apply our hearts unto wisdom,' then we shall be able to say as S. Paul did with holy confidence, 'to me to live is Christ, to die is gain;' and it will not be a sad, but a peaceful thought, that ere another year is flown we may have passed into 'the rest that remaineth for the people of God;' and this day has been appointed to be kept holy by the Church, because it is the anniversary of the Circumcision of our Lord Jesus Christ, Who not only obeyed the whole moral law, and thus became for our salvation, 'the Lord our Righteousness,' but also conformed to all the ceremonies of the Jewish ritual, that the blessings promised to Abraham might descend to us.

Then Miss Norton told the children to turn to the second, third, and fourth chapters of the Epistle to the Romans, and to the second chapter of that to the Colossians, where they found many verses on the subject of Circumcision, which they read attentively, and when they had done so, she took a little book out of her pocket and began to read it to them; for she said it would explain to them more clearly than she could do the subject of the day. So the children looked up and listened with great attention while she read.

"You know what a promise means? A covenant is a double promise; when two persons make an agreement, one on one side, the other on the other side. GOD made both to Abraham. First He made a promise that Abraham should be 'the heir of the world,' or 'inherit all nations,' (Gen. xii. 2, 3, and Romans iv. 13,) which means that to one of Abraham's family all the kingdoms of the world should, sooner or later, belong. Another part of the same promise was, that in Abraham and in his seed, or son, should all the families of the earth be blessed. The whole promise was meant of our LORD JESUS CHRIST, Who is the Seed, or Son of Abraham, (Gal. iii. 16;) and the blessing which was to come on all the world in Him, was not to be through their keeping the Jewish law, but through the righteousness of faith, or believing on Him, (Romans iv. 13.) But GOD made not only a promise, but a covenant between Himself and Abraham, (Gen. xvii. 10.) I have just told you GOD's promise to Abraham, which was the one side of that covenant or agreement, the other side was, that every man-child of Abraham's family should, when eight days old, be circumcised, or go through the solemn form of being made what we now call a Jew, (though the name of Jew was not used till long after Abraham,) so that no one of Abraham's family could ever have all the kingdoms of the world as we know once our LORD JESUS CHRIST shall have; nor be able to bless and save the families of the world, as GOD promised some one should, unless he kept Abraham's side of the covenant and was circumcised. So our SAVIOUR, the LORD JESUS CHRIST, the seed of Abraham, was circumcised for our sakes. But the collect for the day speaks of something more than this.

"Four hundred years after GOD had made that covenant with Abraham, the Israelites, or family of Abraham, came to Mount Sinai, and GOD spake to all from the fiery top of the mountain the ten commandments, and explained them to Moses, (Exodus xx., xxi., xxii., xxiii.) He afterwards called Moses up to the mountain, and told him all the laws of Jewish sacrifices and forms of worship which pointed beforehand to CHRIST; besides writing out for Israel the ten commandments which He had some days before spoken, (Exodus xxiv.) Whoever was circumcised was bound to keep the whole Jewish law, (Gal. v. 3,) and blessings were promised to those that did so. But S. Peter called it a yoke which even the Jews had never been able to bear, (Acts xv. 10.) Now the LORD JESUS, by being circumcised, took that heavy yoke on Him, and was 'made under the law,' or obedient to the law for our sakes. S. Paul saith, 'JESUS CHRIST was made a minister of the circumcision for the truth of GOD; to confirm the promises of GOD made unto the fathers, and that the Gentiles (or people who are not Jews) might glorify GOD for His mercy.' (Romans xv. 10.) And in Him the promises are made sure to us, (2 Cor. i. 20,) the promises of blessings, and mercies, and salvation which are in the Psalms, Prophets, and other parts of the Old Testament, were written and made to Jews, for they only were the old church and family of GOD, circumcised according to Abraham's covenant, and you know that any promise only stands good for those people to whom the promise was made. But we are not Jews, and these promises were not made to us; if the blessed SAVIOUR had not been born as one of Abraham's family, and afterwards circumcised according to GOD's agreement with Abraham, even He would not have had, 'as *Man*,' a right to the written promises in the Old Testament. But in His wonderful love, and mercy, and condescension, He 'took upon Him the seed of Abraham,' and was born an Israelite; He was circumcised, and grafted into the covenant of Abraham, and was obedient to the Jewish law given at Sinai. Thus He had right to all the promises of GOD which are written in the Old Testament; and now He gives all these promises to whomsoever believes on Him, the true Sacrifice that taketh away the sin of the world. And He has appointed the Sacrament of Baptism as an outward and visible sign of the inward and spiritual grace, which is meant by all these promises; and has commanded every one who desires these promised blessings through Him, to be baptized as a means whereby they may receive the same, and a pledge to assure them thereof.

"Remember that this is a day for you to thank GOD that the LORD JESUS CHRIST was circumcised, and so gave you (who have been baptized in His Name) as much right to the Old Testament and its promises as if you were of Abraham's family. But do not stop there, try to believe and trust GOD with faith like Abraham's faith, and then you will receive the blessings which both Old and New Testaments promise."*

By the time that Miss Norton had finished reading, and asking the children questions on what they had heard, the bells began to ring for morning service, and they were soon on their way to the church, walking two and two quietly, and not running and playing as they had done on their way to school, for they knew that they were going to the House of GOD. The text which the Clergyman chose for his sermon that day was taken from the first chapter of the Acts of the Apostles, "It is not for you to know the times and seasons which the FATHER hath put in His own power."

I cannot tell you all that the sermon contained, but I will repeat the last words of it, for they are such as we may all remember with profit to ourselves.

"My brethren," said the Clergyman, "time past is no longer ours; we have indeed sown seeds in it which will bear fruit either for good or evil in this

* From the Children's Monthly Garden, for 1847.

world and in the next, but we cannot call back one of its bygone moments; it is ours only to look back upon with repentance for our sins and shortcomings, and with thankfulness to the Almighty for all our past mercies. Time future is in the hand of GOD, and its events are known only to Him. Time present is His gift to us; it is a talent entrusted to us by our Heavenly King, Who will require an account of it at our hands. Let us, through His grace which is never denied to those who seek it aright, so employ the time now vouchsafed to us, that, walking in the strength of the LORD, we may enter upon the unknown future with peaceful trusting hearts, knowing that all things will work together for our good. And then when that solemn hour draws nigh to each of us, when time shall end in eternity, and when this world is passing away from us like a shadow that departeth, we may commend our immortal spirits with holy confidence into His hands Who has passed before us through the valley of the shadow of death, and opened the gates of Paradise, and Who has prepared for His redeemed people 'many mansions in His FATHER'S house,' where time and change cannot come, for 'there shall be no more death, neither sorrow, nor crying, neither shall there be any more pain, for the former things are passed away.' And He that sits upon the throne hath said, ' Behold, I make all things new.'"

Conversion of S. Paul.

COLLECT.

O God, Who through the preaching of the blessed Apostle Saint Paul, hast caused the light of the Gospel to shine throughout the world; Grant, we beseech Thee, that we, having his wonderful conversion in remembrance, may show forth our thankfulness unto Thee for the same, by following the holy doctrine which he taught; through Jesus Christ our Lord. Amen.

———

THIS is the day set apart by our Church as a holy day, because it is the anniversary of the conversion of S. Paul. Christians may well desire to offer up their praises and prayers in an especial manner on this day; for the miracle which was wrought by God upon the heart of Saul of Tarsus, was for our sakes as well as for his, not only that his soul might be saved, but that he might become Paul, the first Apostle to the Gentiles. By Gentiles we mean all who were not Jews, and in the time of the Apostles the Jews were the only people who worshipped the true God, the other nations of the world being idolaters, or heathens as we now call them. After the death of our blessed Lord, the Apostles were commanded to go first to the lost sheep of the house of Israel, and it was reserved for S. Paul, the unwearied, devoted

Missionary to the heathen, to go out into all lands preaching "CHRIST crucified," also to the Gentiles. He was indeed "in labours abundant, in stripes above measure, thrice beaten with rods, once stoned, thrice suffered shipwreck, a night and a day was in the deep, in journeyings often, in perils of waters, in perils of robbers, in perils by his own countrymen, in perils by the heathen, in perils in the city, in perils in the wilderness, in perils in the sea, in perils among false brethren, in weariness and painfulness, in watchings often, in hunger and thirst, in fastings often, in cold and nakedness," and laden with the care of all the churches of Asia, of Greece, and in fact of the whole Roman Empire into which he had carried the Gospel of JESUS CHRIST. Let us think now of some parts of the life and teaching of S. Paul, that we may draw from them lessons for ourselves, for it is in order that we may do this that our Church sets apart this day. We cannot indeed meditate in one day on all the important truths to be learned from the life of S. Paul, or on the hundredth part of the holy words which he wrote by the inspiration of the HOLY GHOST, and which compose the greater number of the Epistles, in the Holy Bible. But we will try to learn some blessed truth from his history, for we know that it was written for our instruction.

We find the first mention made of S. Paul, in the account of the martyrdom of S. Stephen, where we read that those who stoned the Martyr to death, laid down their clothes at a young man's feet whose name was Saul; and this young man, unlike some of the Disciples, who were simple, unlearned men before GOD called them to be ministers of His grace, and stewards of the mysteries of the Gospel, was instructed in all the learning of the Jewish Rabbis, brought up at the feet of Gamaliel, a doctor of the law, a Jew by his parentage, but a Roman owing to the place of his birth, that is, a free-born and privileged subject of Rome, having been born in one of her provinces; he was a man of power and influence, richly endowed with the good things of this life; but what was he before GOD? his heart was full of unbelief and hardness; he persecuted with the greatest cruelty the Disciples of the LORD JESUS; and as on this day some eighteen hundred years ago, he was on a journey to Damascus with authority to cast into prison, and put to death all the believers in CHRIST JESUS who were to be found in that city. But the LORD, Whom Saul had not yet learned to know, had mercy in store for him: we hear in church the wonderful account of his miraculous conversion, and how as he journeyed the heavens opened, and the voice of the LORD JESUS spoke with almighty power to his soul, saying, "Saul, Saul, why persecutest thou Me?" Afterwards, Saul, rendered blind by the effect of the glorious vision he had beheld, waited in Damascus in obedience to the Divine command, until Ananias was sent to him by GOD to restore his sight by a miracle, and declare to him the Divine Will.

And now was the wonderful effect of the grace of GOD on the sinful nature of man manifested in the life of the Apostle, and we read that he who persecuted now preacheth the faith that once he destroyed; and how earnestly he laboured, and how unceasingly he strove to win souls to CHRIST, we know. From the hour of his conversion he renounced the world, and gave up his whole life to the service of GOD and His Church, "counting all things but dross that he might win CHRIST and be found in Him."

Now all these things happen unto us for an example, as the Apostle tells us. If we turn to the 11th and 12th chapters of the Epistle to the Hebrews, we shall learn what use we are to make of the memory of holy men who have lived and died before us. We read there, "Wherefore, seeing we are compassed about with so great a cloud of witnesses, let us lay aside every weight, and the sin which doth so easily beset us, and let us run with patience the race that is set before us."

In order that you may understand the meaning of these words, I will tell you something about the ancient games from which the Apostle draws his picture of the Christian life. It was a custom among the Greeks, a large and civilized nation at the time when the Apostles lived, to celebrate from time to time in honour of their false gods, who, as you know, were nothing better than idols of wood and stone, public races, in which the racers were men. For this purpose they used to meet in large numbers in a place prepared for the purpose: the men who were to run in these races prepared themselves long beforehand that they might win on these great occasions; they would rather die in the attempt to win than lose the applause of the multitudes of spectators who were assembled to watch them on either side; for those who won in these races were treated with great honour, and after having received a crown of laurel from one who sat as judge at the end of the race, they were triumphantly carried into the city, and looked upon as great men who had deserved every public honour. S. Paul knew that the people to whom he wrote were familiar with every circumstance connected with these games, and he therefore compares the Christian life to them in order that they might understand his argument. Would a man who has to run in these races have encumbered himself with a heavy garment which might entangle his feet and cause him to fall? and shall we be more careless about our precious souls which are to live for ever in joy or misery, and think less of our heavenly reward than they did of the fading crown which they were to receive? O, no, rather, the Apostle continues, "Let us cast off every weight, and the sin which doth so easily beset us." For we, too, are running a race, and if we reach in safety our journey's end, we shall be crowned with an immortal crown of glory, and an entrance shall be given to us into the heavenly city. One by one the victorious runners in these games were crowned and took their places amidst the shouts of the beholders to watch the races of those who were to follow them. And you will believe that if either of those who were running felt faint and weary, the thought of the multitudes who were eagerly watching them, and especially of those who had struggled in the race before them and had received their crowns, and were now looking down on them, and waiting to welcome them to share their victory, would give them fresh strength, and they would strain every nerve, and keeping their eye fixed on the goal to which they were running, and on the judge who sat with the crown in his hand waiting to place it on the head of him who had deserved it, they would forget their weakness and overcome every difficulty, and reach the appointed spot in the right moment. And have we not glorious motives for preseverance in our spiritual race? The Apostle Paul had been speaking of all the servants of GOD, from righteous Abel to the time when he lived, and he said, " Wherefore, seeing we are compassed about with so great a cloud of witnesses." It is thus we are to think of the Saints of GOD, as witnesses of our efforts, as those who have borne the burden before us, have won the race, and obtained the prize; as of a great company who bend from their blessed abodes to watch how we acquit ourselves in the heavenly strife. We must recall their labors, their patience, their faith, and love, and zeal, that we may stir ourselves to follow their example; we must compare our poor cold service with their holy devotedness, and arm ourselves with fresh courage: but it is not in them that we must trust, it is not to them that we must look for help, they will not bestow on us the crown at last. The Grecian runners looked only to the goal, and so are we to find all our strength in fixing the eye of faith upon the Judge of all the earth, Who has first trodden every step of that weary way before us, that He might be touched with the feeling of our infirmities.

"Let us therefore come boldly unto the throne of grace, that we may obtain mercy, and find grace to help in time of need." "And let us run with patience the race that is set before us, looking unto JESUS the Author and Finisher of our faith, Who for the joy that was set before Him, endured the Cross, despising the shame, and is set down at the right hand of the throne of GOD."

The Apostle Paul, when about to end his life and his labours of love by a cruel death, could exclaim with holy confidence, "I have fought a good fight, I have finished my course, I have kept the faith. Henceforth there is laid up for me a crown of righteousness, which the LORD, the righteous Judge shall give me at that day, and not to me only, but unto all them also that love His appearing."

The Apostle has passed now from the race on earth to the rest that remaineth for the people of GOD. He is one of the great cloud of witnesses who look down on us. We meet in church to-day not that we may look to him, but to the same SAVIOUR of Whom he exclaimed, "I can do all things through CHRIST that strengtheneth me;" and praising Him for all His servants departed this life in His faith and fear, beseech Him to give us grace so to follow their good examples, that with them we may be partakers of His heavenly kingdom.

Glory, LORD, to Thee alone,
Who hast glorified Thine own.

The Purification.

COLLECT.

ALMIGHTY and ever-living GOD, we humbly beseech Thy Majesty, that, as Thy only begotten SON was this day presented in the temple in substance of our flesh, so we may be presented unto Thee with pure and clean hearts, by the same Thy SON JESUS CHRIST our LORD. Amen.

IN a little white cottage with a thatched roof, near the entrance of the village of West Cliff, lives Mary Grey. When I left the village I was more sorry to part from Mary than from almost any other parishioner, for I could not help taking a deep interest in one so young, who had known so much sorrow.

But Mary is not the only widowed and childless heart in the world; so I will write a short account of her, in the hope that others suffering like herself, may find the same support under trial that was mercifully given to her. At the age of nineteen Mary came to live in my parish as the wife of William Grey; her modest and industrious behaviour soon won for her the good opinions and kind feelings of the neighbours, who had known her husband since he was a boy, and rejoiced that he had been so happy in his choice of a wife. It would have been a strange thing to have missed Mary and her husband from their place in church, for Mary had married a man who feared GOD, and who was worthy of the love and honour she gave him. It was not only on Sundays that Grey and his wife might be seen walking arm in arm to the House of GOD, they were regular in their attendance on the festivals of the Church, and the other weekly services which were so arranged as not to interfere with the working hours of the greater part of the parishioners. Many a summer's evening have I seen them in church together, and when half an hour later I walked through the village, I have observed them at work, side by side, in their little garden, and have felt sure that the parting blessing they had heard within the hallowed walls was resting on them, and that the peace of GOD which passeth all understanding did indeed keep their hearts and minds through JESUS CHRIST our LORD.

In this world blessings are often sent in a form which we call sorrow and affliction. We know that our LORD has said, "In the world ye shall have tribulation," and that His gracious promise is, "What I do thou knowest not now, but thou *shalt* know hereafter." Whilst I looked upon the Greys as a couple who, by their life and conversation, would glorify GOD, and do good in their generation, and perhaps bring up a family fearing GOD and working righteousness, the sentence had gone forth which was to divide them, and to bring desolation upon their happy home. Who can tell what was the heart-rending sorrow of poor Mary's heart, when one evening the lifeless body of her husband was brought home to her; he had been crushed by the heavy wheel of some machinery, whilst working at his trade. I was soon informed of her heavy affliction, and lost no time in going to see her. I need not attempt to describe the sorrow of this young and loving heart; Mary was indeed overwhelmed, but she never forgot in the moment of her deepest grief, that her trial was appointed by infinite Love and Wisdom, she never doubted that she should one day be enabled to exclaim, "It is good for me that I have been afflicted," and she would say to me amidst her tears, "In another world, sir, I shall know why my beloved husband was taken so early to his rest, and I have been left behind in a life from which all joy and light have fled."

"All joy and light fled! Mary," said I, "can it be so to those who follow Him Whose meat and drink it was to do the Will of Him Who sent Him?" "I did not mean to repine, indeed, sir," said Mary, "I meant that all earthly pleasure seems now to have died with my husband. I know that there is a peace which the world can neither give nor take away, and I trust that peace will still be mine." This conversation took place the morning after her husband's funeral; the next day was Sunday, and I believe that there was not a heart in all West Cliff that did not ache for Mary as she passed alone out of her little cottage, for the first time, and walked slowly towards the church. There was not one who did not wish that they might have it in their power to comfort her; but they respected the fulness of her first deep sorrow, and she walked alone. "Oh, sir," she said to me afterwards, "in church, where I expected most to miss my husband from my side, there I first felt that our separation was not so great: even now we are one in the Communion of Saints, and when I joined in those glorious words, 'Therefore with angels and archangels, and with all the company of heaven,' I felt that I was indeed nearer to him, and that our souls were employed alike whilst I could lift mine up in praise in the midst of my sorrow."

Time passed on, and GOD, Who has promised His people to "send them help from the sanctuary, and to strengthen them out of Zion," poured His peace into Mary's torn heart; all her thoughts were with her husband, she loved to do everything that she had done with *him*, and to keep those things that reminded her of him always in her sight; the little garden was as carefully kept as when he worked in it; and the chair which he used, was in its old place. The neighbours said that Mary would kneel down and bury her face in it at night, and sob as if her heart would break; but however great was the struggle with her natural affections, it was evident, from her calm and resigned demeanour, that her sorrow was sanctified and her heart bent in submission to the Divine will. It was a great effort to her to go out except to church, but she did not shrink from any duty, or indulge her grief selfishly: where distress or sorrow was to be found, there Mary went, to nurse a sick neighbour, and to help in every way that was in her

power. William Grey had subscribed to a fund
while he was in health and receiving good wages, so
that Mary was not in want; and the needlework
which she took in, enabled her not only to supply her
own necessities, but to assist others who were poorer
than herself. The cottage in which she lived had
been bought by her husband, so she had no rent to
pay; some of the neighbours wondered that she did not
leave a place where she had known so much grief,
and return to her own friends; but, knowing her as
I did, I did not at all wonder that she loved better the
place where she had lived with her husband, than all
the world beside. Besides, her own mother was
dead, and her father had married again, so she had
no very strong tie to her old home. There was one
great happiness still in store for Mary in this world;
at the time of her husband's death she expected to
become a mother; and before three months had passed away her little baby was born. It is true, that
there must have been many sad hours when she remembered that the father who would have welcomed
the little one with so much love and joy, was never
to see it in this world; but yet from the time of
the little boy's birth, Mary was a different being
again, there was something of hope and youth in her
voice and step now that she had her child to love,
and the future, which before seemed so dreary, was
full of the pleasing thought that, by the grace of GOD,
she would so train up her beloved child that he
should be like his father in this life, and united to

him for ever at last. Mary was a fond and proud mother, and her neighbors took a kind pleasure in noticing her little one, and assuring her that he was the prettiest boy in the village; and indeed they might say so with truth, for he was a thriving and promising child. When he was some months old, his mother would bring him and sit down with him by his father's grave; it should be the earliest place he knew, she said; and there she loved to offer up earnest prayers for her unconscious little one. And her prayers were heard, though not according to the thoughts of her heart, for the great Shepherd Who sometimes takes the lambs in His arms, as hoping the sheep may follow Him more closely, took this babe to Himself before it was twelve months old. Night and day did Mary watch her child, with breathless anxiety, till it died, after a week's illness, and then the first deep wound in her heart was opened again; and when the little empty cradle was placed by her husband's chair, and the constant offices of love which for so many months had been her joy were no longer needed, she felt doubly desolate; the poor mother was too ill to follow her child's remains to the grave, and was confined to her bed for some weeks afterwards with fever; she recovered slowly, for her broken spirit increased the weakness and disease which oppressed her.

I was surprised one day to see her in church; it was the Feast of the Presentation of CHRIST in the Temple, or the Purification of the Blessed Virgin Mary, and my sermon for that day, dwelling chiefly on the sympathy of our Blessed LORD with the human nature which He had taken upon Him for our sakes, was such as I knew would comfort poor Mary Grey's aching heart, though I little thought, when I wrote it, that she would be one of my hearers: the hymn, too, for the day, spoke the same language, and I believe that the prayers of our little congregation went up with one accord for the widowed mother, who stood once more in her place amongst us, after GOD had laid His chastening hand upon her, and that the remembrance of her sorrow was in every heart, as we sung,

> When our heads are bowed with woe,
> When our bitter tears o'erflow,
> When we mourn the lost, the dear,
> JESU, Son of Mary, hear!
>
> Thou our human flesh hast worn,
> Thou our mortal griefs hast borne,
> Thou hast shed the frequent tear;
> JESU, Son of Mary, hear!
>
> When the heart is sad within,
> With the thought of all its sin,
> When the spirit shrinks with fear,
> JESU, Son of Mary, hear!
>
> Thou the shame of sin hast known,
> Though the sin was not Thine own;
> Thou hast deigned its weight to bear;
> JESU, Son of Mary, hear!

Mary was the last, except myself, to leave the church, and as I followed her at a distance, I saw her, when all the rest of the congregation had passed on, kneel down beside the little newly made grave, which was placed by her husband's. It was noonday, and the neat oak crosses at the head of those she loved cast no shadows across their resting-places. Is it not, I thought, an emblem of religion! the Cross of CHRIST, the profession of our faith, seems all brightness when the flood of life and youth and joy is strong in our path, but it is the experience of few Christians to find it so long; to some in the morning, to others in the evening of life, the light of earthly joy is withdrawn and the shadow of the Cross lengthens over their path.

> "For He Who knew what human hearts would prove,
> How slow to learn the dictates of His love,
> That hard by nature and of stubborn will,
> A life of ease would make them harder still,
> Calls oft a cloud to darken all their years,
> And says, 'Go spend them in the vale of tears.'"

The minister of GOD knows how often trial and sorrow is the appointed lot of the children of GOD: he remembers the words, "These are they which came out of great tribulation, and have washed their robes, and made them white in the Blood of the Lamb;" and he knows that the time will come when "GOD shall wipe away all tears from their eyes."

In the evening of that same day I visited Mary Grey; in answer to my inquiry for her health, and the fear that I expressed that she had overtasked her strength by making the effort to go out too soon, "O sir," she said, "I got nothing but good. I may have been a little tired, but it is not the poor body that ails me most, and my soul received the best comfort. I thought of the earthly sorrow, and of the heavenly joy of the mother of our Blessed Lord, of her so honoured among women, yet of whom it was said that 'a sword should pierce through her heart.' What are my sorrows compared to hers who stood once weeping at the foot of the Cross on which her Divine Son was laid?"

"Yes, Mary," I replied, "and He Who knew and sympathized in her sorrow, and gave to His beloved disciple the charge to watch over her as a son; He Who wept over Lazarus, and restored the son of the widow of Nain to his mother, He has not afflicted you without a cause, He will not lay on you more than you can bear."

"I fear, sir," said Mary, "that I have been giving way almost sinfully since my child's death, I have so longed to follow those dear to me; but in church this morning, many happy thoughts came to my mind, and I felt that a Christian's faith and hope should comfort me even now. Faith that I too shall one day be received into Paradise, and hope to meet there my husband and my baby. I thought of the presentation of the holy Child by His mother in the temple, and of how little she knew the life of pain and the cruel death that awaited Him Who was at once her beloved Son and her adorable Redeemer. But who can tell her blessedness now? she remembers no more the sorrow. And this made me think of the day when I brought my child to be baptized, and how earnestly I prayed 'that he might so pass the waves of this troublesome world, that finally he might come to the land of everlasting life.' And now he is safe, the dangerous voyage is over, no temptation can ever harm him, the dearest wish of my heart for him is granted, and what must the holy angels think if they should look down and see me, his mother, refusing to be comforted, when my treasure is safely laid up for me in heaven?"

I had listened to Mary's words with a rejoicing heart that faith was thus granted to her, and now I said, "Where your treasure is there will your heart be also. This is my comfort for you, Mary. It may be that the loved ones who have been removed from you had twined themselves too closely round your heart for your own soul's good. It may be, that like the disciples on the mount of transfiguration, you might have been ready to exclaim, It is good for us to be here; and if so, He who knows our hearts has dealt gently with you, your joys have only been removed for a time, they have not been turned to bitterness. Even now, through faith, you may call them yours; and thus your best affections, which might have led you from the SAVIOUR, will now draw you heavenwards. 'Whom the LORD loveth He chasteneth.' May this be your blessed experience."

Mary answered me with quiet tears, and I took my leave. As I walked from her cottage to pay my afternoon visit to the school, I could not help thinking how much comfort I had always seen result from a prayerful attention to the teaching of the Church through her holy days and seasons, and I felt more than ever anxious to impress upon the minds of the children the sacred recollections of the day. I explained to them the meaning of the Jewish law with which the Blessed Virgin complied as on this day, and that the offering which redeemed the first-born was a type of our redemption through the Blood of our SAVIOUR. That the infant JESUS was holy, or set apart and dedicated to the service of GOD, according to the Jewish law, which prefigured the Church of the First-born; and that His mother therefore did with Him according to the law of Moses, offering a pair of turtle doves for His redemption, for as yet the great Sacrifice which was shadowed forth in all the ceremonies of the law was not offered up, and the SAVIOUR came not to destroy the law but to fulfil.

Thus was the Eternal SON first presented in His FATHER's house, as it is written, " The LORD Whom ye seek shall suddenly come to His temple ;" but He had made Himself of no reputation and taken upon Him the form of a servant, and only those who were endued with the HOLY SPIRIT might discern the glory of the Godhead through the weakness of humanity and infancy. The children were not very ready in their answers to my questions in this part of the subject, but the youngest of them knew how that Anna the prophetess, who had served GOD so long with fastings and prayers night and day, was enabled to see the Redeemer of Israel in the Son of Mary, and how the aged Simeon, to whom it had been revealed by the HOLY GHOST that he should not die until he had seen the LORD's CHRIST, took the Infant SAVIOUR into his arms, and poured forth his joy in that inspired song which has ever since formed a part of Christian worship, saying, "LORD, now lettest Thou Thy servant depart in peace, according to Thy word, for mine eyes have seen Thy salvation."

I reminded the children how, on a later occasion, the LORD had cleansed the temple, driving from it all those who sold doves and who changed money, and who thus made the sacrifices of the law a pretence for so defiling the holy temple that our LORD said, " My house shall be called a house of prayer, but ye have made it a den of thieves," and again, "Make not My FATHER's house a house of merchandise."

These things were written for our instruction, and how often may we in a measure be guilty of the same sin as the Jews who were driven from the temple by our LORD, if we carry to His house our worldly thoughts and our plans for gain or pleasure.

The hour for school ended before I had spoken all the thoughts which seemed to arise out of the consideration of the Presentation of our Blessed SAVIOUR in the temple; and after a prayer and a hymn sung by the children, they dispersed to their happy homes.

As I passed Mary's cottage on my way, I noticed that some of them tapped gently at her door, to know if they could run on an errand for her, or be useful in any way.

It is now six years since that afternoon, and Mary still lives there alone; her husband's Bible and her child's little toys are as carefully dusted as ever, and are her most cherished possessions. In her little garden the flowers which her husband planted are carefully tended, and the baby's cradle is in its old place. I said she lived alone; but it is hardly so, there is not a little sick child in the village that does not look up and smile at the sound of her voice, not an aged man or woman who does not owe some of their daily comforts to her; if any one is ill, if any trouble is at hand, "Run for Mary Grey," is the first word that is said. But most of all she loves the children; and if a little infant is ill, it is all her pleasure to nurse and soothe it tenderly, so tenderly that it is easy to see how well she remembers the flaxen-headed boy that nestled once against her heart, and soothed her first sorrow with his innocent caresses. Mary never walks through the village but all the children run and catch her by the gown, and claim a kiss; and when on every holy festival she goes to place a wreath of her choicest flowers on the graves of her husband and her child, little loving hearts go with her, and eyes that for her sake are filled with tears as they kneel beside her, and Mary forgets her own sorrow as she turns to teach them to fold their tiny hands in prayer, that when they die they too may be with JESUS.

S. Matthias' Day.

COLLECT.

O ALMIGHTY GOD, Who into the place of the traitor Judas didst choose Thy faithful servant Matthias to be of the number of the twelve Apostles; Grant that Thy Church, being alway preserved from false Apostles, may be ordered and guided by faithful and true pastors; through JESUS CHRIST our LORD. AMEN.

DID you ever live in a district where coal is to be found in large quantities? If so, you will remember well the blackened aspect of the villages and hamlets that are to be found in such neighbourhood; large iron founderies and smelting chimneys are usually near at hand, the very trees and gardens look black and sooty, and the face of the country is far from inviting. It would fill a much larger book than I am going to write now, were I to tell you how that most valuable substance which we call coal, and which GOD has given us in such abundance in our country of England, is formed under the ground, from the decayed trees and leaves which flourished hundreds of years ago, and which have been gradually covered over in the course of time, or of the many clever contrivances by which the labour of digging for it and bringing it to the surface of the earth is shortened by machinery. What I wish to describe to you now, is not so much the history of a coal mine, but a tale of how much good was done in one mining district through the instrumentality of one good man. The village of Colford is situated in one of the dreariest parts of a large northern county in England : at the time of which I am speaking, it could hardly be called a village, for that is a word which generally suggests to our minds a pleasant little family of houses gathered round a venerable Church ; and Colford, some years ago, was but an assemblage of wretched hovels, inhabited by the families of the men who worked in an adjacent mine, varied with a few formal brick houses of more pretensions, belonging to the overseers, to whom the superintendence of the men was intrusted. The owner of the property derived yearly a large sum of money from the sale of the coal found on his estate, but he lived far away, in a more pleasant part of the country, and if he visited Colford, it was to inspect his worldly property, and not to interest himself in the well-being of the inhabitants; there was no Church within eight miles of the place, and in this part of the country there were no houses belonging to those who had the power or inclination to attend to the spiritual or temporal wants of their poorer brethren. It was no wonder then, that when the owner of the estate died, his son, who had been educated by a pious clergyman, who had taught him the importance of the duties and responsibilities which are attached to the possession of large property, found the people in a state resembling rather that of savages than of Christians in this favoured land.

Young Mr. Gordon, for that was his name, knew that money, like every other gift of God, was a talent for which he must give account, and he lost no time in seeking to promote the best interests of those who lived on his estate. He visited himself every cottage in Colford, and made himself acquainted with its inmates, and perhaps I cannot better describe to you the spiritual destitution which he found there, than by quoting his own words in a letter to his brother, a clergyman, who had lately taken holy orders.

"MY DEAR HENRY,—You ask me to tell you something of the state of things in this place. I believe no words of mine could give you a true picture of them. Truly, I can hardly believe that I am in Christian England. There is no church and no clergyman, as you know, consequently no school, no education in anything but vice, no one to visit the sick, to sympathize with the suffering, or to warn the unruly. The wages of the men are high, but they spend them chiefly in drinking, and their wives imitate them in this respect; you can therefore imagine the state of things in their comfortless dwellings; as to the children, the boys accompany their fathers at a very early age, and learn to drink and swear and fight, at a time of life when you could hardly think human nature could be so hardened. The girls are, if possible, proportionately worse; without the same hard work, and with so much evil example around them, they grow up idle and demoralized, and become in their turn bad wives and mothers. It is true, that I have met with some among these people who feel and lament the wickedness among which they live, but they are the exception and not the rule, and can do little good unless some one interferes in behalf of order. This, of course, is now become my duty, and I write to you for advice respecting it: the first step is to build and endow a Church, one sufficiently large to hold our increasing population, and stragglers from the country round. I hope to build one which shall be a feature of beauty in the scenery, to testify my gratitude to the Giver of the many good things I enjoy, a silent finger, pointing to GOD from among the busy abodes of men.

"Then we must have a school-house, and master and mistress, and I hope it will not be difficult to collect a school; there are certainly a large number of infants, who can be taken in at once, and we must try soon to gather older children, and form evening classes for adults. The children are so untaught and ignorant at present, that many of them do not even know the Name of a SAVIOUR, and there is not one who could answer the simplest questions respecting the great truths of salvation; the greater number of them have never been baptized, so that there is much work for a clergyman who remembers our LORD's injunction, 'Feed My lambs.' The question I now write to ask you is, will you be the Incumbent of the new Church? I know that you will think it a privilege and a duty belonging to no one so much as to yourself to labour in this hitherto neglected land, and I should indeed rejoice to see you undertake the work; but when I remember that if you do this, you must give up the hope of living near your wife's family and amongst those who would welcome you as their pastor, and turn your back upon your pleasant house at Greyfield, I feel that I am making a serious request in asking you to come here, where all is hard and dark in the hearts of the poor ignorant people as are the hills around them. Still, I feel nearly sure that you will wish to come. I need not say that I hope to hear from you soon.

"Your affectionate brother,
"ARTHUR GORDON."

The answer to this letter was a long one, but the last part of it contains all that is necessary to continue my story; it was as follows: "You were indeed right in thinking that I should wish to be appointed to the church at Colford, and I shall feel it my highest privilege to devote all my energies to the eternal welfare of the people there. It will be a great mutual pleasure to us to be fellow-workers for our LORD and SAVIOUR in that place: you with your money and influence, and I as a minister in the Church. My dear wife thinks with me, that our path of duty is plain, so we shall not cast a single lingering look at Greyfield. You remember the words of our LORD, 'No man having put his hand to the plough, and looking back, is fit for the kingdom of GOD.'"

Before very many months had elapsed, a beautiful church, in the Early English style of Architecture, was built at Colford: it stood on the side of a hill, and the few trees which grew near it, bounded the churchyard. Close to the church was the parsonage house, and within a stonethrow there were two other new buildings, the spacious schools and the master's comfortable house; but before the first stone of the church was laid, the priest was in the midst of his people, living with his wife and brother in the nearest house of which they could avail themselves; the children were gathered daily into a large room built hastily for the purpose, and another was licensed by the Bishop for the celebration of Divine Service, while the church was building. Even before twelve months had passed, there was a great change in the habits of the people, for whose good these labours of love were intended; they had learnt at last to listen with respect and gratitude to the minister of the most High God, and there were not a few among them who looked forward with hearts almost as full of hope and thankfulness as did Mr. Gordon and his brother, to the day when the church would be consecrated, and the bell should sound over all the hill side, calling them to the house of prayer. This joyful day was fixed for the Feast of Saint Matthias, "for," said Mr. Gordon, "it will be two years on that day since I first walked on this ground and determined, if God spared my life so long, to devote the first fruits of my wealth to His service." " Come then, with me, into my school-room," replied his brother, " and when you see the happy intelligent faces of the children there, and hear their answers to my questions, you will see how God has already blessed our poor endeavours." About thirty neat-looking children rose and curtseyed as the Rev. Mr. Gordon and his brother entered the girls' school-room.

" I am going to ask some questions about next Tuesday," said the clergyman to the school-mistress. "The boys have answered me nicely, and I hope as much from the girls. Can you tell me what day it will be?" said Mr. Gordon, to a very little girl who stood near him.

"The day our church will be made holy for ever," said she.

"I hope so, that is a reason why it will always be a joyful day as the year comes round; but tell me why it is observed by the whole Christian Church as a holy day."

"Because," another child answered, "it is the Feast of St. Matthias."

"Right, and who was S. Matthias?"

"The Apostle who was chosen in the place of the traitor Judas."

"Who were the Apostles?"

"They were twelve of our SAVIOUR'S Disciples, who were chosen by him to be the witnesses and companions of His life, and to be the first ministers in His Church."

"What is the meaning of the word Disciple?"

"One who is taught, or who learns."

"And of the word Apostle?"

"One who is sent, or a messenger: the holy Apostles were sent out into all lands to build the Church of CHRIST, and to ordain ministers."

"What do you mean by the Church of CHRIST, in this sense?"

"I mean all who are baptized in His Name."

"Who are the successors of the Apostles?"

"The Bishops and Priests."

"But was Judas, who came to so awful an end, likewise one of the Apostles?"

"Yes, and in this was fulfilled our LORD'S prophecy, that He should be betrayed by one of His own, for He said, 'He that eateth bread with Me shall betray Me.'"

"It is then," said Mr. Gordon, "a warning to each of us, lest though we may appear good in the sight of men, as the traitor Judas did, while he was in our Blessed LORD's society, yet all the while our holiness should be mere outside show, and our hearts be hard and full of sin; and it also teaches us, that though a minister of the Church of CHRIST may be unworthy to hold his sacred office, yet the holy sacraments which he administers, and the divine words which he reads, will not be less efficacious to those who receive and hear them in faith, for it is the office appointed by the SAVIOUR Himself that will be the channel of the blessing; yet it is a great affliction to the Church when any of her ministers are a cause of grief and offence, and you know that the Collect for S. Matthias's day contains a prayer against this evil.

"What did the eleven Apostles do with respect to the office of Apostleship, from which Judas by transgression fell?"

The children were silent, and Mr. Gordon continued.

"They assembled together for prayer, and having selected two from among the seventy disciples who had seen most of our LORD's miracles, and witnessed His Ascension, they prayed that their LORD and Master, who was now returned into glory, having received good gifts for men, would show them which of the two He had chosen; and having then drawn lots, in faith that their prayer would be answered (according to the Jewish custom), the lot fell upon Matthias, and he was numbered with the Apostles, and received with the other eleven, the gift of the HOLY GHOST upon the day of Pentecost. S. Matthias proved during a life spent in labours to convert first the Jews, and afterwards the Gentile nations who lived eastward of Judæa, that this great gift had not been bestowed on him in vain : his preaching was blessed to the conversion of great numbers of heathen, and he died the death of a martyr, as it is believed, by crucifixion. Our new church will be known by the name of this saint, as it will be consecrated on the day dedicated to his memory.

" How many years is it since our SAVIOUR, having founded His Church on earth, ascended to glory ?"

" More than 1,800 years, sir."

" But is our SAVIOUR less the head of his Church now, than He was then? or does He know all our hearts, as he did that of S. Matthias, when the Apostles prayed to Him to direct them whom to choose ?"

" We know that the SAVIOUR is as near to us now, sir, and that He sees all that we think and do, and orders all things that happen to us; then the LORD JESUS has set over His people at Colford the ministers who will be in future their pastors and teachers, and if any should refuse to hear the word of God by their mouth, it will be as if they had refused to hear CHRIST Himself, Who has sent them, and given them commission to feed His sheep."

After a few more kind words to the children, the two brothers left the school-room, they did not speak until they came in sight of the church, when Mr. Gordon turning to his brother said, " and this is the spot of which, two years ago, I wrote you so melancholy an account, and it has pleased God to grant us already so rich a first-fruits of our labours."

"Do you remember what those children were when you first came?" "I do indeed," replied the clergyman, "blessed be GOD that there is such a change: is it not a proof of what I have just observed to them, that the Divine Head of the Church is not less near than He was to the first Christians? for nothing less than Almighty power and grace could have worked such a reformation; and this church and churchyard, how soon will its hallowed walls be associated with the best feelings of those who, a few years ago, had never entered the house of GOD, but who now bring their weekly pence as a free-will offering, that they may share with us the privilege of erecting it. Next week, seven little infants, besides my own, will be christened there, and James Wilson and Mary Grey are to be married. Old Thomas, who died yesterday, will be the first to lie in the new churchyard: he told me that he blessed GOD he had lived so long as to see this good day for Colford. I must leave you now, brother, for I promised to look in on his poor widow, and you, I see, have business with the carpenters; will they have finished to-morrow, do you think?" "I have little doubt of it, they have been very diligent lately." Mr. Gordon turned towards the long row of cottages, not now so comfortless in appearance as formerly, but still offering a strong contrast to the fair building that rose up by their side: he found the poor woman who had so lately lost her husband, in great grief, but she seemed comforted by the pastor's visit, and took delight in speaking of the departed, and his altered life, since he had, as she said, "the knowledge of the Gospel." "Oh, sir, he would sit for hours looking at the church, when I had moved his chair to the window, that he might see it, and praising God that he had not died years ago in his sins: no, indeed, sir," added she, "he was ever the best man in Colford, though he was dark, as we all were about our souls; this book you gave our little granddaughter, sir, was the last he had in his hand; little Jane read it to him only the morning before he died, and he made a mark against it with his poor trembling fingers, and told her to mind her grandfather's mark when he was dead and gone. It was this verse he marked, sir."

> I love the Church—the holy Church,
> That o'er our life presides,
> The birth, the bridal, and the grave,
> And many an hour besides.
>
> Be mine, through life, to live in her,
> And when the LORD shall call,
> To die in her—the Spouse of CHRIST,
> The Mother of us all.

The Annunciation.

COLLECT.

We beseech Thee, O Lord, pour Thy grace into our hearts; that, as we have known the incarnation of Thy Son Jesus Christ, by the message of an angel, so by His Cross and Passion we may be brought unto the glory of His Resurrection; through the same Jesus Christ our Lord. Amen.

———

IT was the Feast of the Annunciation—a bright spring morning ushered in the anniversary of that day when the Angel Gabriel hailed the lowly Virgin as "highly favoured, and blessed among women." The village children of Braunton were hurrying to school with their Prayer-Books; some conning over the collect, and others, better prepared with their lessons, occasionally stopping to gather a fresh primrose in the bank, or seek for a violet.

"Can any of you tell me why Ellen Merton is not at school this morning?" said the mistress, when the names of the scholars were called over, and Ellen did not answer to hers.

"Please, ma'am, her father is ill, and Mrs. Merton sent Ellen to the town to get some physic, but she told me she should be back before church time," replied Jane Madden.

But Ellen did not return, and after church the

mistress called at her mother's cottage to inquire the reason of the child's absence. She found Ellen in tears, the reason of which Mrs. Merton soon explained by telling her that she had sent the little girl to the neighbouring town for some medicine for her father desiring her to return by the road instead of through the fields, but Ellen had disobeyed her mother, and in getting over a stile she had let the bottle fall, and it was broken.

"I should have gone myself, ma'am," said Mrs. Merton, "but the doctor said my husband ought to take the physic as soon as possible, and I knew Ellen would run faster than I could, but as she did not mind my words about coming home by the road, her father had to wait a long time for the draught, and he was in great pain till he took it."

The child's fresh burst of tears and sorrowful face showed how much she regretted her fault, and Mrs. Roberts, the mistress, seeing that it was not a time to talk to her of it, and expressing a hope that her mother would let her go to school in the afternoon, took her leave.

Ellen was, for her age, one of the most forward girls in the school, and from her general good conduct a favourite with the mistress; but she was not always so obedient as she might have been to her mother, and was often inclined to question her wishes, and if they were not such as she could understand, she would sometimes follow her own in opposition, as in the instance we have mentioned. Mrs. Merton had not told her she feared she might break the bottle and spill the contents in crossing a stile, and as the little girl herself saw no reason why she might not return through the fresh fields, instead of along the dusty road, she chose the former path. If children would always cheerfully and readily obey those who are set over them, without expecting a reason for everything they are desired to do, it would be better for themselves and for those who love them.

There were traces of tears on Ellen's face when she joined her school companions in the afternoon, but as they thought she was sad because her father was ill, they did not ask her any questions. After the school was over, the mistress called the child to her and said :

"I will not now talk of your disobedience to your mother, for I know you have suffered much from the thought of the prolonged pain which it caused your poor father. I am sorry you lost the privilege of joining in the morning service, and hearing the Clergyman explain to the children the reason of the Festival which our Church this day commemorates. Do you know why it is called the Annunciation?"

"Because the Angel Gabriel announced to the Virgin Mary that she was to be the mother of our LORD."

"Yes, Ellen; and though this was a great mystery, which she could not understand, she did not doubt the power and goodness of GOD, but meekly replied, 'Behold the handmaid of the LORD, be it unto me according to thy word.' Do you remember in what portion of Holy Scripture is recorded GOD's first promise to send a Saviour into the world?"

"In the Book of Genesis, when He promised that

the seed of the woman should bruise the serpent's head."

"Yes; and to Abraham it was also said, 'In thy seed shall all generations of the earth be blessed.' To King David also was the promise given that the Saviour should be of his lineage; you know He is often in Scripture called the 'Son of David.' Again we read in the book of the Prophet Isaiah, 'Behold a Virgin shall conceive and bear a Son.' All these prophecies and promises were fulfilled in the miraculous birth of our Blessed LORD, Who, for our sakes, became poor, that we, through His poverty, might be rich. The text of the sermon this morning was, 'Yea, rather, blessed are they that hear the Word of GOD and keep it.' Though the holy mission of the Virgin rendered her blessed, she was still more so in her obedience and faith. To the virgin-mother the holy JESUS, Who in His Divine Person was her GOD, rendered in His human nature the perfect obedience of a son, thus early teaching little children to obey their parents. You may remember reading in the Bible the obedient answer of Mary when the tidings of this day were announced, 'Be it unto me according to Thy word;' that when our LORD was twelve years old He disputed in the temple with the Jewish doctors, who, with 'all who heard Him were astonished at His understanding and answers;' but after that period until He was about thirty years of age, when He began His public ministry, the Holy Scripture only records that He went down with His parents, (that is, with the blessed Virgin and His supposed father, Joseph,) to Nazareth, 'and was subject to them.' Will you try and remember the example of the Saviour when you are tempted to disobey your mother, Ellen? You may not always understand *why* you are desired to do this thing, or go that particular way, but that is no excuse for disobedience; our parents are set over us by GOD, and S. Paul says, ' Children, obey your parents in all things, for this is well pleasing unto the LORD.' Try and not forget this, Ellen, and do all as unto GOD."

When the little girl returned to the cottage she endeavoured to atone for her fault by anticipating every wish of her parents, and secretly determined, by GOD's grace, to practise the great duty of obedience, and well did she keep this resolution; the lesson was hard to learn, (who does not find it so?) but by watchfulness and prayer she conquered her besetting sin.

When Ellen was eighteen she went out to service; constant watchfulness had strengthened the habit of obedience, and her mistress often said that she could always trust Ellen, for she never disobeyed her orders. The little children of the family in which she lived were glad when it was Ellen's turn to stay at home with them on Sunday evening, for she told them pretty scripture stories; and when on one occasion the disobedience of some of her little charges reminded her of her early life, she narrated to the children the history of her own disobedience, and how it might have proved fatal to her father, and then she would have been unhappy all her days; and she told them how by disobedience sin entered into the world, and brought with it the punishment of eternal death, from which nothing less than the perfect obedience of CHRIST could deliver us; and she talked to them of His love and duty to His earthly parents when He was a little child, and Ellen repeated to them the pretty hymn she had learned many years ago.

"But who, O perfect filial heart,
E'er did like Thee a true son's part,
Endearing, firm, serene?

"E'en from the tree He deigned to bow
For her His agonized brow,
Her His sole earthly care."

Christian Year.

S. Mark's Day.

COLLECT.

O ALMIGHTY GOD, Who hast instructed Thy holy Church with the heavenly doctrine of Thy Evangelist Saint Mark; Give us grace, that, being not like children carried away with every blast of vain doctrine, we may be established in the truth of Thy holy Gospel; through JESUS CHRIST our LORD. AMEN.

"MOTHER, will you take me to Church to-day?" said little Amy Morris.

"To-day, child?" replied her mother, who was busy putting away some clothes she had ironed; "why do you want to go to church to-day? I'm too busy to go out, and I can't leave the baby."

"If you could make time, I should be so very glad, mother; I think Susan will be home to take care of baby. It is Saint Mark's Day, to-day."

"Why, how should you know what day it is, with your poor blind eyes?"

"Oh, I remember last year, Saint Mark's Day was the day after my birthday; I went to church with aunt; I wasn't quite blind then, mother, I could see the flowers, if I held them close, and I could see that the hedges were green and gay, as we walked along to church."

Mrs. Morris was very tender and kind to her little blind daughter, so she thought for a moment, and then said, " Well, I'll see what I can do if Susan comes in time, but I'm not dressed."

" Thank you, thank you," said Amy, clapping her hands for joy. " Now I shall have a happy day; it's such a treat, mother, to walk with you; if you'll just put on your bonnet and shawl, your dress will do very well; I can feel that it's as clean as possible," and the little girl threw her arms round her mother. So Amy had her way, and the clothes were put aside, and Susan, the eldest daughter, was left in charge of the baby, and Mrs. Morris put on her bonnet and shawl.

" It's not many pleasures you can have, my girl," she said, " so I must try and spare an hour, every now and then, to take you to church, or get some one else to lead you there. You're become such a church-goer since you were up at your aunt's, but I can't say but it's done you good, for you're a deal livelier than you were."

" When you can go with me yourself, mother, I like it much the best; you know I can help you a little with your work, and nurse baby, and you know the minister said on Sunday, that every half hour even that we spend in prayer to God, is like laying up treasure in heaven. Do you know, mother, I am sure it is true: I'll tell you why; when I first went to aunt, I used to fret a great deal about losing my sight; every day I could see worse, and that made me cross; aunt was very kind, she said nothing, only when I grumbled about not being able to do anything, she said, ' there is one thing you can do.' And she took me often with her to church; at first it seemed strange to me, and at last it seemed quite natural to begin the day that way, and I felt happier; and there were words in the service about being patient and doing God's will, that made me feel less impatient; and then on Saints' days we had a sermon; and one day it was all about our Lord Jesus Christ healing the eyes of the blind, and how He had the same power now to heal the sick; and I asked aunt if she thought the Lord Jesus would let me see again; and she said, if it was for my good He would, but that perhaps blindness was sent as a blessing to me. So then I prayed every day to have my sight again if it was good for me; but now I am quite blind instead, so I know that God saw it was best for me to be so. I shall see again in heaven, you know, mother, and perhaps I should never have thought about getting ready for that glorious place if it were not for my blindness. I used to care about nothing but play, you know."

Amy could not tell that her mother had tears in her eyes, as she spoke, but she felt her press the hand by which she led her tenderly, as she said, "Yes, my child, we know that all that God sends us is for the best, but sometimes we are sinful, and don't believe it; I am thankful that you do, and that it makes you happy."

"Mother," continued Amy, "why did father come to live here? the country was pleasanter."

"Because the railroad was finished at Morcombe, and he could get no more work."

By this time they reached the cathedral, which

was within a short walk of their home; there were other churches open for service at Winchester, where they lived, but Mrs. Morris knew that the sacred music would be a great pleasure to Amy, so she chose the cathedral. They had hardly time to reach the choir part of the cathedral, used for divine service, before the prayers were commenced; and Amy was sorry for this, for she knew it was not right to enter the presence of God in a hurried manner, and she liked to kneel down and repeat a prayer before the minister began to say the exhortation; there were many people in the cathedral that day, but I think that no one there could have had a happier heart than Amy; the loss of sight had removed from her one great temptation to wandering thoughts, and it seemed to her as if her whole soul went up in prayer to God on the wings of the beautiful music. She knew in which parts of the service to stand, and when to kneel; and then the sermon, it was so plain, that the little girl understood it all, and told her father about it that evening. It began with a short history of S. Mark, how he was an Evangelist, or teacher of truth, and one of the four who wrote the holy Gospels, and that he was the companion of S. Peter, whose labours he shared, and from whose lips he heard the account of our blessed Saviour's life, which he wrote in the Gospel which bears his name, and that he at last bore witness to the truth which he had lived to preach, by submitting to a cruel death.

The text which the Clergyman had taken for his sermon, was from the Epistle for the day, out of the fourth chapter of the Epistle to the Ephesians; it was this: "And He gave some Apostles, and some Prophets, and some Evangelists, and some Pastors and Teachers, for the perfecting of the saints, for the work of the ministry, for the edifying of the Body of CHRIST." And when the Clergyman had explained these verses, and taught how by the Body of CHRIST was meant the Church, he went on to speak of the beautiful prayer contained in the Collect, and of our high privileges, to whom, 1800 years after the time when the Apostles and Evangelists lived and wrote, the Gospel of our LORD JESUS CHRIST is preached in its truth and fulness. "We may well thank GOD," he said, " we who assemble year by year to keep the sacred days and seasons in the holy buildings which our fathers of many years ago raised to the glory of GOD, and for the good of man, and we may well pray to be kept from the sin of being carried away from the fellowship of the Church of CHRIST, and the sound of gospel truth by the "vain blasts of some newly invented teaching of man."

When the sermon was over, and the people were all walking away, Amy was pleased to hear her mother say how glad she was that they had gone, and that she would try and take her there very often. And she had another pleasure soon, for when the Clergyman of the parish came to visit them he interested himself much in the little girl, and gave her mother money to take her to a very clever doctor, but there was nothing to be done, the doctor said, which could restore sight to little Amy; she had lost the use of her eyes when she had the small-pox, and her recovery was, humanly speaking, impossible; so the Clergyman asked her mother if she would like Amy to attend a school for the blind, where they were taught to read with their fingers; and very soon the little happy girl was able to read aloud to her mother while she worked, as well as to do many other pleasant and useful things; but you may be sure that what Amy prized above all her other learning was the power of reading her Bible and Prayer-Book; she has learnt to be thankful and content in that state to which it has pleased God to call her, and to praise Him for His goodness in shutting her eyes on the sights of this world, that He might open them on the truths of that glorious world which is around us and above us, and yet of which we think so seldom, and with so little true faith, though they are the things " belonging to our peace."

S. Philip and S. James' Day.

COLLECT.

O ALMIGHTY GOD, Whom truly to know is everlasting life; grant us perfectly to know Thy SON JESUS CHRIST to be the way, the truth, and the life; that, following the steps of Thy holy Apostles, Saint Philip and Saint James, we may steadfastly walk in the way that leadeth to eternal life; through the same Thy SON JESUS CHRIST our LORD. AMEN.

JOHN and Susan Mason were the children of a carpenter who lived at Exeter. William Mason, their father, had been what is called well to do in the world, and when he married, what with his own earnings, and with the washing that his wife took in, they lived very comfortably. Times were altered with them now, for Mrs. Mason had hurt her spine some years ago, and was not only unable to work, but often required a great deal of care and nursing, and her husband had not always work enough, but he was an industrious man, and a good husband and father, and sent his children to school daily, for he said, he would give them a good education while he could work for them, and that when he was old, they should support him. He had four children: John, who was twelve years old, was a clever boy, and forward at his lessons; he promised, too, to be handy at his father's trade: he was an affectionate son, and the neighbours said he had a good heart, because he was always attentive to his mother; but a good heart is a thing that none of us have by nature. And if you had known John Mason well, you would have seen that selfishness and pride, and a desire to be thought well of, were his besetting faults, and that he did not earnestly seek the assistance of the Blessed Holy Spirit Who alone can change our sinful nature.

Susan, the next eldest, was a little girl of ten years old: she was a gentle, thoughtful child, who, from her mother's illness, had learnt to be more useful at home than children of her age often are. It was Susan who nursed her mother, and kept the house clean, and prepared the dinner under her mother's direction. It was Susan who mended her brother's clothes, and darned her father's stockings, and Mrs. Mason often said what a happy mother she was, to have a child who was so willing to learn and to do all that she was told.

Susan was not clever like John, and she was rather backward with her books, but the great difference between them was this, Susan believed and remembered with all her heart, what John only learnt with his head. She did not forget that she was always in the presence of God, and she tried to do what was right because it was pleasing to her Heavenly Father.

Harry, the next in age to Susan, was a lively boy of eight years old; he promised to be something like John in his character: and little Mary, the youngest, was only five.

"I wish, brother Jack," said Harry, one afternoon, "that you would finish cutting out my boat this evening, and come and show me how to sail it on the large pond in the field."

"No, I can't to night," said John, "to-morrow will be a Saint's Day, and I've got some papers to write about the day, I must have them ready to take to school in the morning."

"I wish it were a holiday, instead of a holy day," said Harry, "I mean a day to play, instead of being like a Sunday: I should like to see the chimney sweepers dancing round jack-in-the-green, better than to go to school."

"Oh! Harry," said Susan, "how can you say so? I like the Saints' days so much, because mother always spares me to go to church and to school, and she can't let me go on the other week days."

"I don't know much about to-morrow," said Harry; "I know it is Saint James' Day, I've got the Collect to learn by heart, but I didn't listen while the teacher was telling our class about it; I was looking at Charlie Brown, who was making funny faces behind the teacher's back."

"It is S. Philip and S. James' Day; they are both kept on one day," said John: "if you want to know how to answer at the catechizing, you had better get mother to read my paper to you, for it will be the best in our class, I know; I've taken such pains, and copied out of all the books I could get, besides remembering what the clergyman said about the day."

While the children were talking in this way, Mrs. Mason was lying on the bed, as she was always obliged to do, supported by pillows, and trying to do a little work; she was sorry to hear Harry speak so carelessly, and that he had been so inattentive at school, but she did not scold him, as he had told it openly, for she liked her children to talk freely before her. She was grieved, too, to hear that John praised himself, and seemed proud of having written well, but she did not say anything to them then, only she called Harry to her, and said a few words to him, which made him throw his arms round her neck, and kiss her, and promise to be more attentive another time; and then she said that if John would bring his account of the day and read it aloud after they had had their tea, she would talk about it to them and then Susan and Harry would know more about it.

So John took his papers to the table near the window, and was soon busy writing, and Susan got the tea ready, and then she and Harry learnt the Collect together, and they both knew it perfectly before John exclaimed, " There, I have finished it, and I am sure Mr. Clark will say it is well done, there is not a boy in our school who can write his name so well as I can, mother; look here, Harry, how straight I have written 'John Mason.'"

" There is not a boy, I dare say, whose father has taken such pains to make him improve at school by helping him to prepare at home, John," said his mother, " or who has had so much good schooling, and perhaps I may think, because I am your mother, that there is not a lad who has better abilities; but remember, if it is so, to Whom you owe it, and that the power to learn, and opportunities to improve yourself, are great talents entrusted to you, for which you must one day give account, and that unless you make a good use of them, they will not only increase your temptations, but add to your condemnation. It is of little use to 'know of the doctrine,' unless we 'do the will of GOD,' my boy; but now let us hear your paper. Do you write one for every Saint's Day?"

"We have this year, mother: Mr. Clark said that the first-class boys should write one for every holy day this year, that they might prove that they understood what they were going to commemorate; he told us to be very careful this time, because there are two Apostles who are called S. James. Shall I begin to read what I have written now, mother?" Mrs. Mason said yes, and Susan stood by her brother's side, that she might look over him, for she said she could understand it better if she saw the words, and John put his arm round her waist, for he was very fond of his little sister; and even Harry left off his tricks, and forgot to make little Mary laugh, as he generally did when there was any reading or grave talking going on, for he thought it was a fine thing for John to be reading something he had written himself, just like a book, he said, and he wondered if he should ever be able to do the same. So John began to read as follows:

"The day which is observed by the Church in memory of Saint Philip and Saint James is the first of May.

"The Apostle Philip is the same of whom we read in the first chapter of the Gospel according to Saint John, that 'JESUS findeth him and saith unto him, Follow Me,' and who then went and called Nathaniel and said unto him, 'We have found Him of

Whom Moses in the law, and the Prophets did write, JESUS of Nazareth, the son of Joseph;' but Saint Philip did not quite understand, while the SAVIOUR lived, the Divine Nature and Almighty power of his LORD and Master, for we read in the sixth chapter of Saint John's Gospel, that he wondered how so great a multitude could be satisfied with bread, and again, in the fourteenth chapter, the ninth verse, we read the SAVIOUR's words, 'Have I been so long time with you, and yet hast thou not known Me, Philip?'"

"Did you find these instances in the life of Saint Philip by yourself, John?" said Mrs. Mason.

"No, mother, Mr. Clark pointed them out to us, and we marked the places in our Bibles. I have tried hard to remember all he said."

"That is right," said his mother, and John went on reading. "After the death of the SAVIOUR, and after the HOLY GHOST had descended upon the Apostles, Saint Philip preached and laboured diligently among the heathen nations for many years, until at last, the idolatrous people who lived in a city called Hierapolis, were enraged against him, and put him to a cruel death; it is believed that he was crucified. The Apostle James, whose name is mentioned with Saint Philip, is sometimes called Saint James the less, to distinguish him from James the son of Zebedee, the brother of Saint John the Evangelist, who was put to death by Herod; and sometimes James the brother of our LORD, on account, it is believed, of his relationship to Joseph, the supposed father of our LORD.

"He lived to an advanced age, and was many

years Bishop of Jerusalem. He wrote the inspired Epistle which bears his name, to those of the twelve tribes scattered abroad, that is, to every Hebrew who had embraced Christianity. Many interesting things are told of this holy man, the first Bishop of the Church in Jerusalem, and the manner of his death is thus recorded. The Jews being determined to find some accusation against him, commanded him to declare publicly that the LORD JESUS was not the true MESSIAH, and they brought him to the highest part of the Temple, that he might address the people from thence; and when the Apostle, resisting the threats and temptations of the chiefs of the people, not only refused to deny his SAVIOUR, but declared that they should see the Son of Man coming again in great power and glory, they were so infuriated that they dashed him down from a pinnacle of the Temple. Saint James, whose fall had not quite killed him, had strength enough to raise himself on his knees, and he prayed aloud for his murderers. 'I beseech Thee, O LORD GOD, Heavenly FATHER, forgive them, for they know not what they do.' His enemies, instead of being softened by this act of Christian love, rushed upon him and stoned him till he died. Saint James is supposed to have been about ninety-six years old at the time of his martyrdom."

When John stopped reading, his mother said that she was very glad he had remembered so much, and that he had taken pains to write it so nicely, and

10*

Susan said that she thought she should not forget about the two Saint James' days, and that she should be able to answer some of the questions which would be asked in school.

"Mother," said Harry, who had been wonderfully quiet for him, "what is the use of Saints' days being kept?"

"We might infer that it is right to observe them, even if we could not see their use," replied his mother, "because they are appointed by the Church; but there are many blessings which follow from a right use of them: I will tell you of one, which I think you can understand. Suppose that some great king should say, that to every one who would be a faithful soldier under his son, and who should succeed in conquering a wicked and cruel enemy, while fighting under his son's command, he would give a crown of gold and a rich reward, and take him to live in some far off, glorious palace. Do you not think it would give you courage to go to join in the fight, and to try to deserve the reward, if you knew that your brother John and others that you knew had won the victory before you and obtained the prize? and do you not think that you would like better to picture to yourself all the pleasures of the beautiful palace to which you hoped to go, if you knew that your brother was already there, and would you not hope, as the king had helped him to fight, and received him at last, so he would do for you? And is not this a picture of a Christian's warfare? The King of Heaven has set a glorious combat before us, and called us to be the soldiers and servants of His Son, our LORD JESUS

Christ, and appointed us our eternal reward, and prepared a glorious place for those who overcome in the struggle against sin and Satan."

Then she read to them how that the remembrance of those holy men of old, who were strengthened with such might by the Holy Spirit, that they endured untold sufferings, and submitted joyfully to torture such as we can scarcely bear to think of even, rather than that they should cease to spread the Gospel of the Lord Jesus Christ, the good news of Salvation among their enemies and persecutors; how the memory of these devoted Christians should encourage us to fight manfully, as we promise to do, at our baptism, against sin, the world, and the devil, and to continue Christ's faithful soldiers and servants, unto our life's end; and how these holy men whose names are thus kept in remembrance by our Church, were truly men of like passions with ourselves, fought against the same enemies that we must conquer, they trusted in the same Saviour, they sought the assistance of the same Holy Spirit in Whom we trust, and for Whom we must pray: and as we are encouraged by their lives, and stimulated to fresh zeal, that we may adorn the doctrine of God our Saviour by our lives and conversation, so we may be comforted in our death, by the thought that they are gone before us to the 'rest that remaineth for the people of God,' and that we may look forward to the time when through the infinite mercy of God our names shall be found written with theirs in the Lamb's book of life. And one especial blessing of the Saints' days is, that they bring these holy things near to us. Those Christians who were living when the first Martyr, Stephen, saw the heavens opened, and the SAVIOUR standing at the right hand of GOD the FATHER, who welcomed Saint Peter when he was led forth from prison by an angel's hand, and who saw daily the wonderful works wrought by the Apostles, to whom the LORD had given the power of working miracles, were not likely to forget from day to day, the things belonging to the kingdom of CHRIST; but we, who live eighteen hundred years later, though we have heard all these glorious truths, live mostly in forgetfulness of them, or we think perhaps of them once a week, on Sunday. And then we live the other days, as if these things were a dream, but the Saints' days join us in thought to the time when salvation was first preached through CHRIST Crucified, and serve to bring us nearer to the Cross which was raised on Calvary.

"I hope, indeed, that it will be so with us," said Mrs. Mason, earnestly, "for 'how shall we escape if we neglect so great salvation?' Do you remember what our LORD said about the men of Tyre and Sidon not being so bad as the Jews?"

"Yes, mother," said Susan, reverently, "JESUS said, that it should be more tolerable for the people of Tyre and Sidon, at the day of judgment, than for the unbelieving Jews, for they would have repented at His preaching."

"Yes," said Mrs. Mason, "and the Jews refused to repent when GOD Himself was dwelling among them, speaking unto them through His SON; and we know that in our days there are many thousands who, in this Christian land, harden their hearts in like manner: let us search our own hearts diligently, lest we should be found guilty of the same sin. But we must not talk more now, for it is getting late, and your father will be home soon, and will want his supper." So John put away his book and paper, and little Mary went to bed, for she was almost asleep already, and Susan spread the table for her father's supper: Harry asked his mother to hear him say the Collect for fear he should forget it.

I do not know whether John received as much praise as he expected for having written his paper nicely, when he went to the school the next morning, but I believe he remembered his mother's words, and that he learnt to do what is right from higher motives: for if, like the Pharisees, his only desire in doing good works is that they may be seen of men, he will have no other reward.

Susan went to school and to Church, and listened so attentively to the sermon that she remembered much of it, and was able to tell her mother what the clergyman had said. The text of the sermon was taken from the last part of the first chapter of Saint John's Gospel, where our SAVIOUR tells Nathaniel that He saw him under the fig-tree, before Philip had called him.

"And, mother," said Susan, "the minister said that the LORD JESUS saw him, though He was not in the same place, because He was GOD, and everywhere present, and that the LORD knew his heart, and said he was without guile; and the minister said that the

Saviour knew our hearts, and could see all that we thought, and all that we did, now, as He did while He was upon the earth, and that we ought to remember this, for that it should make us fear to sin, and to think bad thoughts.

"I knew before that God could always see us, but I don't think it ever seemed so plain to me before. I shan't be afraid to go to bed in the dark alone, any more, mother, it makes me feel so safe to think that the Lord Jesus watches over every child: the minister said He did, and that He would send His angels to take care of us."

"I hope you will always remember it, my child, and that it will always be a comfort to you to think that 'the Eye of the Lord is in every place.' It is only to the wicked that this truth must be full of terror. Do you remember the solemn words of the Psalmist in the 91st and 139th Psalms (Prayer Book Version?)"

Susan read them from her Prayer Book. "Are these not beautiful words, mother? may I learn them, some day?"

"Yes," said Mrs. Mason, "but now it is time for you to go to bed, you will not be afraid to-night."

"No, mother, not at all," and the little girl kissed her mother, and went quietly up stairs to the closet off the stairs, where she and her sister Mary slept. Mary was asleep already, and the moonlight streaming into the room, through the small casement window, made everything look so still and strange to Susan, that she would have felt afraid, as children sometimes do, to be all alone, but that she remembered what she had read, and so she soon ceased to feel uncomfortable, and knelt down with a happy heart to say her evening prayer, and her last thought before she slept, was the verse which she always said as soon as she was laid down in bed.

> Glory to Thee, my GOD, this night,
> For all the blessings of the light:
> Keep me, O keep me, King of kings,
> Beneath Thine own Almighty wings.
> Forgive me, LORD, for Thy dear SON,
> The ill that I this day have done;
> That with the world, myself, and Thee,
> I, ere I sleep, at peace may be.

S. Barnabas' Day.

COLLECT.

O LORD GOD ALMIGHTY, Who didst endue Thy holy Apostle Barnabas with singular gifts of the HOLY GHOST; Leave us not, we beseech Thee, destitute of Thy manifold gifts, nor yet of grace to use them alway to Thy honour and glory; through JESUS CHRIST our LORD. AMEN.

DID my little reader ever walk through the poorest streets of London, wondering at the sin and the sorrows of mankind, that have made a part of the world, which was created so fair and beautiful, so miserable now? T—— street is one of these gloomy parts of that mighty city. It is so dark and dirty, that I have thought it looked less wretched on a rainy day in November, when all around was alike cheerless, than when the bright rays of the summer sun pierced the damp and smoky air, and shone upon windows so broken and dirty that they seemed rather to keep out the light than to admit it. Inside most of these windows are piled up heaps of bones, old rags, and bottles, while some of them display through their broken panes, unwholesome food. Children of a wild and squalid appearance, make a continual noise in the street, quarrelling and pelting each other with stones, to the great annoyance of the few respectable people who pass that way, generally with the intention of visiting or relieving some of the inhabitants.

It is indeed one of the worst districts of my parish, and yet in a little room in that gloomy street lives a poor woman, whom I have never visited without a feeling of thankfulness to GOD, for so bright an example of Christian faith and patience; so true it is that—

> "Love is a flower that will not die
> For lack of leafy screen,
> And Christian hope can cheer the eye
> That ne'er saw vernal green."

Some years ago, I was walking through this street for the first time, having met with indifferent or sullen answers from my new parishioners, when I was struck by the appearance of two children who passed me. They were, indeed, hardly better clothed than the ragged boys and girls who called rudely to them from the middle of the road, but their dress was clean and neatly patched; they were little girls of about nine or ten years of age, and as they walked hand in hand, I observed that each carried a Prayer-Book, and that they seemed to possess something which pleased them greatly, and which was wrapped in a piece of newspaper. I followed the children, wondering whether their home could be in such a place as this, until I saw them enter at the open door of a house much neater in appearance than any of the others. The windows nearest the ground were clean, and mended neatly with paper where they were cracked, and the floor of the passage was swept; I noticed, too, through the window, that a geranium which seemed carefully watered, was in flower, and gave a pleasant token that some one lived there who loved to make their home as bright as they could. I walked into the house after the children, and knocked at the door of a room in which I plainly heard their cheerful voices. It was opened to me by a neat, but poorly dressed woman, who curtseyed to me, and welcomed me gladly, calling to one of the children to set a chair for me; there were but two in the room, which contained little furniture except a bed, a cot, a few boxes, a table, a little shelf, on which a few books were carefully dusted, and a larger one, which held the scanty supply of cooking materials, plates, and cups belonging to the little family. A fine little boy, about four years old, stood quietly by his mother's side for a few minutes, but he soon began to be impatient, and in spite of his sisters' caution to " be quiet while the gentleman was talking to mother," he pulled them by their frocks and seemed eager to obtain something from them.

"Give him his cake, Mary," said Mrs. Thompson, for that was the poor woman's name. "I beg your pardon, sir," she said, turning to me, "I'm almost afraid Jemmy's a spoilt lad between his sisters and myself, since his poor father died. It's not often we see any of the gentlefolks except the Clergyman, and Mr. A——, that was here before you, sir, used to notice him so much that he is not afraid of you, I fancy."

"I should be sorry to see him afraid of me," I replied, and as I held out my hand the child came timidly up to me. "Where did your sister get that nice cake for you?" I said.

"At the school, sir; I'm going there too, when I'm old enough," replied the little fellow.

"Do they go every day to school?"

"Yes, sir," answered the little girls at once.

"And why do you get cake to-day?"

"It is a Saint's day; S. Barnabas' Day, sir."

"And so you have been to the parish school, and are two of my little scholars then?"

"Yes, sir."

"And you have had a feast in the school-room after the holy service was over?"

"Yes, sir; such a feast, meat and pudding!"

Their poor mother smiled at the happy faces of her children; she knew how seldom they tasted meat at home, and she added, "They have brought their cake home for Jemmy and their mother; they always do, sir."

"And can you tell me," I asked, "why we have a school feast and other rejoicings in our parish on this Saint's day?"

"Yes, sir; our church was consecrated on this day several years ago."

I asked them what it meant to consecrate a church, and they answered that it meant that it was set apart for the service of GOD, and made a holy place for ever. They also replied very nicely to some questions which I put to them about S. Barnabas, and told me how he was rich, but devoted all his worldly goods to the service of the poor and persecuted Christians in his time, and that he was called Barnabas, which means the son of consolation, for this reason; and that after labouring with S. Paul for many years he was at last stoned to death by the Jews on account of his religion.

I was glad to find that the little girls remembered so well what they were taught in the school, and still more pleased to observe that they showed in their conduct the good effects of their religious education, that they were gentle to each other, and obedient to their mother, who seemed to find all her earthly comfort in her children.

I asked her whether it would not be possible for her to remove to a more healthy and favourable situation than the street in which I found her, and she then told me the sad story of her privations and hardships. She had been a servant in a gentleman's family, and had saved together a little money, which she added to her husband's stock when they married, in order to purchase a small but promising business in the city; one misfortune after another reduced her and her husband to the lowest poverty, and she found herself, at his death, possessed of nothing she could call her own, but the house in which she now lived, which was given to her in part payment of a debt by one who owed her husband a large sum. Unable to sell it for anything, and too poor to rent a room in a better part of the city, she decided on letting it out for lodgings, keeping only one room herself; she was but poorly paid, she said, but she contrived to get her living by this means, and by taking in work for a large general shop in the neighbourhood; her greatest trial, she said, was that her children should grow up in such a place, where all the sights and sounds were evil, but she thanked God that hitherto, and she had been there nearly a year, she had been able to keep them from joining in bad company, and their regular attendance at school was the greatest comfort to her; the poor woman seemed to have little hope of ever being rich enough to leave the place herself, until, if it should please GOD, her boy should grow up to work for her; but she hoped in a few years' time to obtain for her girls employment which would remove them to better homes; she dreaded, she said, especially for them, the scenes of fighting and bad language which frequently disturbed them in the rooms occupied by her lodgers. I reminded her that where GOD had placed her path, there she would find grace sufficient for her; she had not, like Lot of old, willingly chosen to live in the tents of wickedness, she had not put herself in the way of temptation, and therefore she might pray in faith to be delivered from evil.

After this visit, I frequently went to see Mrs. Thompson and her children; her lowly room was indeed a green spot in the desert of iniquity around her; for many many months she walked alone with her children to all the services of the church, the only family in all that street that did so; but at last, one and another of her neighbours, won over by the consistency of her conduct, and softened by trouble in which the widow had been a friend and a neighbour to them, were induced to accompany her, and I rejoiced to see in her life the fulfilment of the divine command and promise:

"Let your light shine before men, that they may see your good works and glorify your FATHER which is in Heaven.'

S. John Baptist's Day.

COLLECT.

ALMIGHTY GOD, by Whose Providence Thy servant John Baptist was wonderfully born, and sent to prepare the way of Thy SON, our SAVIOUR, by preaching repentance; Make us so to follow his doctrine and holy life, that we may truly repent according to his preaching; and after his example constantly speak the truth, boldly rebuke vice, and patiently suffer for the truth's sake; through JESUS CHRIST our LORD. AMEN.

DO you know who S. John the Baptist was? O yes, all Christian children must have read the history of his life in the New Testament. This is the anniversary, or return according to the time of year, of the day when it is supposed he was born; the Christian Church has set apart this day as a holy day, upon which we are especially to remember the doctrines which this man "who was sent from GOD" taught, and to think of what his work upon earth was, and what we have to do with his preaching, and to thank GOD for giving us all His prophets and teachers, and upon this day, more especially, for the life and death of John the Baptist, the great Forerunner of our LORD, the preacher of repentance, he of whom our SAVIOUR said that, "among those that are born of women, there is not a greater prophet than John the Baptist." The day which we call S. John's Day, in remembrance of the Apostle John, is in winter, just after Christmas Day, but S. John Baptist's Day is in the middle of summer; in the morning and afternoon we shall go to church, and in the evening we will walk in the pleasant fields. And now I will talk to you of S. John the Baptist, that every thing relating to him may be fresh in your minds before you go to church to-morrow and hear of him.

His birth was foretold many years before he came into the world; the Prophet Isaiah, who lived several hundred years before, speaks of him when he says in Isaiah xl. 3, " The voice of him that crieth in the wilderness, Prepare ye the way of the LORD, make straight in the desert a highway for our GOD; " and Malachi the Prophet refers to him when he says, speaking by the Spirit and in the Name of GOD, " Behold, I will send My messenger and he shall prepare My way before Me."—Mal. iii. 1. And again, iv. 5, 6, " Behold, I will send you Elijah the Prophet before the coming of the great and dreadful day of the LORD. And he shall turn the heart of the fathers to the children, and the heart of the children to their fathers, lest I come and smite the earth with a curse."

Our LORD plainly tells us that this prophecy related to John the Baptist, when He says in S. Matt. xi. 14, " This is that Elias which was for to come; " and in S. Matt. iii. 3, we read, " For this is he that was spoken of by the Prophet Esaias, saying, The voice of one crying in the wilderness." S. John was the last teacher who was sent under the old covenant, or the time when the Church of GOD, which then consisted of the Jewish nation alone, was governed by the laws of Moses; the time was fast approaching when He, Who was shadowed forth in all the types and ceremonies of the law, was to appear upon earth and commence a new government, even JESUS of Nazareth, " of Whom Moses in the law and the Prophets spake," was to establish a new and better covenant of grace, and make known the Gospel of the kingdom. S. John, then, was more highly honoured than any of the prophets who had gone before him, for he was the immediate forerunner of Him to Whom all prophecy had testified; to him was confided the preaching of repentance, which was to make ready a people prepared for their LORD, by teaching them their sinfulness, and consequent need of a SAVIOUR; accordingly, in order to prepare the minds of his countrymen to receive the teaching of John, the circumstances of his birth were miraculous, that all might look upon him as a prophet sent from GOD; his birth was foretold to his father Zacharias by the Angel Gabriel, and the truth of his words confirmed by a sign, for Zacharias was struck dumb, and did not recover the use of his speech until after the birth of the child, whom his father, obedient to the words of the angel, had named John. Zacharias and Elizabeth, the father and mother of John, had no other children, and they were already old, and therefore had given up all hope of having a child, when the Angel was sent to promise them this wonderful child. We read that they were "righteous before GOD, walking in all the commandments and ordinances of the LORD, blameless." Zacharias was engaged in the performance of his duty as a priest when the Angel appeared to him; it is always to those who are engaged in the way of duty, and serving God according to their knowledge of His will, that the blessing of the Almighty is given.

We may believe that it was a joyful time for Elizabeth when the Virgin Mary came to visit her, and it was revealed to her by the HOLY SPIRIT that the "mother of her LORD was come unto her," and when the holy Mary, speaking as the Spirit of God dictated, poured forth that beautiful hymn of rejoicing which we always sing at our evening service in church, which begins with the words, "My soul doth magnify the LORD;" and when Zacharias, filled too with the HOLY GHOST, said of his infant son, "And thou, child, shalt be called the Prophet of the Highest; for thou shalt go before the face of the LORD, to prepare His ways." We do not know whether it was likewise revealed to Zacharias that his son should close a life of self-denial by a cruel death, but doubtless if it were, the HOLY SPIRIT of GOD, Who showed him things to come, would have revealed to him also the eternal glory into which his son would be received, for the merit's sake of the REDEEMER, Whose messenger he was; and that for the joy set before him, he would cheerfully endure death, despising the shame.

We read that "the child grew and waxed strong in Spirit, and was in the desert until the time of his showing unto Israel," that is, until the time appointed by God for the commencement of his ministry. When he was about the age of thirty years, "In those days," says S. Matthew, "came John the Baptist, preaching in the wilderness of Judea, and saying, Repent ye, for the kingdom of heaven is at hand!" He preached to the multitude who came to hear him of their need of repentance and change of life; he charged all who came to be baptized of him, that they should forsake those sins to which they were particularly tempted; he enjoined upon them the exercise of charity, and warned them against a false security on the ground that they were the children of Abraham, while in their lives they did not resemble him. To all those who confessed their sins, and thus gave promise of sincere repentance, John administered the rite of Baptism. From this circumstance he derives his name, and because also he was honoured by being permitted to administer the ordinance of Baptism to his Divine Master, to Whom he said truly, "I have need to be baptized of Thee, and comest Thou to me?" John knew well, by the inspiration of the HOLY SPIRIT, that JESUS of Nazareth was the expected MESSIAH, and pointing him out to one of his disciples he said, "Behold the Lamb of GOD Who taketh away the sin of the world."

Think, then, what he must have felt when his LORD and SAVIOUR came to be baptized of him, and thus fulfil all righteousness. Our SAVIOUR was now about to commence the work of our salvation by His public ministry, and His baptism was accompanied by the visible descent of the HOLY SPIRIT, in the form of a dove, lighting upon Him, by Whom He was led through all the sufferings of His perfect work on earth, until He offered Himself, through the same Eternal Spirit, without spot to GOD, and died for man. At the same time the voice of GOD the FATHER was heard from Heaven, saying, "This is My beloved Son in Whom I am well pleased." Our Saviour had, doubtless, another purpose in receiving this holy ordinance, namely, that He should leave us an example that we should follow His steps; you know that we have all been baptized, and thus admitted into the Church of Christ. The holy Apostles, who were inspired by the Spirit of God, and their successors, the first Bishops and Priests of the Church, baptized little infants, as well as the other members of the families of those who became Christians, and from this time it has been a custom in the Church to baptize every little child soon after its birth, remembering Who has said, "Suffer little children to come unto me."

Soon after the baptism of our Lord, John was thrown into prison by the wicked king Herod. We read, first that Herod had heard John gladly when he preached to him of repentance and righteousness; so true it is that many will go willingly to hear the Gospel preached, who yet refuse to obey its precepts. John had reproved Herod for living in great and open sin, (for Herod had taken his brother's wife to live with him,) and the king commanded him to be seized and thrown into prison, on account of this faithful reproof. Herod, probably, had never intended to put him to death, but one sin indulged in generally leads to the commission of a greater. The daughter of Herodias, the wife of Herod's brother, having obtained from the king a promise that he would grant her any request which she should make, asked him to give her the head of John the Baptist; and Herod, though he was sorry to do the thing, for he had some respect or fear of John, yet granted her sinful petition, rather than break his rash oath.

We may well shudder at the thought of a young maiden desiring to hold in her hand the head of the victim of her wicked malice. There is indeed no bound to the hardness and depravity of the human heart, when it is once given up to the service of Satan.

While John was in prison, his disciples asked him whether JESUS was the true MESSIAH promised to their nation. John the Baptist sent them to the LORD with this question. He well knew that JESUS was the CHRIST, being enlightened by the HOLY GHOST, but the SAVIOUR was not believed in by the Jewish nation generally, because of the hardness of their hearts, and as yet He had not openly declared Himself to be the MESSIAH, except by His works, which proved His divine origin to as many as would believe and be saved. " He came unto His own, but His own received Him not; but as many as believed in Him to them gave He power to become the sons of GOD." Our SAVIOUR did not, therefore, directly reply to the question of the disciples of John, but having performed several miracles before them, He sent them unto John, telling them to repeat in answer to the question the marvellous works which they had seen, for as they surely knew, no man could do such miracles except it were given him from above. Do we wonder that any of those who beheld the miracles of our LORD JESUS, yet remained in unbelief? how is it now in our own days? we read of all that the LORD performed, we have the writings of the inspired Apostles to tell us of His death, resurrection, and ascension, and to instruct us in the way of godliness, and yet how many of us live in practical unbelief, refusing to forsake our sins and flee from the wrath to come, seeking first the kingdom of Heaven which Jesus came to preach.

Surely we, too, have need of the repentance which John the Baptist came to preach; we must, as the Jews of old, be convinced of our sinful nature, and of our many transgressions against the laws of God, that we may feel, each of us, our personal need of a Saviour. Those who had confessed their sins, and received the baptism of John as a sign of their repentance, believed in the Lord Jesus and glorified God—but the Pharisees and self-righteous lawyers, trusting in their own good works, hardened their hearts in unbelief. O let us be careful to which of these classes we belong—to the humble penitents, or the self-righteous Pharisees. At our Baptism, the Holy Ghost was vouchsafed to us, that by His gracious influence we might be led to Christ, and grow in Christian holiness; let us not then stifle His voice in our hearts, lest we be more guilty than the Jews, who had not the same blessed privileges.

There are many lessons which we ought to learn from the life of John the Baptist. He left his home and all its comforts, that he might serve and obey God, and labour for the good of others; his raiment was a rough coat of camel's hair, and his meat was locusts and wild honey, the scanty provision furnished for him by nature in the wilderness. How will our selfish, idle habits of life bear to be compared with this? we who seldom give up any comfort or indulgence for the sake of others, or deny ourselves one hour's sleep that we may give the time to God. How small is the amount of pleasure we have ever renounced for Christ's sake; how short the time set apart for prayer and self-examination; how imperfect is our repentance; how cold our zeal. Why are we so different from the early followers of Christ? Is it not that the concerns of earth have too large a place in our hearts, that the good seed is choked with the cares, and riches, and pleasures of this life, and we bring no fruit to perfection?

There is not one among us, no, not the youngest child to whom I am now speaking, who has not need of repentance, and who, if he will be saved, must not bring forth fruits meet for repentance.

Sorrow for sin, if it is sincere, always leads us to Christ, and makes us seek after holiness. Let each of us, then, from this day forth, try to remember that this world is not our home, that we have a work to do here, a soul to be saved, Heaven to win; here we are pilgrims far from our Father's house, in the wilderness of life; we must not love ease and comfort too much, or fix our hearts on the pleasures of time, "For he that soweth to the flesh, shall of the flesh reap corruption; but he that soweth to the Spirit, shall of the Spirit reap life everlasting."

S. Peter's Day.

COLLECT.

O ALMIGHTY GOD, Who by thy SON JESUS CHRIST didst give to Thy Apostle Saint Peter, many excellent gifts, and commandedst him earnestly to feed Thy flock; Make, we beseech Thee, all Bishops and Pastors diligently to preach Thy holy Word, and the people obediently to follow the same, that they may receive the crown of everlasting glory; through JESUS CHRIST our LORD. AMEN.

> "That gracious chiding look, Thy call,
> To win him to himself and Thee,
> Sweetening the sorrow of his fall,
> Which else were rued too bitterly."
> *Christian Year.*

"GOOD-BYE, and GOD bless you, my boy, since it is His will that you should leave your home; do not forget the good lessons you have learnt at school, and go to church whenever you have an opportunity of so doing without neglecting your duties to your master and mistress."

Such were the parting words of John Maynard to his eldest son, Philip, who was about to leave his home to enter as a footboy in the service of a gentleman in London.

"Never fear, father," replied the boy, "I shall not soon forget our kind pastor's instruction, or your good advice; I have made some good resolutions, and intend to keep them."

"Not in your own strength, Philip, that were not

possible; in your new station you will be in many dangers, but remember our LORD's words, 'Watch and pray, that ye enter not into temptation.'"

Just then the coach which was to convey Philip from the village of Endsleigh, drew up, and with a hearty shake of the hand from his father, a few tears and kisses from his mother and little sisters, the boy set off on his journey.

And now we must take you back a few years to give some account of Philip's parents.—His father, John Maynard, was for some years in the service of the late Squire of Endsleigh, Mr. Graham, and was much respected by his master and the family for his good conduct. When Mr. Graham died, John found himself handsomely remembered, and this legacy, added to his own savings, enabled him to stock a small farm. He married an amiable young woman, to whom he had been long attached, and for some years everything prospered with him. They had four children: Philip, the subject of this story, two daughters, Susan and Jane, and Henry, a blue-eyed boy five years old, and the pet and plaything of the family.

A short time before the period at which this story commences, John Maynard had bound himself for a friend, who being unable to discharge his debt, poor John's stock was taken, and with it his means of subsistence. The squire (the son of John's old master) offered to procure for the farmer's eldest son a situation in London, and it was thankfully accepted, for though John had often anticipated with pleasure the time when his son could manage the farm for him, he did not murmur at the will of GOD Who permitted this trial to befall him.

How anxiously did the little family look for Philip's first letter. It soon arrived, and told them that he liked his place very much, his master and mistress were kind, and so were the servants.

"London is a fine place, father," wrote Philip, "but the streets are not paved with gold as grandmother used to tell me, and I have hardly seen a tree yet, and the air is not so fresh as at Endsleigh."

Philip soon became acquainted with a boy of his own age, who lived as page in a family next door to Mr. Carus, Philip's new master. This boy, John Croft, was in many respects a contrast to Philip; both boys had been well brought up by religious parents, but John was now an orphan, his father and mother having died within a few days of each other of an epidemic which raged in the town in which they lived. This sad circumstance had left a deep impression on the little orphan, and given a thoughtful tone to his mind; he was not strong in health, and his disposition was gentle and rather timid. Philip, on the contrary, was high-spirited, rather impetuous and self-confident, but, notwithstanding the differences of disposition, the boys were great friends. For some time Philip went on very steadily, and gave great satisfaction to his master, he was also a favourite with his fellow servants on account of his obliging disposition; the consciousness of this made him very happy, and he began to wonder what his father could have meant by the "dangers" to which he would be exposed in London.

When Philip had been there a year, the butler, under whom he was placed, left, and his situation was filled by a person very unlike him in principles. This man, James, was in the habit of frequenting a low gambling-house, and it was not long ere he invited Philip to accompany him thither, telling him that he need not mention it to the housekeeper, who might bring them into trouble. The boy knew that gambling was a vice, and that it would be wrong to go with James if he were required to keep it a secret from the housekeeper, who was a conscientious, good woman, and very kind to Philip, so he told the butler he did not want to join him.

The man laughed, and sneeringly remarked, that "If Master Page was afraid to look at a dice-box or a pack of cards, he did not care to take him."

This was Philip's weak point, he did not like to be thought a coward. Poor boy! he forgot that manfully to resist evil is true courage, and that he who cannot face the jeers of the wicked is a real coward; so he told James he was not afraid, and to prove it, he would accompany him the first time he could obtain leave to spend the evening out.

He told his friend John, who earnestly endeavoured to dissuade him from his purpose, but without avail.

"Why," said Philip, "you need not fear, I don't intend to touch the dice or cards, I shall only go this once, because James said I was a coward, and he shan't call me that again."

"But you are running into temptation," replied John, "and you know we daily pray, 'Lead us not into temptation.' I wish you would tell James you cannot go with him because you think it wrong, and if he does laugh at you, think which is worse to offend, God or man."

"I will only go this once, John; I am not afraid of being tempted to do wrong; but now good-bye, master will be wanting me directly."

Philip soon obtained permission to absent himself for an evening, and accompanied James to the gambling-house; the boy was fond of excitement, and therefore soon became interested in the fortunes of the players; but he refused to join them, and was rather proud the next day to tell his friend how well he had kept his resolution, and declined being anything but a looker-on. Philip had yet to learn that the first step in a wrong path inevitably conducts him who pursues it to sin and sorrow.

The butler's next invitation was at first hesitatingly declined, and then accepted: a few more visits, and Philip became accustomed to the language and recklessness of the men with whom James associated, and was soon induced to stake a small sum—he won —played again and again with varied success, but ere long fortune turned against him, and in the course of a short time all his money was gone. He had promised to send a portion of his wages to his father when they became due, to assist in discharging some expenses caused by the severe illness of little Henry; but how could he now manage it? He already owed the money to one of his wicked associates, from whom he could expect no mercy.

Ashamed to confess his fault to his father, or his friend John, he begged James to lend him the required sum, but he refused, at the same time suggesting that it would be no harm to borrow the money from that which his master had given him for the payment of some little bills. At first Philip was shocked at this proposition, but James told him that it would harm no one, the tradespeople could well afford to wait a little longer for their money, and that Philip might pay them before his master knew anything of the circumstance.

When sin is not steadily resisted with earnest prayer for God's assistance, the conscience becomes blunted, and we cannot easily discern right from wrong. Of this our poor Philip was a sad instance, for he now with little hesitation committed an act of fraud from which, but a few months since, he would have shrunk.

Philip sent the money to his father, and the bills remained unpaid, but the boy was not happy, and in constant dread of his dishonesty being discovered; a hasty summons from his master would cause him to turn pale, and he never went into the parlour without fear.

One week day he was desired to attend some of Mr. Carus' family to church; it was a long time since he had entered the temple of God, except once on Sundays, though he had frequent opportunities of enjoying this privilege. It was S. Peter's Day, and the prayers were followed by a sermon, the text was, "Watch and pray, that ye enter not into temptation." These words of Divine admonition reminded Philip of the time when he last heard them; and the good resolutions he had then made, and the life he had since led, rose before him—his father had solemnly repeated this text in reply to his boasted confidence in his own strength; he had relied on this strength, and it had failed him. Philip listened attentively to the sermon, part of which was as follows:—

"All Scripture is written for our instruction, and doubtless it was for this reason that the fall of the holy Apostle, the anniversary of whose martyrdom we this day commemorate, is recorded; S. Peter relied on his own strength, and he denied his LORD. Contrast his vehement expression, 'Though I should die with Thee, yet will I not deny Thee,' with his subsequent denial of CHRIST. He Who foreknew all things, admonished the zealous Disciple to watchfulness and prayer, without which the strongest faith becomes weak, and the most fervent love cold; and we, my brethren, trust to our own strength, and act as if we could of ourselves do the will of GOD, and work out our own salvation.

"Remember the Parable of the Wheat and the Tares, it was 'while men slept' that the enemy sowed tares amongst the wheat; we are never in so great danger as when we fancy ourselves secure. We must ever be watchful of our conduct, and earnestly pray for GOD's good guidance. S. Peter shed bitter tears of penitence, and after his Divine Master had ascended into heaven, and fulfilled His gracious promise to His Disciples by sending to them the Comforter, the Apostle testified boldly to the truth, despising imprisonment, shame, and even a cruel death. S. Peter was crucified with his head downwards, declaring he was not worthy to die the same death as his SAVIOUR.

"Let us endeavour to follow the example of the Apostle after his repentance. We have all denied, and daily deny CHRIST; we deny Him when we fear the mocking laugh of the unrighteous and evil doer, and again by refusing to watch and pray we deny His power to assist and guide us. Remember that if we are ashamed to acknowledge our LORD on earth, He will not confess us before the Angels in Heaven."

This sermon made Philip very unhappy, he felt how sinfully he had acted in neglecting to "watch and pray" against temptation, and before he left the church he had earnestly prayed for forgiveness and a more humble spirit.

The boy was very frightened when he thought of confessing to his master the fraud he had practised, but he knew it was a positive duty.

Master will be sure to send me away, thought Philip, and then I shall be a burthen upon father instead of helping him; my character is gone, and it will break poor mother's heart to know that her boy is dishonest. These were bitter reflections to him as he returned from church, but earnestly praying in his heart to GOD to give him strength, he determined to confess all to Mr. Carus when he next saw him.

An opportunity occurred the following morning, and Philip told his master the whole truth. Mr. Carus looked very grave, but he was a good man, and seeing that Philip's repentance was sincere, he told him he would not dismiss him from his service, " but," said Mr. Carus, " you have lost my confidence, Philip, and whether you regain it must depend on your own conduct: write to your father, and give him a full account of your misconduct; I know this will be to you a painful task, but we must not shrink from the earthly punishment due to sin, but thank God for chastising us in this world, that our souls may be saved in the last day."

Philip was more affected by his master's kindness than if Mr. Carus had sent him away in anger, and he determined, by the aid of God's Holy Spirit, to regain his character. Earnestly did the boy strive, and as he became day by day more watchful, prayerful, and less self-confident, so was God's strength made perfect in his weakness.

He continued many years in the service of Mr. Carus, whose good opinion he regained by his steady conduct; and when at the age of thirty he married and set up a small shop, the kindness of his master and the family followed Philip to his new station in life.

John Maynard and his wife died a few years before their son quitted service, but their last hours were rendered happy by the knowledge of his improved conduct.

S. James's Day.

COLLECT.

GRANT, O merciful GOD, that as Thine holy Apostle Saint James, leaving his father and all that he had, without delay, was obedient unto the calling of Thy SON JESUS CHRIST, and followed Him; so we, forsaking all worldly and carnal affections, may be evermore ready to follow Thy holy commandments; through JESUS CHRIST our LORD. AMEN.

IN the second class train from London to Oxford, sat a young man, apparently not more than twenty years of age; his dress, his sunburnt face, and still more his careless, happy manner, spoke him to be a sailor. William Burton, for such was his name, was returning home after an absence of nearly eight years, which he had spent at sea or in foreign countries. As he drew nearer and nearer to his native village, and recognized familiar names and places, his heart was so overflowing with happiness that he could not refrain from sharing it with his fellow travellers. An old gentleman who sat opposite to him, pleased with his frank nature, entered into conversation with him, and William soon put him in possession of his history. He told him that his father was a farmer, and had seen better days, but that little by little his property decreased, and when William was twelve years old, his parents were so poor that they did not think it right to refuse for their son an offer made by the captain of a merchant ship, who liked the lad, to take him on board his ship. It cost them much, no doubt, to part from their only son, and it must have been a hard trial to William to leave his father, his mother, and only sister, for he spoke of it now with tears in his eyes; but they were very happy tears, for, as he said, in less than an hour he hoped to be with them. And he had no thought of leaving them again, for he had been well paid, and had saved a good bit of money; and he had received a letter from his father, a year ago, telling him that he had inherited several hundred pounds by the death of a relative, that his farm was well stocked, and larger by many acres than in former times, and that he looked forward anxiously to the time when his son should return and help him to manage it. And now, said the youth, I *am* come, thank GOD, with forty pounds of my own earnings to add to the stock. I have never said a word to father of that, it will be such a surprise to him; and I have brought him a gold watch, and some foreign seeds, and all sorts of curious things for my mother, and rare shells and this for my sister, added he, showing a fine parrot which he carried in a cage.

It was impossible not to share in the pleasure of the youth, and when he left the train at the station half a mile from his home, his fellow-travellers wished him joy with all their hearts.

Poor William Burton! he was dreaming indeed only of joy, and his heart was little prepared for the sorrow which was coming upon him. As he approached the village every object was familiar to him; here was a tree which he had climbed when a boy, and there a brook over which he always lifted his little sister; and now the church spire is seen above the trees, and he feels as if it were but yesterday that he had heard the sweet music of the church bells of his home. He walked faster and faster, thinking of the joyful meeting which awaited him, of his father's blessing, and his mother's tears of joy, and of his little sister now grown into a woman.

The sight of a stranger would have attracted attention in the little village of Westham, even if he had not carried a talking bird in his hand. William was soon followed by a troop of little children whom he was almost too eager to notice; but when he saw on the opposite side of the road his old acquaintance the village schoolmaster, he crossed over and made himself known to him. The good man shook him warmly by the hand, but in answer to William's eager inquiry whether they were all well at home, he shook his head sorrowfully. The poor youth had been so happy a moment before, that he could not believe or understand sorrow.

"Is any one ill, father or mother?" he said.

"No, not ill; but now," continued the other gravely, "come in with me; you must not hear bad news in the street."

William followed him mechanically, he had a dreadful fear at his heart, but he could scarcely give it a name.

"Life is short, my boy," said the schoolmaster, when they had entered his cottage, "and eternity is long ; you must think of that. You will not see your parents again here, but I trust you will *there*," pointing up to heaven as he spoke. "Death did not find them unprepared, and they died blessing you, and leaving many a word of good advice for you. If we had known where to find you, we should have written to you to spare you this shock."

Words cannot describe poor William's grief, he could not realize his loss, for the sudden change from joy to sorrow had overpowered him. In a few moments, however, he rose, and said that he would go to his sister.

"Mary," said the schoolmaster, "is married; she went to the north with her husband three months before her mother died."

Then William sat down and listened to all the particulars, for he had no one waiting for him now, and his own dear village was more desolate than the wide sea to him.

He heard that soon after his sister had married a grazier from Yorkshire, his mother had died of cholera; her daughter, who was sent for, did not arrive till she was dead, but she was in time to attend the death-bed of her father, who only survived his wife ten days. The kind neighbours had taken care of the property for the poor lad until he should return; and the minister had the charge of his father's will, in which everything was left to his son, Mary having had her share at her marriage. She had returned to her husband, and they had lately heard that she had a little girl.

"Now, don't be thinking of going to the old place

to-night," said the kind-hearted man to William; "there is no one there but old Susan; you know her, she used to help your mother in busy times, and she is there to look after things, and her son has minded the farm for you. You'll only be fretting yourself all night long if you go there."

William thanked him, but said he had rather go, at least he should realize his sorrow when he looked upon the vacant seats of his parents, and even that would be some relief to him. They accordingly set off together; as they went through the village William had many a look and word of true sympathy from his old neighbours, who, as they said, pitied the poor lonesome lad from their hearts. He had hardly courage to open the door of the house and look around him, and was truly thankful when his considerate companion called old Susan away, and busied himself with her in making preparations for his supper and his night's rest, thus leaving him alone to give vent to his full heart. He threw himself on his knees beside his mother's chair and wept bitterly. Every little recollection of his childhood came fresh upon his mind, he saw his father's Bible in its old place, with the spectacles upon it, as they had always been; and there was a broken piece of an old rocking-horse, and a cricket bat, kept, no doubt, by his dear mother because they had belonged to her boy. Sad as all these thoughts made poor William, it was a relief to him to give way to his sorrow, and when his friend came in again he found him more composed; he fixed on an hour in the following day, when his own duties should be over, to accompany William to the Clergyman, and then took leave of him, as he said he wished to be alone. It was then that the poor boy first felt how truly desolate he was on earth, when the evening grew into night, and he was alone with his gloomy thoughts; he went to bed, and after lying awake for many hours, he slept, and dreamt that he had returned home in happiness, and awoke to find it only a dream. In the morning he sat brooding over his grief and disappointment, until he was aroused by the church bells.

At that familiar sound he rose up and took his hat; he had never been allowed to neglect that sacred call to prayer in the house of GOD when a boy, and often when far away, he had dwelt with pleasure on the thought of again walking with his mother to church. Now he should pass the grave of both his parents, and he set off early that he might visit it unobserved. When he entered the church he went to that part of it where he had sat with his father and mother, and kneeling down, prayed as he he had never done before. I do not mean that William was an irreligious lad, far from it; he had been trained in the right way, and he had never entirely departed from it. Morning and evening he said his prayers, and the Bible and Prayer-Book his mother gave him at parting had been well used, and carefully treasured by him; but, like many of us, he had looked upon prayer as a duty only before, now his heavy heart made it a necessity. It was well for him that the language of prayer was not strange to him, and that reverence for the house of GOD was a feeling long implanted in his heart, or how could the holy service have comforted him now? He saw the light stream through the coloured window on to the seat, as it had done when he was a little child, and his mother had chidden him for playing with it. His happy home, father, mother, all were gone; every child he had known was grown almost beyond his knowledge, the old people were dead, and their names on the tombstones he had passed; the Clergyman he had known was gone, and his place supplied by another; the church alone was unchanged, and as he sat there he felt as if he were a child again. He remembered the last time he had been there it was with his mother and sister, and he recollected that it was S. James's Day, and that he had learned the collect for the day for the last time, to say to his father.

At last the service commenced, and though poor William's loss mixed itself with all his thoughts and prayers, yet he found in the very effort to bring his sorrow before the throne of GOD, and to join in praise and prayer for spiritual mercies with others, that his heart was strengthened and comforted. Every word of the Litany seemed as if it had been written for him, just as when he had been happy it had seemed all praise and thanksgiving; he felt no longer utterly desolate, and the thought of the calm rest into which he trusted his beloved parents had been received, filled his heart with peace. He was startled when the collect was read to find that it was again S. James's Day; the same feast of the Church come round again after all his years of separation, the very day on which he had last accompanied his mother to that church; he had not observed the saints' days since he left England, and with the words of the Prayer-Book, like an old remembered tune, came back on his mind a tide of long forgotten and endearing recollections. He thought of the stories of the holy Apostles which his mother used to tell him on Sunday evenings, and of how the first Christians had passed through much tribulation to their rest, and that we, their followers, must not wonder if God should likewise teach us by affliction that this world is not our own; that we must not make earthly happiness our idol, but remember that we are like children at school, learning the lessons in this world which are to fit us for a residence in our Father's house.

All these words of his beloved mother passed through William's mind when the service was concluded. And he had lingered behind the rest of the congregation to visit once more the grave of his parents. He was not allowed to go home to dinner, for many kind neighbours came to ask him to return with them and share their best, and a hearty welcome.

When the bell rang for afternoon service, William was again in his place at church. After the second lesson, the Clergyman questioned the school children, and William heard similar answers to those which he had given, when a child, to the same questions. The Clergyman said that, doubtless, the day which we observed in commemoration of S. James, was the day of his death by the hand of Herod. S. James was the brother of the Apostle John; the Gospel for the day gives the account of their first coming to JESUS, when their mother asked for them that they should sit, one on the right hand and one on the left of their LORD, in the Kingdom of CHRIST. S. James was one of that favoured few whom we oftenest find in the company of their Divine Master; from the day when he "left all to follow JESUS" until his death is recorded by S. Luke, who says that Herod killed James, the brother of John, with the sword. The Clergyman then referred to a hymn which the children had learnt at school. They did not repeat it then, but I will give it for the sake of those of my readers who do not know it.

> Two brothers freely cast their lot
>   With David's royal Son;
> The cost of conquest counting not,
>   They deem the battle won.
>
> Brothers in heart they hope to gain
>   An undivided joy,
> That man may one with man remain,
>   As boy was one with boy.
>
> CHRIST heard, and willed that James should fall,
>   First prey of Satan's rage;
> John linger out his fellows all,
>   And die in bloodless age.
>
> Now they join hands once more above,
>   Before the Conqueror's throne;
> Thus GOD grants prayer, but in His love
>   Makes times and ways His own.

The Clergyman said that it was a common mistake to think that prayer was denied because it was not answered when and how we asked and expected. The mother of the Apostles, James and John, was thinking probably of earthly honours for her sons, but

CHRIST heard her prayer, and enrolled them among that number of faithful men, who were partakers of His sufferings here, and will share his glory hereafter. In our days, many a parent may deem her prayers for a beloved child refused, because, perhaps, its early death afflicts her heart; while in reality her prayers for the salvation of that child were heard by our heavenly FATHER, Who foreknoweth all things, and removed the son of her love from a life of temptation, which might have been the death of his soul.

Or, again, a dutiful child may be returning homeward, full of prayer and hope that he might brighten the declining years of his parents, and live with them in peace and happiness, causing them joy by walking in the right way in which he had been trained, and GOD may answer this prayer too, though in a manner very different from that which poor earthly love had planned; the parents may be taken to their eternal rest, and the child left to honour their memory, and fulfil their wishes, while he submits without a murmur to the decree of his FATHER which is in Heaven, and tries *so* to live here that he may rejoin the parents he has lost for a time in a blessed and never ending eternity.

William's tears fell fast while the Minister was speaking; holy and happy thoughts came into his heart, and his life, which had seemed so dark and dreary the evening before, appeared now like a happy preparation time for heaven. When the prayer was said for that "peace which the world can neither give nor take away," he felt as if he had never experienced it before, so true it is that such peace is only to be found by fixing the heart upon those things which are above, far, far above the shifting scenes of this life. When William left the church he did not leave his consolation behind him, but the blessing of GOD the FATHER, the SON, and the HOLY GHOST, which he had prayed for, and the Minister had pronounced in GOD's Name, went with him; he returned home, not to give way to his sorrow, though not to forget it, not to repine because GOD had seen fit to send him affliction, but to pray that it might be sanctified to him.

When the good schoolmaster came that evening, he was thankful to see how much more resigned he was; he went with him to the Clergyman, and there left him, for, as he said, no one can speak so well to you as the parson, and I had best leave you alone with him.

William found indeed a kind friend and counsellor in his Parish Priest, who never lost sight of him, and seldom allowed many days to pass without calling at his little farm, where he retained old Susan and her son as his assistants; he was quite inexperienced in the management of land and cattle, having been trained to such a different life, but he found every farmer in the village willing to do him a kind turn, and lend him a helping hand. In the house of GOD he found the support and teaching which he needed in order to bear his trial rightly. And morning and afternoon, before service, on Sundays and holy days, he assisted in the school, hearing the youngest children repeat their lessons.

By the Clergyman's advice, he wrote to his sister, and asked her to come, with her husband and child, on a visit to him, so that when Christmas Day came round, the first Christmas he spent in England, and to which he had so long looked forward, his home was not entirely lonely. In the course of time William married, and became a happy as well as useful member of society; happier, no doubt, in the joys and affections of this life, because he had learnt to look through them, and above them, to Him Who will hallow the Christian's joy, and sanctify his sorrow. The Church was to him a sacred spot, where all that was dear on earth, and all his brightest hopes of heaven were centred; there, by his mother's side, he had lisped his first prayer, and there, when his father and mother had forsaken him, he found heavenly comfort; there, soon after his return, he received the rite of Confirmation, and was admitted to the Holy Communion; before that altar he was married, and each little one with which GOD blessed him, was solemnly dedicated to its SAVIOUR there, and made an heir of the kingdom of Heaven in holy Baptism. Beneath the shade of the old church tower, and near his parents' graves, he was soon called to lay his firstborn little son, in full hope of a joyful resurrection.

When last I saw him, he was surrounded by his children, and his children's children, and his silvery locks and stooping form, reminded me that, before many years had passed, he too would be carried to his last rest in that green church-yard; but it must have been severe weather indeed which robbed him of his daily service in the house of God.

> "For he loved the sole thing that knew no change
> In the soul of the boy or man,
> And the last dear thing he was fond to love,
> Was that holy service high,
> Which lifted his heart to joys above,
> And pleasures which do not die." *

* Ballads by the Rev. A. C. Coxe.

S. Bartholomew's Day.

COLLECT.

O ALMIGHTY and everlasting GOD, Who didst give to Thine Apostle Bartholomew grace truly to believe and preach Thy Word; Grant, we beseech Thee, unto Thy Church, to love that Word which he believed, and both to preach and receive the same; through JESUS CHRIST our LORD. AMEN.

"When first earth's rulers welcomed home
 The Church, their zeal impressed
Upon the Seasons, as they come,
 The image of their guest.

"Men's words and works, their hopes and fears,
 Henceforth forbid to rove,
Paused, when a Martyr claimed her tears,
 Or Saint inspired her love.

"But craving wealth and feverish power
 Such service now discard;
 The loss of one excited hour
 A sacrifice too hard!" *Lyra Apostolica.*

"AUNT JANE, Aunt Jane, where are you? We want you so much; we want to ask you for leave for a very great treat."

"And what is this very great treat to be, that makes you all so eager," said Mrs. Miller to her little nieces and nephew, Alice, Sarah, and Henry Brown.

"O Aunt, Martha Lewis has been here to invite us all to go to the fair with her to-morrow at nine o'clock; her brothers are going to take her and a great many other children in one of Mr. Lewis's farm carts, and we shall have such fun! O do let us go, dear aunt; and may we spend our new shillings that grandfather gave us?"

"You know you said we should go to the fair," said Alice, eagerly, for she half feared from her aunt's grave looks, that they would not obtain the desired permission.

"I said that you should go to the fair, my dear children," said Mrs. Miller, "and I hope to be able to keep my promise, and take you there in the afternoon; your uncle is going to buy a horse, and I have some purchases to make, and I am very glad to be able to give you the pleasure. I cannot consent to your going with Martha Lewis, there are many reasons why I should not do so; but I will tell you of one which would be quite sufficient, even were there no other objection: to-morrow is S. Bartholomew's Day, and we shall go to church in the morning. So now go and play again, for I am very busy at present, but when the clock strikes five come in to tea, and we will talk about to-morrow and all its pleasures."

Henry and Sarah thanked their aunt, and ran off to play hide-and-seek among the raspberry bushes. They were sorry not to have a long day at the fair, but they knew that their aunt never said a thing which she did not mean, and they did not think of being ill-tempered because they could not have exactly their own way; but Alice stood still, looking gloomy and cross, until her aunt spoke again, and said:

"Alice, my dear, go and play with your brother and sister, thank Martha kindly for her invitation, but say that I have fixed to take you myself in the afternoon."

Alice did not move, but at last she said, "If you would only let me go, aunt, I am older than the others, and I would be very steady: you know I can go to church any day, but the fair will be only once a year, and I have never been to one."

Mrs. Miller looked grave, but she only said, "I have given you my answer, Alice, I will talk to you by-and-by." So Alice left the room slowly, but instead of joining her brother and sister, she climbed upon a heap of stones and leant over the garden wall, and told Patty James, who lived next door, and who was going with Martha Lewis to the fair, how cross her aunt was, and how she would not let her go, just because she wished it so much.

Alice knew how wrong she was, and her heart pricked her all the time, for her aunt had adopted her and her brother and sister, when their parents died, and they were without a home in the world, and she and her husband loved them as if they were their own children.

Mr. Miller was a gardener, and supplied the neighbouring town with fruit and flowers, so that he could afford to give a hearty welcome and a happy home to his sister's children. And the little Browns loved both uncle and aunt dearly, as it was natural they should do, but Alice was now in a naughty temper, and very bad, ungrateful thoughts arose in her mind. She heard her little brother and sister calling her, but she took no notice of them, and when the clock struck five, she turned slowly towards the house, and seated herself at the tea-table without offering to help her aunt to spread the bread and butter for the younger ones, or to lift the kettle, or make herself useful in any way, which it was generally a pleasure to her to do.

Mrs. Miller saw that the little girl was giving way to wrong feelings, but she did not notice it then; her husband came in to tea, and Henry and Sally, who were quite full of their expected treat, talked eagerly to him about how far it was to Shoreham, where the fair was to be held, and of how long a time they should have to spend in the town. They were very much occupied, too, in deciding what they should buy, and their uncle said that if they could purchase half the things they talked of with their money, Shoreham fair would be the most wonderful place in the world!

"But what is the matter with Alice, that she looks so grave, is she not to be one of the party?" he asked kindly.

Alice said nothing, but hung down her head, and her aunt replied, "Alice is discontented because I cannot let her go to the fair with Martha Lewis, and I fear she is indulging self-willed thoughts."

Alice was very sorry to see her kind uncle and aunt look grave and displeased with her, and she longed to say how unhappy she was, and to confess all her naughtiness, but she could not make up her mind to do this at once, for she recollected that when she had climbed up the wall to talk to Patty, she had disobeyed her aunt, who had forbidden her children to do it, because she feared that they might slip and hurt themselves.

And she knew that she should be punished for an act of wilful disobedience, she feared that her aunt might think it right to keep her from the fair, if she knew how naughty she had been; so she made up her mind to say nothing about having climbed the wall this time, and never to do so any more; and then, thought she, there can be no harm in not telling of it this once. So she tried to put away her ill temper, and the remembrance of her fault together: she spoke cheerfully, and said:

"Aunt, may we not go out to play now?"

"Yes, if you like, my love," replied Mrs. Miller, "and I will follow you soon, that we may have a little conversation about to-morrow."

Now Alice had taken a step in the right direction when she tried to overcome her temper, but she was doing very wrong in determining to conceal her fault, and her conscience began to tell her this presently. At first she tried not to listen to it, and she ran very fast and was very noisy, but she could not be happy, and it was well for her that it was so, and that she had not learnt to harden her heart against this inward monitor. She felt very miserable, and at last she stopped and said a prayer to GOD in her heart, to help her to act rightly; and then she no longer doubted what she ought to do.

She went at once into the house, and said, "If you please, aunt, may I speak to you? I am very unhappy, and I have been very naughty."

Mrs. Miller sat down and drew the little girl close to her, and listened gently while Alice told her all. She was very glad that she confessed it openly, and when she cried and hid her face in her lap, and asked to be forgiven, she talked to her of One far greater than herself Whom she had offended, and of Whom she must seek pardon, even her Heavenly FATHER.

"You know, my dear child," she said, "that I forgive you with all my heart, but do you not remember what I said when little Henry climbed the wall the other day?"

"Yes, aunt, you said that if we were disobedient you must punish us," and Alice spoke firmly now, for she was really humble, and she was more sorry to have done wrong than that she must submit to the consequences of her fault.

Mrs. Miller thought for a minute, and then she said, "This is Monday, Alice, I shall not give you leave to play in the garden again till Thursday; I am sorry to deprive you of pleasure, but you know why I do it."

"Yes," said Alice, " and indeed I will try to remember, and not to disobey you again. I cannot think how I could be so wicked as to say such ungrateful things. I did not mean them, indeed I did not."

"When we give way wilfully to one fault, we generally commit a great many, my child; you indulged a wayward temper, and Satan tempted you to disobey and to speak many things which your heart told you were untrue, and you were cross with your little brother and sister, and refused to share their pleasure:

and all these things grew out of the first naughty thought that you did not try to overcome."

Just then the children's merry voices were heard, begging their aunt to come into the garden. Little Sally saw that her sister had been crying, so she forgot that Alice had been cross to her, and threw her arms round her neck, saying, "Do come too, Ally, I want to show you my gooseberry bush; it is so full of fruit;" but Alice kissed her and said gently, "I must not come to-night, dear, because I have done what aunt told us not to do, and it is my punishment."

Alice did not know that her aunt was within hearing, for she was talking to Henry at the window, but she did hear, and was pleased to find that Alice owned her fault frankly; she walked a little while with the younger children, and then she brought them in with her, and sat down to talk with them, putting a chair next herself for Alice.

"O, aunt, will you tell us a story?" exclaimed Henry and Sally.

"I am going to talk to you, but I do not know that you will call what I shall say, a story," said Mrs. Miller; "tell me what day to-morrow will be."

"S. Bartholomew's Day, you said, aunt."

"And who was S. Bartholomew?"

"He was one of the twelve Apostles."

"Do you remember what I told you on S. James's Day, about the commemoration of the Saints on especial days?"

"Yes," replied Alice, "you told us that the Church set apart these days that we might thank GOD Who sent forth His servants to preach the good news of Salvation to all lands, and that we might remember the doctrine that they taught, and try to follow their holy example."

"To-morrow will be one of these days, and do you think it would be right for those who are not prevented by other duties, from spending an hour in prayer and praise in the house of GOD, and trying to keep the day holy as the Church appoints, to prefer instead to pass the whole day in idle amusement?"

"No, aunt."

"I know what you mean," said Henry, "you are thinking that we wanted to go to the fair instead of to church."

Mrs. Miller smiled, and said she was glad they understood her meaning, and then she went on: "If the Squire's lady were to invite you to play in her garden, and to spend the day with her children, do you think that you would refuse; would you say, 'I cannot come, because Patty James has asked us to play with her, and we like it better; we will come, if you please, another day?'"

"O, aunt, how can you think of such a thing? the Squire's lady would not invite us; if she did, of course we should go."

"Or if the Queen were to send for you to the court, do you think you could say that you had another pleasure you liked better to accept?"

The children laughed outright when their aunt said this, all but Alice, who looked thoughtful, for she knew that her aunt was thinking of her words.

"The King of kings has a house in this village,"

continued Mrs. Miller, " and He has sent us an invitation through His servant, the minister, to enter His courts to-morrow, but I know a little girl who would have stayed away for the sake of following her own fancies, and who thought that any day would do to go to church; do not look sad, Alice. I am not reproving you, my child: we are all too apt to think and say the same, grown-up people as well as children, I fear; but what I wish to show you is, that we cannot please God by going to His house, unless we love to serve Him, with all our hearts, and with all our souls, and with all our strength. And though by nature we are far from feeling this, yet we must not stay away and wait till we have grace to love to pray and to praise God.

"We must go and ask for the Holy Spirit in the place where God has promised to bestow it, and then we may expect a blessing, and be sure that God will teach us to love His courts on earth, and prepare us to enter into His presence hereafter. We read in the Psalms, the inspired words of David, 'In Thy presence is fulness of joy, at Thy right hand there is pleasure for evermore.' But it is only the heart which has been taught by the Holy Spirit, which will find delight in the employments of the Blessed in Heaven. We cannot become good all at once, still less can we make ourselves so, but if we try in everything to do the will of God, He will graciously teach us to serve Him aright.

" Do you remember what we are told in the Bible about seeking first the kingdom of God?"

" Yes," said Alice, " our Saviour says, 'Seek ye

first the kingdom of GOD and His righteousness, and all these things shall be added unto you.'"

"Those things of which our Blessed LORD speaks, are food and clothing, and all the comforts which we call necessaries of life, yet we are told not to put them before the concerns of our souls. The wants of the body will cease in a few short years, but the soul will live for ever, in happiness or misery; and if we are not to seek first what we shall eat, or what we shall drink, or wherewithal we shall be clothed, much less should we neglect our souls for the sake of these worldly amusements."

Mrs. Miller stopped when she had said this, for she saw that though Alice was listening attentively, Henry and Sally were beginning to look sleepy, so she said, "It will soon be bed-time, but we will talk a little about S. Bartholomew before you go. You remember that he is believed to have been the same with that Disciple of whom we read, under the name of Nathaniel. What did our LORD say when S. Philip brought Nathaniel to Him?"

"He said, 'Behold an Israelite indeed, in whom is no guile,' and JESUS said," continued Alice, reverently, "that He saw Nathaniel under the fig tree, before Philip called him."

"Let us always remember then, my dear children, that the LORD JESUS reads our hearts and sees our thoughts as well as our actions, and let us try to be without guile, guile means deceit or any kind of falsehood. The Apostle Bartholomew laboured diligently after the death of the SAVIOUR to spread abroad in the world the knowledge of His glorious Gospel; he preached the truth through many heathen nations, and was put to a most cruel death, as it is believed, in Africa: he died comforting the converts to Christianity who stood around him, and exhorting them to steadfastness in the faith.

"Now we will not talk longer, for I see you are tired." So the children kissed their aunt, and went to bed; Alice stayed behind the others to ask once more for forgiveness, and to hear a few more kind words.

The children were dressed early the next morning, and ran to tell their uncle that it was very fine, though he had feared from the clouds the night before, that there was a storm in the air. Henry and Sally were very busy in the garden, before breakfast, helping him to gather fruit and flowers, and Alice, who knew that she might not join in this pleasure, made herself as useful as she could in many little ways in the house, and then sat down to learn the Collect for the day, by heart; the knowledge that she was trying to do what was right, and that her aunt was pleased with her, made her so happy, that when the cart passed by in which Martha Lewis and her companions were seated, laughing and talking very loud, she wondered that she had cared so very much to go with them.

It was soon time to prepare for church, and a pleasant walk it was down the shady lane. There were many people walking the same way, and some were hurrying in the contrary direction, in order to take the road to Shoreham, which was already thronged with carts and foot passengers on their way to the fair.

There was a sermon after the prayers in church, the little Browns were very attentive to it, and Alice recollected the text perfectly, and repeated it to her aunt as they walked home, though it was a long one. It was this, " Enter ye in at the strait gate : for wide is the gate, and broad is the way, that leadeth to destruction, and many there be which go in thereat: because strait is the gate, and narrow is the way which leadeth unto life; and few there be that find it."

It was dinner time when they reached home, and directly afterwards they set off for Shoreham. They were a cheerful party, and had a very merry drive; little Henry sat in front with his uncle, and as he held the whip, he fancied that he was of great use in driving, though he turned round so often to laugh and talk with his sisters, that it was well for them all that their uncle held the reins.

The children had each a bright shilling to spend, besides which their uncle had given them another in pence. They began to spend the money well, for they each gave a penny to a poor blind man, whose little boy held a gate open, through which they had to pass; when they arrived at Shoreham they were quite bewildered with the many gay sights on either side of the road. There were booths of toys and fruit, cakes, and china ware, besides Punch and Judy. A show of wild beasts, dancing figures, and a juggler; then there were panoramas and puppet shows, tight-rope dancers, and children on stilts, and the streets were so noisy as well as crowded, that Alice thought to herself that she should have been quite frightened if she had been there alone.

When their uncle left them to go to that part of the fair where the cattle were kept, Mrs. Miller took the children to see a great many pretty things: they went first to a panorama of London, and then to a wild beast show, and afterwards to some gardens where were swings and merry go-rounds, and a pond. Mr. Miller joined them here, and took them in a boat; you may be sure that altogether they spent a very happy afternoon, especially as they met some of their little friends from the village in the gardens.

When all the sight seeing was over, they went to the stalls where many pretty things were sold, and after a great deal of consideration, Henry laid out his money in a little boat for himself, and a doll for Sally, who wisely chose to spend hers in a pretty book of good pictures, which they could look at every Sunday. Alice bought a neat little work-basket for herself, and a flower-pot for her aunt.

Their uncle said, laughingly, that as no one had bought a toy for him, he must get some cakes as a fairing for himself: so he purchased some which they ate on their way home, for the afternoon's enjoyment had given them a good appetite. Alice had looked out often for Martha Lewis and her party, and at last, just as they were preparing to return, she saw Martha and her companions standing near a juggler who was performing some curious tricks; Martha's frock was torn, and she was talking and laughing in a very loud and not at all becoming manner, and the children who were with her were romping in a rude way, and some of them were quarrelling. They seemed quite to have forgotten themselves in the excitement of the scene. The children noticed this, and Sally said she supposed it was because they had no one to take care of them, and they had been there all day alone.

Mrs. Miller made no remark to Alice, for she felt sure that the little girl was learning the lesson which she hoped the day's experience would teach her: that the path of obedience is the happiest as well as the safest.

The evening closed in fast before they reached home, and Sally was fast asleep in her aunt's lap the last few miles; not so Henry, he was as full of fun as when they had set out, and chatted away of all they had seen, to his uncle.

"Dear aunt," said Alice, "I am so glad that you did not give me my own way, and that we went to church in the morning."

"And I am very glad that my dear niece should learn early in life, that no happiness can satisfy our hearts, if we follow it too eagerly, and forget GOD while we seek it," replied Mrs. Miller.

"There is a beautiful verse which says,

'Why should we fear, youth's draught of joy,
   If pure, should sparkle less?
Why should the cup the sooner cloy,
   Which GOD has deigned to bless?'

"I will read you to-morrow, the hymn in the 'Christian Year,' in which it is found: but see, here we are at home, and John is ready to hold the horse and old Susan is waiting to give us our supper, and to hear all our news."

When the little Browns were fast asleep in bed, an hour later, their kind uncle and aunt walked together in the garden talking of them, and of how they hoped that they might be able to train them in the right way.

"I feel," said Mrs. Miller, "that it is, if possible, a more sacred duty, than if they were our own children: I can never forget their dear mother's last look at them, as she prayed to meet them again in heaven."

"God grant it," said Mr. Miller, fervently, "they have been very happy this afternoon; that is as it should be; I like to see duty and pleasure go hand in hand with children, and I hope that they will always remember S. Bartholomew's Day with profit."

S. Matthew's Day.

COLLECT.

O ALMIGHTY GOD, Who by Thy blessed Son didst call Matthew from the receipt of custom to be an Apostle and Evangelist; Grant us grace to forsake all covetous desires, and inordinate love of riches, and to follow the same Thy Son JESUS CHRIST, Who liveth and reigneth with Thee and the HOLY GHOST, one GOD, world without end. AMEN.

"In Dreamland once I saw a Church,
    Amid the trees it stood;
And reared its little steeple-cross
    Above the sweet green wood."

Christian Ballads.

T was a bright autumnal day when the parishioners of the pretty village of Ranford, in the south of Devon, might have been seen returning from church. Mr. Graham, the Rector, was much beloved by all, for he was ever ready to minister to the temporal and spiritual wants of his poorer brethren; he was a widower, his wife having died two years previous to the date of my narrative, leaving a little girl ten years old, to deplore with her father their sad loss.

Little Mary (she bore her mother's name) waited in the church for her father; she did not speak to him there, for she knew it was the house of GOD, and that she must behave in it with reverence; but during their walk home, she asked why her papa told the sexton to be so careful of the old red baptistery cushion; "for papa," remarked Mary, "I heard you say to James Wilson, that you looked with more pleasure on that cushion than on anything else in the Church, and it was but the other day that you told me that you loved the little south window because the school children of their own accord saved their pence to buy it; and you said God loved little children who offered to Him in a spirit of love and humility. Did any child give the red cushion, papa?"

"No, my child, it was the widow's mite; and you remember what our Blessed Lord said of that offering."

"Oh, yes, papa; He said she had cast in more than all the rich who gave of their abundance. Will you tell me about this poor widow, dear papa?"

"Yes, my child; but did you not promise Jenny Brown to tell her about the sermon of to-day, since she is ill and thus kept from church? and you told me you had two nice fresh eggs for her dinner."

"I intend to go there, papa; but may I not hear the story first?"

"First tell me what feast do we this day commemorate, Mary?"

"The feast of S. Matthew."

"And what great lesson does the life of this holy Apostle teach us?"

"Self-denial; and you said in your sermon that as S. Matthew left all and followed Jesus, so we must leave our own wishes and desires if they are contrary to His commands."

"Yes, Mary, we must take up our cross daily and follow our Saviour; living (as by God's grace we do), in a Christian land, we are not called upon to suffer great things, as the blessed Martyrs who sealed their faith with their blood; but self-denial is still our duty, and we may, during each day, find many ways of exercising it. The most pleasant path is rarely the safest. And now will my little girl hear the story first, or go at once to Jenny Brown?"

"Thank you, papa, I will not stay a minute longer, but will wait your leisure to tell me the story," and the little girl ran off with a light heart and step. She was soon at the neat cottage of her humble friend, and the old woman looked so pleased to see her young lady, as she always called the kind pastor's daughter, that Mary was more than rewarded for her little act of self-denial.

"See, Jenny, I have brought you some fresh eggs: my hens only gave me two this morning, and the housekeeper made you this little cake; she will bring the syrup for your cough in the evening."

"Thank you kindly, miss; it is very good of you to think of, and come and see a poor old woman; as my sight is bad, would it tire you to read to me the Epistle and Gospel for to-day, my dear young lady?"

Mary willingly complied, and then told old Jenny the text, and all she could remember of the sermon. The text was part of the ninth verse of the ninth chapter of S. Matthew's Gospel: "And He arose and followed Him."

"You know, Jenny," said the little girl, "papa said that S. Matthew was a Publican, and that his business made him very rich, but Publicans were always hated by the Jews, because they gained money by making others poor, and also they were employed by the Romans to gather the taxes, and the Jews thought it wrong to have anything to do with the Gentiles. And papa told us that we must be like S. Matthew, when Christ calls us, and follow Him at once, as the holy Apostle did, for he never waited to consider how much of this world's goods he should lose by following the Saviour, but obeyed at once with a cheerful heart and willing mind; and we must not be covetous and love money for its own sake, or it will become a snare to us, but use the riches of this world in God's service; and papa says that time is as much a talent as money, and that our Heavenly Father will require from us an account of how we have spent it; and though we are not all rich, the poorest have time to use in God's service; and papa told me the other day, that even I, though a little girl, can glorify God by following Christ."

"True, indeed, miss," replied Jenny, "we all have time, and many is the hour I have wasted that I would now gladly have to go over again; it is little I can do now, but I try to be patient when God afflicts me, and thank Him for His many mercies."

Little Mary was so glad to please Jenny that she quite forgot the time, until the old clock warned her that it was time to return to the rectory; so wishing poor Jenny good day, and promising to see her again soon, she hastened home.

When she walked with her papa in the afternoon, he told her he had not forgotten her wish to hear of the old cushion, and related the story thus:

"Many years ago, Mary, before you were born, there was no beautiful little church in the village, like we have now, and the poor were obliged to walk some miles to attend Divine Service; but a good man passing through Ranford, was shocked to see no church here, and Mr. Hayward (that was his name) having some money, and wishing to devote it to God's service, determined to build a temple to Him in this village. I was appointed the clergyman, and one day, a very old woman called at the Parsonage, and told me it had grieved her that she had nothing to give to the church, for almost all the poor had contributed according to their ability; but she was very poor, and could afford nothing but her earnest prayers that God's blessing might prosper the good work.

"I told her that as God had withheld from her the talent of riches, He would not require an offering of them from her, but that her prayers would be accepted for Christ's sake. I reminded her that God could not really receive anything from us, as all were His free gifts, but a willing heart and ready mind were always a precious offering in His sight. The old woman, Betty Morris, thanked me and went away, but when I called at her cottage, a few days after, she told me she had thought of a small offering she could make, if I would not refuse it. 'It is this, sir,' said Betty, producing the hood of her red cloak, 'I can spare this bit of cloth, if your reverence can turn it to any use in the church.'

"I willingly accepted the widow's mite, and it is the Baptistery cushion which excited your curiosity, Mary; do you not now understand why I regard it with feelings of pleasure, my child?"

"Oh! yes, papa; and I shall always love to look at it and think of the poor widow; but I hope you gave her a new cloak?"

"No, Mary, that would have destroyed the act of self-denial; her offering was to God, and she required no earthly recompense. If when you had decided to perform your promise to Jenny Brown before hearing my story, I had called you back, and told you that you should be rewarded for your intention to do right by following your own wishes, would you feel that you had practised self-denial?"

"Oh! no, papa; I understand what you mean."

"My dear child," said Mr. Graham, can you tell me why our Saviour so commended the widow's mite?"

"Because she gave all she had, was it not, papa?"

"Yes, Mary; doubtless there were many both rich and poor who cast largely into the treasury of their substance, and to many I dare say it was an act of self-denial; but the poor widow gave all she had, and so we must, in like manner, give all to God; our worldly substance, our thoughts, our desires, and our best affections. We must not consider how little we may devote to God, but try how much we can offer to Him. How does the Catechism tell you you must love God, Mary?"

"With all my heart, with all my mind, with all my soul, and with all my strength," replied the little girl.

"I am glad you have remembered this so well, my dear child, and may God ever give you grace to perform this great duty. Do you know to whom these lines refer?

> 'At once he rose, and left his gold,
>   His treasure and his heart
> Transferr'd, where he shall safe behold
>   Earth and her idols part;
>
> 'While he beside his endless store
> Shall sit and floods unceasing pour
> Of CHRIST's true riches o'er all time and space,
> First angel of His Church, first steward of His grace.'"

"To S. Matthew, papa; I read them in my hymn for to-day; but why is the Apostle called 'First angel of His Church?' I thought angels were holy spirits, and S. Matthew was a man."

"The word Angel means a messenger, and as S. Matthew was the first of the four Evangelists, which also signifies a messenger of good tidings, he is called in this beautiful hymn an angel. But now, Mary, we are at the Rectory gate, and I cannot talk to my little girl any more until the evening."

S. Michael and All Angels,

OR,
MICHAELMAS DAY.

COLLECT.

O Everlasting God, Who hast ordained and constituted the services of Angels and men in a wonderful order; mercifully grant, that as Thy holy Angels always do Thee service in heaven, so, by Thy appointment, they may succour and defend us on earth; through Jesus Christ our Lord. Amen.

"IT is my birthday, I am four years old, father," said little Willy, the youngest son of Farmer Morris, as he ran down to breakfast one morning.

"You are my little Michaelmas goose," said his father, tossing the child into the air, and giving him a kiss as he put him down. "What a nice new frock mother has made you!"

"I think we may take him to church to-day, James," said Mrs. Morris to her husband, "if he will promise to be very good."

Little Willy made many promises of good behaviour, and his father said he should go to church, and also go with him afterwards to fetch the four children of Widow Brown to dine with him.

This was as much pleasure as Willy's heart could hold, and he could scarcely eat his breakfast for joy.

"You are going to give us a goose, to-day, mother," said the farmer presently.

"Yes, to be sure I am," said Mrs. Morris, laughing, as she looked at the eager faces of the little ones, "a goose almost as large as Willy himself."

"Then don't you think that neighbour Brown could step as far, and dine with us?" said the kind-hearted farmer, who always liked to see those around his table who were not so well off at home as he was.

"I'm afraid not," replied his wife; "she is very weak; but Sally and Mary shall carry her a bit hot."

"That we will," said the little girls at once, "and take her some flowers too."

"Why did the church bells ring this morning, father?" said little Willy.

"Because it is a holy day, the feast of Saint Michael and All Angels. When you are a little older, and go to school with brother Jack, you will know all about it, but you can understand, now, that we go to church to thank God for sending His holy Angels to take care of us, and that we keep a day to remember this mercy, just as we keep one day, the day when you were born, as your birthday. We shall hear a great deal about the Angels in church; Saint Michael is the name of one of those holy beings, of whom we hear most in the Bible, so we call this day after him, the feast of Saint Michael and All Angels, or Michaelmas Day."

"What does a feast of the Church mean, Mary?"

"A holy happy day, father."

"I wonder which of you can tell me why we often

have goose for dinner, on Michaelmas Day," said the farmer.

"Because Queen Elizabeth was eating goose one Michaelmas Day, when she heard that a number of ships, called the Spanish Armada, that were coming to make war upon England, were destroyed : and she said, ' Let English people eat goose on this day for ever.' I learnt that in school," said Jack.

"Well," said his father, "I think that you and your sisters had better be thinking of school now." The three children accordingly set off, Jack to the boys' and his sisters to the girls' school, where we will follow them for a little while. When the opening prayer was concluded, and they had taken their places, and repeated their lessons, their teacher said, " I will now try to explain to you the subject of our prayers and praises to GOD this day. We meet in public worship to pray that the holy angels may, by GOD's appointment, succour and defend us on earth. Look at the Epistle, and you will see why we call the day by Saint Michael's name. It is because we read of Saint Michael as an Archangel, or the chief of angels : very little is told us respecting these glorious beings, enough, however, to teach us to believe in their existence, and to show us that they serve their Creator by ministering to us, His weak and sinful, yet redeemed creatures. Now turn to the Gospel, and you will see why it was chosen for to-day ; because it contains those words of our SAVIOUR, which tell us that the angels watch over little children. The first lesson which will be read in Church, will relate that part of the history of Jacob when the angel of the LORD appeared to him. You know that our Lord Jesus Christ, the Lord of angels, and of all created beings, is sometimes called by this name in the Old Testament. The second lesson is the account of the miraculous deliverance of S. Peter from prison, when the Lord sent an angel to rescue him from the power of Herod. The first lesson in the evening will be, the account of the vision of the Prophet Daniel, when an angel appeared to foretell future events to him; and the second lesson will be part of the Epistle of S. Jude, in which the Apostle speaks of the angels who fell from heaven and became evil spirits, and in which Michael the Archangel is also mentioned. I hope you will be very attentive to these chapters when they are read, and will be able to answer the questions which you will be asked on Sunday. Have you found all the places in your Bibles?"

The children said that they had, and one of the youngest of them asked if they could see these angels.

Their teacher told them that all Christians, without seeking to see, must believe that we are not only surrounded by evil spirits, who tempt us to sin, but that we are watched by the company of Holy Angels. The Holy Spirit, speaking by S. Paul, tells us in the first chapter of the Epistle to the Hebrews, that they are "ministering spirits sent forth to minister to those who shall be heirs of salvation." If then we are Christians in heart, as well as outwardly, our redeemed spirits will, after our death, be carried by angels to that blessed abode, where with them we shall behold the face of our Father which is in Heaven.

"Now, as you have all been attentive," continued

their kind instructress, "I will give each of you a pretty card, with a hymn on it, which you can learn, and repeat to me next week."

The hymn was a very beautiful one, as you will see from the first verse, which was,

> They slumber not, nor sleep,
> Whom Thou dost send, O GOD of light,
> Around Thine own the livelong night,
> Their watch and ward to keep.

The children were delighted with their cards, but they did not open their bags to look at them during the time of divine service, for they remembered that they were in the House of GOD, and they tried to behave with reverence. But now to return to little Willy. His mother dressed him by half-past ten o'clock. And he walked between her and his father to church. Farmer Morris called out to his eldest son, as he left the house, to look well after the farm, and that he should take his turn to go to church in the afternoon, as well as some of the men.

Little Willy nodded to his sisters, and his brother Jack, who passed him with their companions, walking two and two to their places in church, and he saw them again when he was lifted on to the bench by his father, while the Psalms were sung. He behaved very well, and had a happy birthday; and every year, as the day returns, he will remember how he first went to church, and what beautiful stories his mother told him about the angels, as he sat on her knee before he said his prayers that night.

S. Luke the Evangelist's Day.

COLLECT.

ALMIGHTY GOD, Who calledst Luke the Physician, whose praise is in the Gospel, to be an Evangelist, and Physician of the soul; May it please Thee, that by the wholesome medicines of the doctrine delivered by him, all the diseases of our souls may be healed; through the merits of THY SON JESUS CHRIST, our LORD. Amen.

IN a gloomy cell of one of the large prisons of London, a man was seated on the ground. He was a young man, and if you looked at him well it was easy to see that the fierce air and countenance which he bore at present had not been stamped upon his face from childhood, for there was something of a better nature to be traced in his features. Young as he was, William Raikes, for such was his name, was awaiting his trial for felony, and would probably be sentenced to transportation. He had given no proof of repentance or of a softened heart since he had been in the prison, though the Chaplain who visited him had constantly read and talked with him, and prayed for him with persuasive earnestness. Even when a letter came from the young man's widowed mother, saying that with a breaking heart and enfeebled body she should yet make one more effort to see her poor boy, as she called him, he had not wept; but to-day a chord had been touched in his heart which brought back the memory of happy and innocent days, and the hard man's heart was moved.

The Clergyman had said that it was S. Luke's Day, and had read the second lesson for the day.

S. Luke's Day, thought William, I remember it well; it was the first day I went to church, I was five years old; and William's memory travelled back to the old village, and his father's cottage under the elm trees, and to the field through which they walked to church; he could almost feel the breath of the bright summer air upon his cheek again, as he thought of how he used to leave his mother's side to pluck bright flowers in that field, and of how she carried them home for him that he might weave them into garlands with his little sister who died.

William said nothing of these thoughts to the Clergyman, but when the door was locked after him and he was again alone, he threw himself on the ground and wept. They were the first tears he had shed, and now they flowed bitterly, while for the first time during many years of guilt and misery, William suffered himself to dwell on the peaceful recollection of his childhood. There had been times indeed when the thought of his mother and the remembrance of her prayers, and of his pious education, had arisen in his mind; but he had stifled these thoughts and put them far from him, and had generally hastened to drown the stings of conscience in an intoxicating draught; but the faithfulness and long-suffering of God were greater even than his sin, and the voice of the Holy Spirit graciously vouchsafed to him in his Baptism, but so long forgotten and sinned against, was once more heard in his heart.

Yes, thought William, it was S. Luke's Day, I remember it well. I see it all as if it were yesterday. Father going out to work, and shouting to me as he went, to be a good lad in church : he used to go himself in the evenings, and I ran after him for a kiss, and he lifted me up and carried me on his shoulder and put me down over the hedge into the garden; there was my little row in the garden. I wonder if it is there now? I used to gather a posy for mother on Sundays, and I gathered one that day. I remember grandmother, and mother, and I went into the orchard and gathered apples to make a pudding for dinner. Mother shook the branches into his pinafore, the little boy with rosy cheeks and large eyes, little Willy they called me; and then the bells began to ring for church, they made my heart beat, I was so proud to go; that was a happy day. When I said my prayers by my little cot at night, I could not think of any thing naughty I had done except that I had played with the ribbons in my straw hat in church when mother had taken it off. And then next year I went to school, that was the summer, sister and I used to play in the hay-fields, and we went to the school-feast together, and the next summer she died.

I remember what grandmother said when mother cried so, and I could not stop her tears though I kissed her and begged her not to grieve; she said, "See, Willy, how mother loved little Mary, she loves you quite as well: if you grow up a good boy you will make her heart glad, but if you do not, she will shed worse tears for you than for the little one who is safe in Paradise."

At the thought of how bitterly these words had

been realized poor William wept afresh. He was roused by the opening of the door, and the entrance of the jailer who brought him his food; the man seeing his grief, looked kindly at him, and William encouraged by his manner, asked if Mr. Wright, the Chaplain, had left the prison; and being told that he was still there, he said, " O ask him if he will be so good as to come to me once more to-day, for I am wretched."

Mr. Wright heard with pleasure that his presence was desired by the poor young man, and was soon seated by William's side listening kindly while he told him of the happy home he had rendered desolate, and of how he had wilfully sinned against the holy precepts in which he had been trained.

Mr. Wright told him that to feel and acknowledge how great his sin had been was the first step towards true repentance, and seeing that nothing seemed to touch his heart so much as the remembrance of his childhood, he encouraged him to talk over the recollections which the mention of the day had awakened.

" My father died, sir," said William in answer to a question from Mr. Wright, " when I was about seven years old; he was a good man, and my mother loved him tenderly, and grieved a long while: she never married again, but all her pleasure was in her children. I was her only son, sir, and after father died I went on well for a long time, I was rather quick at my books, and had mostly a good character at the school. I shall never forget how happy I was one year. I was ten years old then, when I carried home a Prayer Book as a prize for good conduct, and mother was so pleased and proud, and made me a cover for it.

"The next day was a Saint's Day, S. Luke's Day. You reminded me of it by naming the day this morning, sir; our church was called after S. Luke, and we had our school feast on that day. We all walked to the church in the morning, and then we dined in a field belonging to the Vicar, where there was a large barn in which the tables were spread in case of bad weather. O, what a happy day that was! and I sat next mother at tea in the evening, for the parents of the school children were invited to tea, and as I walked home with her she told me she was a happy mother to have a good boy.

"Things went on well with me till I was about twelve years old, and then I was apprenticed to a carpenter who had two sons about my age, both idle, good-for-nothing lads; but they were not so much to blame as I was, for they had never been taught better, they had no mother, and their father was a drinking man; they had never been sent to school or to church, and used to pass the Sundays in playing pitch and toss in the lane, or drinking at the public-house. The younger one used sometimes to sing hymns in the gallery of a meeting-house, for he had a good voice, and then he would turn them into ridicule with his bad companions afterwards; but, as I said before, sir, they never came to church, though the Vicar talked to them about it from the time they first came into our village; they were good-natured lads, and I was soon great friends with them. My mother began to be frightened about me when she found what a character they bore, but as I was steady for some time, and used to go regularly to church and school, though they laughed at me for it, she began to hope I should not follow their example.

"I told you, sir, that it made me very sad to think how happy I had been on this very day in years that are gone. I remember well how I spent S. Luke's Day when I was in my fifteenth year. My master had finished some work which brought him in a large sum of money, and as I had helped him steadily with it and worked over-hours, he gave me a whole holiday. I did not spend it with his sons as I sometimes did now, but went to church with my mother that day, and to the school feast; as I was only a Sunday scholar then, I did not go in the week except on Saints' Days, when any boy who could get leave from his employers might attend the school. I had been more than usually attentive to my duties at that time, for the day was approaching when I was to go up with other young people from our village to receive Confirmation, and the solemn words which the Clergyman said about receiving God's grace in vain, had taken some hold on my mind. I resolved to break off from all my idle companions, and to be more with my mother, instead of leaving her alone, and passing whole evenings, even on Sunday, on the village green with others who were worse than myself. I determined, too, to read the lessons for each day, and to say my prayers more carefully, (for I had begun to neglect both,) and to forsake the use of bad words. I went to church with these thoughts on my mind, and it seemed to me as if the Vicar could see into my heart, for he preached a sermon that seemed all about me. The text was from the words of S. Paul, I have not forgotten it even to this day. 'Demas hath forsaken me, having loved this present world, only Luke is with me.' The sermon was addressed especially to those who were preparing for Confirmation. I shall never forget what I felt when the Minister said, 'Choose ye this day whom ye will serve; if the LORD be GOD, follow Him;' and how he pointed out two paths, the broad and easy, and the narrow and steep, and told us to pray for constant hearts to cleave to the way of salvation, as S. Luke had done, even through persecution; and he said, that though it would not be our privilege to preach the Gospel in heathen countries, and to overcome idolatry, and to endure persecution even unto death, or to hand down the knowledge of the truth to all ages, as the Evangelist S. Luke had done in his inspired account of the ministry of our LORD, which he had heard from the lips of S. Paul, yet that we had sin to overcome, and the religion of our LORD to glorify by our lives, and our neighbours to edify, and good works to do in faith and love, and that if we persevered unto the end, we, like S. Luke, should be of the number of those who would hear those joyful words of our LORD, 'Come, ye blessed of my FATHER, inherit the kingdom prepared for you from the foundation of the world.'

"I could not keep back my tears in church that morning, and I think my mother noticed them and understood my thoughts, for she gave me my father's Bible that evening, and talked seriously to me, and I was sincere when I promised her to try to lead a new life, and to prepare for Confirmation and my first Communion; but I did not receive either, sir; I shut myself out from these blessings and from all that was good.

"A few weeks after this, my master accused me unjustly of having sold some of his tools. I had not done it; but though I guessed who had, and that was his own son, I would not betray my friend, and as I was too proud and angry to defend myself the suspicion rested on me. My master did not hesitate to accuse me of it openly, and this enraged me so much that the next time he said a word of it, I flew at him and knocked him down, and he fell with his head against a sharp corner of the tool-house, and as he lay stunned, and as I feared dead, I was afraid to remain, and determined to set off before he could be discovered, and hide myself in some large town. My master owed me wages, so, as I wanted money, I took some, for I knew where he kept it. I did not stop to think of how I should break my mother's heart, or of how my character would now be justly blackened. A thought crossed me once that I would go to the kind Vicar and confess the truth, but my master looked so like one dead, and I had struck him in passion, so I was afraid of being taken up for murder. I took the money, and ran off along a road on which I knew I could get a lift on a coach that would soon place miles between me and my home; that was the first step, sir, on the road to my ruin, the moment when I took the money without even stopping to count it. It was soon spent, and I wandered about the streets of London, for it was there I went in search of any means of earning my bread.

"I soon fell in with some men, who promised to

get work and money for me, and as they let me live with them and share their food, I did not question them as to how I was to gain my living with them, for I soon saw that such words were an offence to them. I became accustomed before long to their language and their bad ways, and was not much shocked even when I found at last that I was expected to help them to steal and to break into houses at night; and I have done so, sir, and have gone on from bad to worse.

"At first I used to think of my mother sometimes, and of my vows to serve GOD that I had so fearfully broken; but these thoughts were so dreadful that I put them away, and till to-day they have never come back to my mind so strongly. O, sir, what shall I do? How shall I face my mother?"

"Rather say," replied Mr. Wright, solemnly, "how shall I face my heavenly FATHER, the GOD Whose laws I have broken, Whose grace I have resisted, and Whose mercies I have put from me with my own hand."

"It is true, it is indeed true," said William, " I have done all this and much more. O, sir, you do not know how wicked I have been."

When the Clergyman saw that William was really feeling how great his sin had been, and trusting that he was beginning to experience true repentance, he talked to him of the mercy of GOD in our LORD JESUS CHRIST, and of the atonement that had been made for sin on Calvary, and he prayed by his side that it would please GOD to lead the poor sinner to true penitence, and to pardon his sin for the LORD JESUS CHRIST's sake.

"O, sir, said William, afterwards, 'the words of the Church prayers that you use seem to rise up to condemn me."

"Rather say," said Mr. Wright, "that they speak to you of the long-suffering of that SAVIOUR Who is the great Physician of the soul, as S. Luke is called in the collect, and Who is willing to heal your soul from its many sicknesses. You have indeed fearfully destroyed that health of soul, your baptismal grace, but there is a never-failing medicine for sin and uncleanness by which even yet all the diseases of your soul may be healed, even the Blood of the Lamb.

"If you remember what you learnt at school," he continued, "you cannot have forgotten how many proofs of the pardoning mercy of our SAVIOUR are to be found in the writings of the Evangelist whom we commemorate to-day."

Mr. Wright then opened the Bible at the fifteenth chapter of St. Luke's Gospel, and read the parable of the Prodigal Son.

"These words," he said, "were spoken by our Divine Master Himself to tell repentant sinners in every age and clime of the pardon freely offered to them. You, William, like the prodigal son, have left your heavenly FATHER's care, and wasted the blessings He provided for you, and have reduced yourself to misery and destitution of soul and body; but if through his infinite grace you return unto Him, you will not be sent empty away. 'There is joy in the presence of the Angels of GOD over one sinner that repenteth,' and 'Let the wicked forsake his way, and the unrighteous man his thoughts, and let him return unto the LORD and He will have mercy upon him, and to our GOD, for He will abundantly pardon him.'"

Day after day did Mr. Wright sit with William from this time, and each visit confirmed his hope of the sincere penitence of the prisoner. On one occasion he found his mother with him; the poor woman was greatly comforted under her heavy sorrow about her son, when she found that he repented of his evil courses, though her heart sank within her at the thought that he had only been restored to her to be parted from her for ever in this world (for there was little hope that his sentence would be short of transportation.)

"I have indeed deserved my punishment, sir," said William to Mr. Wright, "I would not be a dutiful son to my mother, and now I am not allowed the consolation of soothing her last years."

The day of the trial came on, and, contrary to the expectations, and beyond even the most sanguine hopes of those who took an interest in the young man and his widowed mother, William, though he was proved guilty of having assisted to rob a house, was sentenced only to prison and hard labour for three months; the evidence went to prove that he had not taken a principal part, and his youth, and the fact of his having fallen when so young among the gang of thieves with whom he had been connected, were urged for a lenient sentence in his case. I cannot describe the joy of the mother, and the thankfulness of her son when this decision was made known to them; Mr. Wright, too, rejoiced sincerely that the youth in whose welfare he had taken so much interest, would not be exposed to the temptations and bad influence of a convict settlement.

Three months passed away, during which William went through the punishment he had so justly deserved with soberness and humility; he left the prison with a good character for his conduct while there, and the next day he went with his mother to see his kind and faithful friend, Mr. Wright. They soon began to speak of William's plans for the future, and his mother said,

"I tell my boy, sir, that I think it may be hard for him to go to the old place where his faults are so well known, and that I will live with him anywhere that he can make an honest living, for we will never part again."

"And what does William say?" asked Mr. Wright.

"That I could not think of such a thing, sir, as to take my mother from the old home she has loved so long, just to spare my own false pride; besides, sir, there where I have broken the laws of God and man, there I would desire to live to His glory, and to prove the sincerity of my repentance. I know what trials I shall have at first, sir; the neighbours will shun me as a thief, but it is not more than I deserve, and I will try to win their better opinion at last."

I need not say that Mr. Wright fully approved of William's determination; he sent a letter by him to the Clergyman of his village, who joyfully received the wanderer into the fold once more. And in the old church, which he had not hoped to see again, William, having proved the sincerity of his repentance by his altered life, received, after a long course of preparation, the holy rite of Confirmation, and partook of the most holy Sacrament of CHRIST's Body and Blood.

He walked once more by his mother's side through the fresh fields, supporting her feeble steps, and talking of the goodness and mercy which had thus brought healing to his soul by means of the wholesome medicines of the doctrine delivered by a successor of S. Luke.

It is true that the heavy cloud resting on his early years cast a shadow over his joys, for the fruit of sin is sorrow. William was a humble and a grave man all his days, and never forgot his fall, though few of those who knew him remembered it against him; but he lived in the joyful hope that his sins would not be found written in the book of judgment against him at the last day, but that He Who died to save him, had " blotted out the hand-writing that was against, him and taken it away, nailing it to His Cross."

S. Simon and S. Jude's Day.

COLLECT.

O ALMIGHTY GOD, Who hast built Thy Church upon the foundation of the Apostles and Prophets, JESUS CHRIST Himself being the head corner-stone; Grant us so to be joined together in unity of spirit by their doctrine, that we may be made an holy temple acceptable unto Thee; through JESUS CHRIST our LORD. AMEN.

"GOOD day, neighbour Charlton, where are you going so early? you don't often leave your work at this time of day."

"Where should I be going but to church, Derry?" replied his friend; "do you not know that this is the Feast of S. Simon and S. Jude?"

"Well, I did hear the bells ringing, but I can't find time for church except on Sundays, and I don't know how you manage it, for I heard you say yesterday that you had so much to do, you did not know which way to turn."

"So I have," said Charlton, "but I'll tell you my plan; if I am very busy when a Saint's Day comes round, I get up half an hour earlier, and work half an hour later, and that gives me time for church; and I don't find I lose anything by it, and if I did, it is hard if we can't sacrifice something to the Giver of so many rich blessings."

"I always think week-day services are for the rich, and not for us poor hard-working people," said Derry.

"But we have souls as well as rich people, haven't we, neighbour? and the Minister told us in his sermon last Sunday, that religion was not only to be a Sunday duty, but the business of our lives, and that we must carry it into every action if we would really serve God as Christians."

"I dare say what you tell me is very right, Charlton, but I don't profess to be so good as many people, and if I do as much as I think right, God will be merciful to me."

"But," said Charlton, "Holy Scripture tells us that much will be required of those who have received much, and we Christians have so many high privileges,—but here is my good wife coming to meet me, and we are opposite the Church; you'll come too, won't you, Derry?"

"I can't to-day, Robert; I've got a job to finish at the shop hard by, and I promised to be there by this time, so good-bye."

Robert Charlton was a blacksmith, and being the only one in the village of Coombe, he had plenty of work; he was a very respectable man, and highly regarded by all his neighbours, to whom he was ever ready to lend a helping hand. Both Robert and his wife feared God, and endeavoured to bring up their only child Martha in the right path.

James Derry was a widower, with three children; a little girl called Ann, aged fourteen, and her brothers Willie and Tom, the former nine, and the latter six years old; their father was a carpenter, and as he was at his shop a great part of each day, and did not send his children to school, they ran about where they pleased and often got into mischief. Little children should feel very grateful to their kind parents who send them to school, and do their duty by training them to serve GOD in this world, that they may in the next praise Him with the holy angels to all eternity.

"Mother, mother," cried Martha Charlton, as she ran into the cottage after divine service, for Martha went to church with the other school children, "see what I have got! after church the squire's lady came into the school and heard the Minister catechise us, and then she gave us each a pretty hymn; is it not on a beautiful card, mother? The Minister told me it was like the old Prayer-Books when printing was first invented; are not the colours bright? he called it illuminated, and then he told us all about S. Simon and S. Jude, and how they converted the heathens, and were martyrs to our holy faith.

"Look, father, at my beautiful card," said the child, as Charlton entered the cottage, "may I read the hymn?"

"Yes, my child, I should like to hear it."

And Martha read:—

> "He Whom the FATHER from above
> Sent down on earth to dwell,
> Hath sent the Apostles of His love,
> That love through earth to tell.
>
> "The banner of the cross unfurled,
> To all of human race,
> His heralds carry through the world
> The sign of JESU'S grace.

> "How beauteous are their passing feet
> Upon the mountain height,
> As with the words of truth they greet
> Those plunged in error's night.
>
> "CHRIST they proclaim, and all around
> Sink back the gates of hell,
> As at the mystic trumpet's sound
> The heathen towers fell."

"Is it not pretty, father?"

"Yes, indeed it is, my dear; you know our forefathers were once heathens, as the poor savages in many parts of the world now are; it is believed that the Apostle S. Paul converted the Britons. It is thought that S. Simon and S. Jude preached the Gospel in Asia."

"O, father, I should so like to go and convert the heathen, and do some good like the holy Apostles."

"My dear child," replied her father, "you can follow the steps of the Apostles, though you cannot convert the heathen nations; and you may not be, as the Martyrs were, suffered to die in defence of the truth; you know, Martha, GOD has given to each of us our appointed post, and we must not think we could better serve Him at any other.

"What would you say if I were one day to tell mother and you that I did not think I could do anything to please GOD while I remained at the forge, and that I should go about the country preaching?"

"O, father, that would be very silly," said Martha, "for what should mother and I do if you left off working for us? besides it would be wrong, because the other day you told me that all GOD's true Ministers were ordained by the Bishop, and you could not be a real minister because you are not ordained."

"Yes, Martha, it would be very wrong of me to leave 'that station in life to which it has pleased God to call me;' and how cannot my little girl understand that she also has duties which she must leave undone if she chose for herself a new path? Is there nothing you can do for CHRIST'S sake, no kindness you can show to a poor sick neighbour?"

"O yes, father, I can nurse Mary Morgan's baby when she is busy washing, and I can read to Widow Rake, who has been so long bedridden," and the child enumerated many acts of Christian love which it was in her power to show her neighbours, "but that seems so little, father."

"It would be little, my child, if GOD saw as men see, but He searcheth the heart, and requires of us obedience, and not that we should question His commands. The SAVIOUR has said, that if we but give a cup of water to a disciple for His sake, we shall not lose our reward. But there is some one at the door, Martha; go and see who knocks."

It was Derry, who, almost breathless with running, begged Charlton to go with him and help carry little Tom, who had clambered up a wall and fallen several feet.

"He's badly hurt, Charlton, and I fear his leg is broken," said the father, "if he had been at school this would not have happened; perhaps he'll die, and it will be all my fault for letting him run so wild."

When they reached the spot where the poor child

lay, he appeared in great pain and was moaning sadly, for, besides a broken leg, he had some severe bruises; he was carefully carried home, and the doctor set the broken limb, but told Derry the child must remain perfectly quiet for some weeks.

As Derry could not stay from his work to nurse little Tom, he told Ann to take care of her brother; but she had never been taught to give up her own fancies to please others, and when Tom, who was in great pain, became fretful, she left him and went out in the lane to play. Whilst she was there, Martha passed and asked for the little sufferer, and finding that his sister had left him, she inquired if the doctor had forbidden him to see any one.

"O no," said Ann, "but he is so cross, and I'm tired of spinning his top, and he wants me to tell him stories, and I can't. You may go in," she continued, as Martha looked at the door.

Now it was a bright October morning, the sun shone and the air was fresh, and Martha was going with her father to the neighbouring town; she knew it would be kind to stay with little Tom, but then she should lose the pleasure of a walk with her father, and then it was Ann's duty to take care of her brother; besides, thought Martha, if he is so cross and fretful, perhaps I shall not be able to amuse him, and then I can do no good—but she suddenly remembered the Festival of S. Simon and S. Jude, and her father's words, and decided to go and see Tom; so turning to Ann, she said, "If you will go and tell father where I am, I will stay a little time with Tom." Ann willingly undertook to carry the message, for the selfish child was glad to have the charge of her brother taken from her.

Tom was suffering much, and very fretful, and it was a long time before Martha could soothe him, but her manner was so gentle, and her voice so kind, that she at last succeeded. She told him several pretty stories, and the child was so amused he almost forgot his pain, and when she rose to return home, he cried, and begged her to come the next day.

"You are so kind and gentle," said Tom, "and don't scold me like Ann does when I am in pain, and indeed it is very bad, and I can't help crying sometimes."

Martha kissed the poor child, and promised to see him again soon. Many long hours did she spend by Tom's bedside, using her utmost efforts to please and divert him, and though the young girl knew it not, she was converting those who, in this Christian land, were no better than heathens, for little Tom had never been taught about GOD and the blessed SAVIOUR. Martha often read him Scripture stories of holy children of old, and of blessed Martyrs who suffered for CHRIST's sake, and of little children who early learned to serve Him by self-denial. Sometimes Willie came in while Martha was relating these stories, and then he would sit quietly and listen, and by degrees he became as fond of staying with the kind little girl as poor Tom was of having her to sit by him.

Derry was very grateful to Martha for her kindness to his poor child, and often told Ann he wished she would try and be more like Martha.

"Tom is never cross with her, Ann," said her fa

ther, "she has a way of pleasing him, and yet she does not seem as if it were a trouble to her."

Martha sometimes talked to Tom of the Holy JESUS, Who was once a little child, and was made man for our sakes, and Who suffered a cruel death to save us from eternal punishment. "And, Tom," said the little girl, "the Minister tells us we can all suffer something for CHRIST's sake, and that we should when in pain or sorrow, remember Who sends us affliction. Will you think of this when you feel fretful and in pain?"

Tom gradually recovered, but it was a long time before he could walk; he one day astonished his father by asking if he might go to school with Martha.

"I should learn to read there, daddy, and be able to tell you such pretty stories. Do, please, let me go?"

Derry willingly consented, and Ann and Willie feeling a little ashamed at their own ignorance, for Ann was older than Martha, asked if they might also go to school.

In the course of a year the three children were greatly improved; Ann had learned to sew, and kept her father's cottage neat and comfortable, for she was not now always to be seen playing in the road; and Willie was beginning to write pretty well; little Tom was very happy and proud when he could show his father a new Prayer-Book which the Rector's lady had given him for being attentive in church.

Robert Charlton and his wife looked fondly on their child, as they remarked to each other how soon her earnest wish to serve GOD in her generation had been fulfilled.

All Saints' Day.

COLLECT.

O ALMIGHTY GOD, who hast knit together Thine elect in one communion and fellowship, in the mystical body of Thy Son CHRIST our LORD; Grant us grace so to follow Thy blessed Saints in all virtuous and godly living, that we may come to those unspeakable joys which Thou hast prepared for those who unfeignedly love Thee; through JESUS CHRIST our LORD. Amen.

THE subject of the following pages was the only child of Thomas Spencer, the coachman of Squire Jones, who lived in the largest house of East Hampton, of which place I was once the vicar: his memory is connected, in my own mind, with the Feast of All Saints, and it was in speaking on this festival with my children that I gave them the following account of my little parishioner. They were much interested in his story, and I now publish it, in the hope that others may likewise learn from it, that the Cross of CHRIST sheds sweetness and peace over the death of a Christian child, as it does holiness and happiness in life.

When first I knew little Robert Spencer, he was a merry healthy child, with red cheeks, and bright blue eyes: he was always an attentive scholar, and behaved better than many boys of his age at church and school. But when he was about ten years old, I noticed that he became gradually thinner and paler, and of a more thoughtful disposition, and I thought that his mother was not mistaken when she told me one day, with tears in her eyes, of how good and gentle Robert was become, and that she thought GOD was teaching her child by His HOLY SPIRIT, and preparing him for a better world. In truth, before many months had passed, Robert was too poorly to attend the school, and before he was twelve years old, he was in a rapid decline. I visited him very often, and observed with thankfulness, that as he approached nearer to the time of his death, he was more and more occupied with heavenly things.

I called to see him one evening, after a cold but bright day in November. I found him seated in an easy chair by the fire, while his mother busied herself to shelter him from the night air by carefully closing the window curtains. Upon my asking how he was, the little invalid answered with a smile that he was very comfortable, and that he was glad I was come, as he hoped I would persuade his mother to grant him a great favour. "I am afraid it is something imprudent, Robert," I replied, "if your mother does not consent willingly."

"Indeed, sir," she said, "I am afraid it is; he wants to be taken to church to-morrow, and I am frightened to think of it, but I do not like to deny him anything either."

"I am sure that Robert will not wish to go if it is not right that he should, would you, my dear boy?' I said.

"O no, sir, indeed I would not, I would not vex mother by asking to go if she is afraid, but I want her to think about it first: you see, sir," continued he, " it was my cough which kept me from church, and now that is quite gone, and the doctor says it is not likely to come again, and he says that nothing will hurt me now, and mother has often drawn me out in the wheel chair when the sun was shining, so I think I might get as far as the church if the day is fine, I wish so much to go there once more. Do not cry, mother dear," said the boy, putting his thin hand on hers, " you know I am only going a little while before you."

His poor mother repressed her tears lest she should agitate the little sufferer, for the colour was rising fast to his pale cheeks.

" I will go and ask the doctor, my dear child," she said, "whether you may have your way, if Mr. —— will be so very kind as to stay with you till I come back."

I promised to do this, and Robert assured me that he would not think more of going to church if the doctor thought he would be running any risk in doing so, " but mother," he said, as she was preparing to go, " you know the Squire's family are all away, and I might sit in their pew, where there are cushions, don't forget to tell the doctor that."

When we were left alone I asked him why he was so anxious to go to church to-morrow, though I guessed the reason readily.

" O, sir, it will be All Saints' Day, and I always loved to go to church on that day. It used to bring such glorious thoughts to my mind, of all the happy spirits that are saved and gone before us. Last All

Saints' Day, I remember how I thought what Paradise would be like, and now, it is such a solemn thought; but I hope to be there so soon: I trust so," he added, as tears of earnest feeling rolled down his face, "for the LORD JESUS CHRIST's sake. I do pray very often as I lie down, or sit here, but I long once more to say with all the congregation, 'Make me to be numbered with Thy Saints, in glory everlasting.'" He did not speak for some moments afterwards, for Robert was overcome by his feelings, and I did not like to disturb him. Presently, when I had given him some water, he said to me, "Often, sir, when the pain in my side is very bad, and I cannot breathe, and sinful, impatient thoughts come into my mind, I say over to myself those lines you marked in my Hymn Book,

'Meet it is we raise our eyes—
Up from earth towards the skies;
Thinking of the Saints that rest,
After toil, in Abraham's breast,
Lest we faint in our distress,
Through exceeding heaviness.

'Strengthen us to run our race
With a portion of their grace,
That when Thou shalt come with dread
Judging both the quick and dead;
They with us, and we with them
May attain Thy diadem.'"

He could not speak longer together without difficulty, but he said the first lines of the verse, and was pleased when I finished them. His mother returned soon, and brought the welcome news, that if he were pretty well he might have his wish.

"O thank you, dear mother," he said, "I am *so* happy; I shall go with you to the dear old church once more. My poor mother," he continued, as his mother left the room to prepare his bed, " is very sad when she thinks of my death. When I am gone, sir, I know you will often come and talk to her: will you tell her from me, with my dearest love, not to grieve more than she can help, for I shall be quite happy then, and freed from sin and pain for ever ? "

I took leave of little Robert, but the next morning when I woke I thought of him, for the weather had changed during the night, and winter was setting in with a cold east wind. I sent him a message as early as I could, to say that I was sorry that he was disappointed in his hope of going out, by the weather, but that I would come and see him in the course of the day. In the afternoon I went accordingly. " Well, my boy," I said, " I was sorry not to see you where you so much wished to be, this morning, but 'man proposes, yet God disposes,' you know."

" Yes, sir, I was very sorry too," he said, " but I have had a happy day: mother read all the Church Services to me, we began at eleven o'clock, and I could follow you with my heart, all along, only not the sermon, sir: if you have time will you tell me something of that ? " I said I would, and asked him what part of the service he had most enjoyed: he seemed to have found rich comfort in all, for he named each part successively, the Lessons, the Collect, the Epistle and Gospel, and then the Creed.

" O, sir," said he, " it is such a comfort to me to say, 'I believe,' with all my heart to those glorious words, 'The communion of Saints, the forgiveness of sins, the resurrection of the body, and the life ever lasting.' He was much pleased when I said that those sentences had been the text of my morning's sermon.

"It is enough," he said, "to make me happy now, and happy when I die, to believe that all my sins will be forgiven, and I shall have everlasting life.

"I can see the words of the belief written over the altar, quite plainly in my mind; with the sun shining on them through the window, and the willows waving close by, against the blue sky, just as I used to see it, and I liked to think to-day,

> 'The faith for which Thy saints endured
> The dungeon and the stake,
> That very faith with hearts assured,
> Upon our lips we take.'"

"What do you understand, Robert," I asked, "by the communion of Saints?"

"Does it not mean, sir, that all Christians have fellowship together, and love one another, wherever they may be?"

"It does, my boy," I answered, "it means the fulfilment of our SAVIOUR'S prayer for us, 'that they all may be *one*,' one in the LORD JESUS, children of the same FATHER, baptized into one Church, sanctified by one HOLY SPIRIT, and journeying towards one blessed home. The communion of Saints is the relationship of Christians in this world, and in the next, to each other."

"Do you think, sir, that Saints in heaven see us, and hear us? and can they pray for us, and help us?"

"There is but one Mediator between GOD and man, the LORD JESUS CHRIST," I repeated, "it is enough for us that He hears all our prayers, and intercedes for us. We do not know what may be the employments of the departed faithful; we know that they are 'present with the LORD,' (2 Cor. v. 8,) that no sin or sorrow can ever reach them more: we know too, that they will welcome us if we are admitted to share their joys at our death; but whether they are permitted to minister to us, as Angels are, we are not told: if we were, no doubt our weak natures would fall into the sin of 'honouring the creature, more than the Creator,' and addressing prayers to them."

"We do not read much in the Bible, do we, sir, about the state of the soul after death?"

"Not much, my boy, but we may gather more than perhaps you think, if we look attentively into the Scriptures, and there are several passages which would lead us to infer that the spirits of the departed faithful do indeed, from their blessed abode, look down and watch over those who have still 'to work out their own salvation with fear and trembling.' In the twelfth chapter of the Epistle to the Hebrews, this thought seems given to us as a solemn encouragement. 'Seeing, then, that we are compassed about with so great a cloud of witnesses,' writes S. Paul, after he has been enumerating those, who through faith have glorified GOD in their lives and by their deaths, ' let us lay aside every weight, and let us run with patience the race which is set before us.' The Apostle here draws his figure from the ancient games, of which I have before told you, and speaks of departed believers, as of spectators of our efforts, and having raised our hearts to the glorious thought of the ' general assembly, and Church of the first-born which are written in heaven,' to the spirits of just men made perfect; into whose presence we are spiritually come, he adds, lest we should rest even on this great mystery too long, 'looking unto JESUS, in whom we all have fellowship with the FATHER.' But we will think of some other passages; can you remember any?"

"The Parable of the Rich Man and the Beggar," suggested Robert.

"Yes, that is one. Our LORD tells us that the beggar was carried by angels to Abraham's bosom, viz., the company of the faithful. The death of Stephen, too, who saw heaven opened and the glorified REDEEMER, into whose presence his ransomed spirit was about to be received. And there are many others which give abundant proof of the truth of those words, 'Blessed are the dead which die in the LORD.' The strongest assurance of the immediate happiness of the soul of the Christian after death, is, I think, to be found in the promise of our LORD JESUS CHRIST to the dying thief, 'To-day thou shalt be with Me in Paradise:' for we must understand by Paradise that place where the soul of our LORD tarried with the spirits of departed believers before His resurrection, where they await a day of still greater glory; for of them it is written, 'that they should rest yet for a little season, until their fellow-servants also and their brethren, which should be killed as they were, should be fulfilled.' (Rev. vi. 11.) 'For they without us cannot be made perfect.' (Hebrews xi. 40.) Then, when this corruptible shall put on incorruption, when the glorified body shall be reunited to the already sanctified spirit, shall be brought to pass the saying which is written, 'Death is swallowed up in victory.'" (1 Cor. xv. 54.)

I did not say all this to little Robert at once, but it was the chief subject of our conversation : little I call him, from my remembrance of what he was when I first knew him; he was grown tall and very thin now, and his earthly house was fast wasting away; he lived nearly three months after the day of which I have been speaking, and during that time I visited him very often. His mother told me that a murmur, or an impatient word never passed his lips, though his sufferings at times were fearful to witness. He was anxious for the return of his father, who was absent with his master's family, and sent him many affectionate messages; but he would not press his return, lest it should pain him if unable to comply with his request. Every day, as his bodily weakness increased, he seemed to grow in the love of the LORD JESUS CHRIST, even his dearest earthly ties seemed weak in comparison of his spiritual affections, the love of GOD was indeed shed abroad in his heart, and his dying bed was a place of holiness and peace; he remembered and confessed with sorrow and humility sinful words or actions of which he had been guilty when in health, and sent little tokens of his love to many of his companions, when he was too weak to see them. The joy of his father's sudden return proved too much for his exhausted frame, and the evening of the day on which he arrived he burst a blood-vessel, and survived only a few moments. I entered the room in time to see his last look of affection at his mother.

Upon seeing me, he raised one hand as if to point to heaven, with an upward look of peace and hope, one moment's struggle for breath, and all was over,—his warfare was accomplished, and his emancipated spirit we may humbly and firmly trust had joined the blessed company of the redeemed, the Apostles and Saints of old, with whom he had so earnestly prayed to be numbered. As I gazed upon his tranquil form for the last time, I thought of one of his favourite verses,—

"They need, O LORD, Thy special grace
Who fight in this world's view,
But in the sick room face to face
Is Satan vanquished too.

"Both need the same protecting grace
To keep them undefiled,
And both shall in Thy presence stand
Thy Martyr, and Thy child."

THE END.

www.ingramcontent.com/pod-product-compliance
Lightning Source LLC
Chambersburg PA
CBHW021151230426
43667CB00006B/349